About Island Press

Since 1984, the nonprofit Island Press has been stimulating, shaping, and communicating the ideas that are essential for solving environmental problems worldwide. With more than 800 titles in print and some 40 new releases each year, we are the nation's leading publisher on environmental issues. We identify innovative thinkers and emerging trends in the environmental field. We work with world-renowned experts and authors to develop cross-disciplinary solutions to environmental challenges.

Island Press designs and implements coordinated book publication campaigns in order to communicate our critical messages in print, in person, and online using the latest technologies, programs, and the media. Our goal: to reach targeted audiences—scientists, policymakers, environmental advocates, the media, and concerned citizens—who can and will take action to protect the plants and animals that enrich our world, the ecosystems we need to survive, the water we drink, and the air we breathe.

Island Press gratefully acknowledges the support of its work by the Agua Fund, Inc., Annenberg Foundation, The Christensen Fund, The Nathan Cummings Foundation, The Geraldine R. Dodge Foundation, Doris Duke Charitable Foundation, The Educational Foundation of America, Betsy and Jesse Fink Foundation, The William and Flora Hewlett Foundation, The Kendeda Fund, The Andrew W. Mellon Foundation, The Curtis and Edith Munson Foundation, Oak Foundation, The Overbrook Foundation, the David and Lucile Packard Foundation, The Summit Fund of Washington, Trust for Architectural Easements, Wallace Global Fund, The Winslow Foundation, and other generous donors.

The opinions expressed in this book are those of the author(s) and do not necessarily reflect the views of our donors.

THE AGILE CITY

JAMES S. RUSSELL

THE AGILE CITY

Building Well-being and Wealth in
an Era of Climate Change

 **ISLAND**PRESS

Washington | Covelo | London

ISLAND PRESS is a trademark of the Center for Resource Economics.

Library of Congress Cataloging-in-Publication Data

Russell, James S.
    The agile city : building well-being and wealth in an era of climate change /
By James S. Russell.
        p.   cm.
    Includes bibliographical references and index.
    ISBN-13: 978-1-59726-724-3 (cloth : alk. paper)
    ISBN-10: 1-59726-724-4 (cloth : alk. paper)
    ISBN-13: 978-1-59726-725-0 (pbk. : alk. paper)
    ISBN-10: 1-59726-725-2 (pbk. : alk. paper)
    1. Climatic changes. 2. Climatic changes—Government policy. 3. Economic development. 4. Sustainable development. 5.Financial crises—History—21st century.
I. Title.
    QC903.R87   2011
    363.738'74561—dc22

                                        2011005024

Printed on recycled, acid-free paper

Manufactured in the United States of America
10 9 8 7 6 5 4 3 2 1

KEYWORDS: Carbon neutrality, climate change adaptation, climate change mitigation, community planning, energy efficiency, environmental design and planning, green architecture, green building, green infrastructure, grey infrastructure, megaburbs, neoburbs, New Orleans rebuilding, sustainable communities, sustainable transportation, water resources

To Mary and Ralph

CONTENTS

ACKNOWLEDGMENTS

Elements of this book gestated over a long time, and many people have been of inestimable help. The late Astra Zarina, who founded the Architecture in Rome program at the University of Washington, introduced me to the ways a great city works. I was able to document the lay of the American urban landscape thanks to insightful editors at *Architectural Record*: Mildred Schmertz, Stephen Kliment, and Robert Ivy. Manuela Hoelterhoff has been a staunch champion of architecture at Bloomberg. Jeff Weinstein has focused my written vagaries at three different publications.

The New York State Council on the Arts, Bermard Tschumi at Columbia University's Graduate School of Architecture Planning and Preservation, and Sal LaRosa and Ron Bentley have offered welcome financial (and at times moral) support.

It has been a privilege to work with Michael Gallis and benefit from his astounding insights. I have cited many people in the book whose research or experience has enriched the argument, but some I've relied on again and again: Michael Gallis, Christopher Leinberger, Clark Stevens in Montana, Jeanne Nathan and Robert Tannen in New Orleans, Robert Bruegmann in Chicago, and the Lincoln Institute for Land Policy in Cambridge. Thanks also go to Tracy Metz in Amsterdam, David Cohn in Madrid, Peter Slatin, Cathleen McGuigan, Nancy Levinson, Roberta Brandes Gratz, Kenneth Frampton, Amanda Burden, Barry Bergdoll, and Ada Louise Huxtable. At Island Press, heartfelt thanks to editor Heather Boyer and to Courtney Lix and Rebecca Bright.

I could not have gotten this book done without Robert Hughes, Hillary Brown, S.J. Rozan, Monty Freeman, Amy Schatz, and Max Rudin. I am the lucky beneficiary of unflagging love, support, and inspiration from Steven Blier.

PROLOGUE
Carbon-neutral Now

The blond stone walls and handsome vaulted roof of Kroon Hall have an un-assuming barnlike presence amid neo-Gothic neighbors at Yale University. An intimate plaza, a pleasing meeting place for the School of Forestry and Environmental Studies, welcomes you. Hefty wooden louvers on the tall, narrow entrance side cut afternoon sun (figure P.1). Inside, sun filters down the wood-paneled main stair, inviting you to climb to the top-floor reading room, with its gracefully vaulting ceiling. There, photovoltaic panels over skylights shower celestial light, perfectly balanced by stripes of sunlight seeping through the louvered end wall. You might notice the little green and red lights next to the windows that signal when natural breezes can be used instead of heating and cooling, but you probably do not know that five very-low-energy systems heat and cool the building. It's not obvious that Kroon's long narrow shape mini-mizes absorption of summer heat while gathering the low winter sun and grabbing passing breezes for ventilation. Though the building fits as comfort-ably as an old pair of jeans, Hopkins Architects, of London, working with the locally based Centerbrook Architects and Planners, have calibrated every de-tail of this new office and seminar-room building to produce, husband, or har-vest energy (figure P.2).

A few years ago, a building could garner headlines because it cut energy use 20 or 30 percent from today's norms. Kroon aimed much higher, at "carbon neutrality": reducing to zero the heat-trapping gases that warm the planet.[1]

Zero. A few years ago, experts would have said you can't get there. But improvements in building design, technology, and construction now make carbon-neutral buildings an increasingly reachable goal. Electric cars can be

Figure P.1 Kroon Hall, Yale University. The louvers on the east-facing side of this building are one of many tactics designed by Hopkins Architects with Centerbrook Architects to achieve near zero-carbon emissions. Credit: © Robert Benson

Figure P.2 The daylighted top-floor reading room and café at Kroon Hall, Yale University. Photovoltaic panels over skylights generate energy and filter the sun, which balances sidelight seeping through the building's protective exterior louvers. Credit: © Robert Benson

considered zero emission only if the power that charges them comes from relatively rare renewable sources. Workable zero-emission coal-fired power plants and zero-emission gas-driven ones look far away in time.

As global warming effects become more evident, and the debate over what to do about it becomes more difficult, it's important to know that buildings can get to zero. After all, they are responsible for almost 40 percent of US greenhouse gas emissions.

A geothermal well system draws heat from the earth in winter and cools in the summer. A displacement-ventilation system relies on the buoyancy of warm air to ventilate the building with only minimal fan use. These devices cost more, and are unusual but not exotic. "The only way to make really efficient buildings is to employ as many different strategies as possible," Hopkins's director, Michael Taylor, says. "We reduced energy demand by 50 percent, and then met 25 percent of the energy needs with a 100-kilowatt photovoltaic array, so we have a resulting 62.5 percent reduction in our carbon footprint." This isn't zero but comprises the state of the carbon-reduction art at this writing.

Pull the focus out to the scale of communities, though, and you can see how much more can be accomplished.

At the western edge of North America, on the southern tip of the mountainous and densely forested Vancouver Island, Dockside Green has already become carbon positive. The mix of town houses, mid-rise apartments, and commercial buildings is rising in phases on a narrow, fifteen-acre former industrial site just above the famous Inner Harbor of Victoria, British Columbia (figure P.3).

Dockside Green harnesses economies of scale to affordably build in carbon-reduction measures that are impractical for single buildings. From an apartment rooftop, where owners tend rows of lettuce, you can look down on a stream, planted with native wetland grasses, that burbles in front of the outdoor terraces of town houses (figure P.4). The stream is clean enough that crayfish thrive and ducks nest even though it mixes runoff from rain-harvesting gardens and water treated in an on-site sewage plant. Vancouver architecture firm Busby Perkins + Will (master planner of the site) designed the first eight buildings to cross ventilate and to capture warmth from the low winter sun, as Kroon does. Awnings automatically unfurl to cut unwanted heat. These tactics, with 100 percent fresh-air mechanical ventilation, make the elimination of air-conditioning possible in Victoria's temperate climate. Meters in each apartment provide real-time information on water use, heating bills, and elec-

Figure P.3 Overview of the early phases of Dockside Green, in Victoria, British Columbia. Its location near downtown allows residents to get to destinations along a bike path that runs along the Inner Harbor and on a passenger ferry that crosses it. Credit: Courtesy Dockside Green

trical use. The flickering data mesmerize owners, who scamper about, snuffing phantom kilowatts. With familiar devices, such as compact-fluorescent lighting and Energy Star appliances, Dockside Green cuts its energy use by more than 50 percent below Canada's building-code standards.

As the project got under way, Joe Van Belleghem, a partner at Windmill West (Dockside Green's codeveloper, with Vancity, a credit union), got plenty of local attention when he promised to write the city a $1 million check if any of the buildings fell below Platinum-level certification (the highest tier) of the LEED (Leadership in Energy and Environmental Design) green-building rating system. So far, he has not had to pay up. Dockside Green will eventually include twenty-six buildings and be home to about twenty-five hundred people in three neighborhoods. At that scale, the developers were able to afford to build a biomass gasification plant, which accelerates the decomposition of construction-waste wood into a clean-burning biogas that supplies hot water and hydronic heating to the entire development. Van Belleghem collects fees from residents for the heat and hot water he provides, which will largely pay for the plant's construction. By producing its own heating fuel and supplying the excess output to an adjacent hotel, according to architect Peter Busby,

Figure P.4 At Dockside Green, storm runoff and water treated in an on-site sewage plant combine in a naturalized stream that creates an amenity for residents as it keeps polluted water out of Victoria's sparkling Inner Harbor. Credit: Courtesy Dockside Green

Dockside Green makes up for the carbon content of the electricity it needs from the grid to power lights and appliances. That's how it is carbon positive.

Dockside Green goes a step further by helping to reduce auto dependency, which saves more energy and reduces the carbon footprint of everyday activities. Its location links residents to four bus lines, a tiny passenger ferry—cute as a toy—that chugs to various locations around the bay, and the Galloping Goose bike path, which has become a commuting artery. The developer also subsidizes membership in a local car cooperative. "We encourage you to become a member and get in the habit of not using your own car," Van Belleghem says. The developer will pay $25,000 to buy back the parking space built for each unit.[2]

Kroon and Dockside are both pioneering and quotidian. They use advanced but proven technologies. Neither is noticeably an "eco building," ostentatiously showing off solar panels, nor do they demand lifestyle changes (through Dockside makes biking to work easy). Both the building and the community are more appealing and functional than conventional versions.

In the total absence of a coherent American approach to climate change, both Kroon and Dockside Green go deeply green, showing how quickly such strategies are progressing. If you want to achieve carbon neutrality today, even the most efficient designs must augment with solar, wind, biofuel, or hydro-power, and these sources demand special conditions (a breeze, a dammed stream nearby) or a considerable amount of space (solar), and usually cost much more per square foot than conservation measures do (as was the case at Kroon). Indeed, Yale balked at the cost and land area needed to fully meet Kroon's energy needs on-site. (It purchased carbon credits to get to zero.) Had the university chosen to build a district power plant that used renewable fuel, as Dockside Green does, Yale would not have needed to purchase the credits, and it would have reduced the carbon footprint of any building hooked onto the system.

Most buildings and settings cannot yet cost-effectively lower their energy and carbon impact to such a great degree. You begin to see that the barriers are not overwhelming, however. *The Agile City* is about how buildings and communities help the United States rapidly close its yawning green performance gap while making places that work better and realize our dreams.

INTRODUCTION

The Concrete Metropolis in a Dynamic Era

In a very short time the United States has realized that global warming poses real challenges to the nation's future. *The Agile City* engages the fundamental question of what to do about it.

The big talk is of "alternative energy": hydrogen-powered cars and biofuels; clean coal, reinvented nuclear, and elaborate, yet-to-be-perfected means to store huge amounts of carbon while we figure out what to do with it. Advocates hope to plug one or more of these clean technologies into the grid and declare the problem solved. Though appealing, these are speculative technologies that demand enormous investment and that can work only with very large subsidies. They have large environmental effects we ignore at our peril, and they may not even prove viable.

As Kroon Hall and Dockside Green show, we can achieve carbon neutrality today in buildings and communities with efficiency measures that are already proven and with a dollop of renewable energy. We can retrofit our communities to drastically reduce the amount of driving we need to do, and therefore reduce transportation carbon emissions, one of the two largest sources of greenhouse gases in our economy (the other is buildings). Rethinking construction and our communities has additional benefits. The word *agile* appears in this book's title because we must adapt our lives to a world that climate change is altering before our eyes. Clean energy alone is not enough. We face disruptions of weather patterns and agriculture, acidifying seas, storms, floods, and droughts. Given the irreversible warming already set in motion, we'll have to keep changing. In other words, we'll need to develop an urban culture of agility.

1

Unlike high-tech alternative energy technologies, *The Agile City* focuses on reducing emissions *and* coping with climate-change effects.

In much of the global warming debate, energy efficiency is treated almost condescendingly, as something nice to do but of marginal usefulness. *The Agile City* shows that change undertaken at the building and community levels can reach carbon-reduction goals rapidly, perhaps much quicker and at lower cost than shoving the economy into carbon submission with a disruptive range of carbon taxes (then waiting for markets to sort out the problem) or praying that a big-technology silver bullet will save us and avoid our personal inconvenience.

It may be that we must ultimately resort to high-tech alternative energy, nuclear, biofuels, and every conservation measure, as many experts argue. Others say it hardly matters what Americans do if the big and growing emitters—such as China—don't take steps to drastically cut the carbon they pour into the atmosphere. But why shouldn't we exploit the rich potential of conservation as fast as possible? Why should other countries take action in the absence of a serious US commitment? At this writing, the United States is the world laggard, unable to move ahead on commonsense conservation strategies that don't cost much. Comparatively speaking, conservation and adaptation are the low-hanging fruit.

Adapting buildings and communities not only promises rapid progress in reducing America's carbon footprint but also offers numerous other benefits that tax gimmicks and massive alternative-energy investments can't match.

Adapting to the future is as much about changing hidebound attitudes and examining underlying assumptions as it is about technology and policy. *The Agile City* helps the reader identify changes that make large impacts at low costs. We'll be wise to think about habitual development patterns, brain-dead regulatory regimes, and obsolete incentives built in by tax policy. Fixing them can be frustrating: we have to fight political battles about them, steer rigid bureaucracies in new directions, collaborate with those who are used to guarding turf. But the real costs of these kinds of changes are actually small—and the benefits large—not just in terms of the environment but because we'll be tuning communities to realize broader aspirations: to build wealth more responsibly and to make places that are pleasing to live in. Many strategies are low-tech and low cost (such as making bicycles a bigger part of our lives), and others offer handsome paybacks on investment—but only if we confront ingrained habit about what we build and how we pay for it.

Why Buildings?

The structures that we live and work in generate almost 40 percent of greenhouse gas emissions—and buildings tend to use the dirtiest energy: electricity generated from coal.[1] About 35 percent of the nation's assets are invested in real estate and infrastructure, and we're adding up to 2 percent a year to that base. Every square foot built by conventional means is already obsolete—and may have to be remodeled or abandoned in just a few years. Waiting to take action will prove costly.[2] A wide variety of tested tactics exist today to dramatically reduce the impacts of buildings on the environment, from old-fashioned awnings to new ways to light buildings with the sun and ventilate them with breezes. We're just leaving them on the table.

Why Communities?

Rather than devote enormous amounts of time and treasure to build SUVs that get fifty miles per gallon on the way to the discount superstore thirty miles away, *The Agile City* argues that intelligently designing our towns could reduce that trip to a few miles or eliminate it entirely. That's just one way that building (and upgrading) communities can dramatically reduce the land we plow under, the energy we consume, and the aggravation we endure in the course of daily tasks.

Why Buildings and Communities?

Environment-enhancing investments pay back more quickly when building strategies are coordinated with neighborhood layouts and urban networks. For example, a group of buildings can amortize the up-front costs of a shared geothermal well much more quickly than sinking wells for each structure. Thinking about the design of an entire city block at once, rather than one building at a time, means that every room in each building can be flooded with daylight so that few rooms need to rely on electric lights. Or, one structure can shade another from the heat of the afternoon sun. Cities can be remade to cope with the greater frequency of flooding, drought, forest fires, and wildfires, rather than await the enormous costs of catastrophe.

Coping with climate change cannot be compartmentalized when the urban places we share face so many other challenges. Good jobs have involved steadily longer and more congested commutes to affordable neighborhoods. Housing costs rise while communities decline and schools struggle. Fast-growing places deliver more traffic than opportunity. Broadly speaking, *The Agile City* shows how communities can develop the capacity to adapt to circumstance—whatever those circumstances may be. Real progress can be made only if tactics that engage global warming offer collateral benefits, as many do.

If we focus on arranging related urban functions close together, we multiply benefits. Think about locating a hospital not on just any old empty piece of land but close to doctors and labs and aligned to key transit routes. Then many staffers can get to work, patients can get care, and service businesses can access customers without driving. In this way, we reduce traffic, pollution, energy, time wasted, and the need for huge parking lots all at once.

Is Undertaking Large-scale Change Worth It?

We'll shiver under layers of organic-wool sweaters living colorless lives confined to our dimly lit homes, say the skeptics, as we sabotage our economy by struggling to get to jobs in speed-limited biofueled buses. The skeptics have rarely done their homework. On the other hand, advocates often seem to turn every purchasing decision and lifestyle choice into a moral dilemma—for example, paper or plastic, which is worse? If we layer on rules and taxes and command lifestyle choices in a single-minded drive toward carbon neutrality, we could well damage our economy and fuel a backlash instead of an evolution toward sustainability.

We won't recognize the true potential of sustainability by analyzing it in today's narrow economic terms, by describing economic paybacks for energy conservation, for example, solely in terms of electricity costs avoided at current prices. Saving energy does save money, while also reducing greenhouse gases and other kinds of air pollution. It also reduces the strain on electricity-delivery infrastructure. It cuts the amount of energy we must import, thereby reducing the nation's payment imbalance. It presses energy prices downward by freeing supply, and it reduces the power of global-energy oligopolies. Those benefits can be more difficult to calculate but are no less real. It is clear that alternatives—including business as usual—offer far less useful paybacks. *The Agile City* reveals tactics that create such multiplier effects, which means that ecologically driven change can shore up economic opportunity, make more productive workplaces, and help revive neglected communities. These are not Pollyanna blandishments. Being able to look at multiple effects and multiple benefits of political choices and private investments is essential to ensuring wealth and well-being in the future.

A ROADMAP

In part 1, *The Agile City* considers land, our attitudes toward it, and our methods of dividing it up and building on it for human use. Coming to terms with climate change means that people must proactively make choices about what is built where. That's a culture change for Americans, who have long seen land, and what's done with it, as equating freedom. And that has meant that America has passively left the making of cities in the hands of owners and speculators. Communities have already become deeply unhappy about the simplistic choices they seem to face: Accept the increasingly destructive consequences of growth through the heedless accumulation of individual investments? Or, try to recognize community values by entwining development with an increasingly complex, costly, and often ineffective regulatory apparatus?

The Agile City shows how to get beyond those simplistic, lose-lose dualities by engaging America's conflicting but deeply held values relating to the role of private property in society. New ideas about ownership help us come to terms with environmental issues without losing the freedom of action that old ideas were supposed to preserve. Ignoring what the future portends will only make land conflicts wrenchingly difficult to resolve—as they proved to be after the tragedy of Hurricane Katrina, when disaster relief too often meant rebuilding in unsafe places. Concepts of ownership evolved in the past as the United States transformed itself from a small-town agrarian nation to a big-city, industrial powerhouse. We can learn from that history as we renegotiate our relationship to land.

As chapter 2 will show, the needed conversation has already begun. In precious landscapes all over the United States, people are uniting once-warring constituencies as they sensitively integrate human activities into more resilient environments, from played-out ranches in the Rocky Mountain West to eroding coastal beaches everywhere. Barriers aplenty obstruct a future that must value innovation, adaptability, and diverse scales of economic endeavor. But many are cultural and political, not financial or technical.

Communities cannot dynamically adapt to the future if the drivers of wealth and growth are at cross purposes—as they are in America. We may work in a factory or keyboard on a computer, but it is the city itself that is the field of growth and wealth creation. Cities thrive or stagnate by the way real estate is financed, by the way housing subsidies are distributed, by the way transportation is provided, and by the way water is obtained, distributed, and disposed of. Part 2 shows how these "growth machine" forces powerfully and dysfunctionally shape communities, and how this fragmented, unintegrated assortment of stimuli fails.

Growth machine distortions caused suburbia to go viral, creating the megaburb, a new kind of city that only looks suburban but integrates cities, suburbs, and semirural exurbs. (Since all these places are now urban, even if low density, *The Agile City* refers to them as cities.) Megaburbs metastasized on a model of supposedly affordable urban growth that demanded families move to newer communities ever farther out, locking in a land-hungry, energy-intensive lifestyle of vast driving distances between Oz-like suburban downtowns. Though our suburban conurbations may create great wealth and contain many communities that seek to preserve closeness to nature, these politically fragmented landscapes have few tools to act in concert to further their interests. Growth machine forces tend to suburbanize country idylls while sapping denser, otherwise desirable older towns and cities of vitality. Megaburbs, however, may prove more adaptable than we yet know, since they encompass so much space that's wasted or ignored.

After all, global warming is only one reason we need to understand better how our communities get created—why some grow and others stagnate. Many of us find ourselves increasingly ready to move out of cities that seem always headed in the wrong direction: more congested, more expensive, farther from the fields and forests promised by the suburban dream, with too many hours stuck in a car and taxes always rising. American cities today grow and change reactively—and they take mystifying new forms because we haven't taken the future in hand.

Part 3 considers the kinds of places an agile growth machine could create. Homes, workplaces, and public places not only can reduce their impact on the planet but can do so by updating traditional technologies, such as the lowly yet versatile window shutter. Buildings and neighborhoods can evocatively express the uniqueness of their places and climates: harvesting natural sources of sun, daylight, shade, fresh air, and cooling to do what we've spent a couple of generations engineering expensive and complex mechanical systems to do.

As building design and construction rapidly evolves (no man-to-the-moon effort necessary), the United States can transcend its habit of making cities almost entirely as an assemblage of ventures that leave no room for any value other than profit. *The Agile City* is not a call for faith-based greening. Rather than pile on too many do-gooder agendas, it shows how to build well-being and wealth at the same time. Along the way, this generation can pass on its best values, as past generations whose buildings we venerate have, and enrich the places we share rather than simply aggrandize who each of us thinks we are.

Adaptation is an urgent cause in some communities: climate-change effects like flooding and coastal erosion already threaten their survival. Such communities face wrenching choices, but even less vulnerable cities and towns are recognizing that today's diffuse, low-density, one-size-fits-all development model no longer works. Diversifying development patterns—creating a range of densities—is becoming necessary for economic success in a more closely integrated world, and it can go hand in hand with reducing environmental impact. Linking communities at a variety of densities with suitable transportation, for example, diversifies economic potential while reducing dependency on driving. Economic engines, such as universities, medical research centers, and suburban downtowns, already find they need to cluster more, thriving near high-density residential neighborhoods. High-intensity business and residential cores work better when they're walkable, bikable, and well served by transit. Intensifying transportation modes (roads, commuter rail, high-speed rail, and enhanced freight rail) along natural movement corridors will reduce congestion and carbon emissions while linking more people, more businesses, and more customers.

In this way, cities will also create the scale and diversity needed to compete in a global economy of megacities. We'll create incentives to rebuild overlooked swaths of cities and suburbs that have been ignored, rather than mortgage our future on energy-intense communities, built to last only one generation, that are flung into new landscapes that we can no longer afford to maintain. Cities as diverse as Portland (Oregon), Vancouver (British Columbia), and Berlin show how to harvest public consensus and individual leadership to comprehensively nurture adaptive development and urban revitalization—forging a contemporary identity that merges business and citizen commitment.

We'll find more efficiencies by planning our communities at the metropolitan and metro-region scale—matching the scale of economic exchange and environmental potential today. We'll need to rapidly foster innovation and to mainstream winning ideas; for example, the US Green Building Council's LEED (Leadership in Energy and Environmental Design) rating system has already become a widely emulated model for crowd-sourcing innovation at the building and community scale. It's just one way to create agility in the seemingly immutable "permanent" communities we make.

While many states have been creating green-technology incentives, the national political debate has long been locked into false choices. The presumption too often goes unchallenged that carbon taxes or mobility taxes will simply deprive people of income. Properly designed, of course, they will shift incentives and disincentives to encourage investments that are more productive environmentally and economically. That's how we begin to create both an environmental and an economic ethos of dynamism that's entrepreneurial, receptive to the new, and perpetually adaptable. That's what America's supposedly loosely regulated and individualist land ethos is supposed to provide but doesn't, except in landscapes beyond the urban edge that are affordable only because of distortions introduced by the growth machine. But "loose-fit" urban conditions—ample developable property, easy access, and the most minimal regulations necessary—can be, and need to be, created in mature places as well as on empty land. *The Agile City* shows how to create the urban-planning equivalent of open-source computer code. An agile, loose-fit city will deploy regulations straightforwardly, balancing them with incentives. Rules will reward performance (energy, water, and emissions saved) rather than prescribing what lightbulbs we'll use and what cars we'll drive.

The mortgage meltdown that began in 2007 should have brought an end to bubble economics—desperate means to jump-start sluggish economies by bribing consumers (through subsidies and tax gimmicks) to buy more stuff made from artificially cheap resources that are becoming scarcer and more costly as they get exploited beyond recovery, from forests to fisheries, from oil to copper. The Great Recession, the collapse of global natural systems, and the rapidly increasing development of huge nations such as India and China require us to ask where genuinely sustainable wealth and well-being will come from. To a surprising extent, chapter 10 argues, wealth may well flow from green investments. Many green measures offer unique economic values that conventional accounting tends to miss. Few anticipated that cleaning the nation's air and water in the 1970s would restore enormous real estate value to cities, rural places, and coastlines. Skillfully designed green investments often boost well-being while repairing natural systems, which gross domestic product (GDP) fails to measure. Capturing these advantages can make restoring the natural workings of nature vital to the bottom line.

NATURE BITES US BACK

Climate change is the focus of *The Agile City*, but the world's web of natural systems is so tightly interlocked—and the human impact on it now so great—that we can no longer afford to look at any problem as *the* environmental issue of the day. Climate change nests within several major, interrelated environmental challenges, all of which are amenable to a variety of solutions at the level of the urban systems with which we've laced the world. In this book, responding to climate change means responding to these interrelated issues to the extent possible.

An era of hypergrowth that has had profound environmental consequences began when the capitalist world began to draw in the vast territories of Russia, its satellites, and China after the fall of the Iron Curtain of Communism around 1990, later joined by India, Brazil, and others.[3] Every country in the world became more economically entwined with the global economic juggernaut.[4] The developing world will continue to fuel most of the world's growth, as hundreds of millions of Brazilians, Indians, Russians, and Chinese vault from abject poverty into the global middle class, probably joined by such populous nations as Mexico and Indonesia. One estimate predicts that US gross domestic product will triple by 2050, but India will catch up with America and China will generate more than twice America's output.[5]

Is such massive growth even possible? Many environmental advocates, and an increasing number of economists, think not. After all, a better life for billions has more than doubled demands on nature in the past forty-five years.[6] Already this unprecedented consumption burdens global ecologies to a degree unimaginable just a decade or so ago. The environmental triumphs of the past, such as slashing tailpipe emissions and transforming rivers from sewers to swimmable sanctuaries, look small compared to the cleanup tasks in many parts of the world.

Ecosystems over time have often proved resilient to human use, capable of healing. But human actions no longer harm a forest here and there or pollute the air only around big cities. We're altering vast landscapes at a regional and continental scale. In too many places, people have gone too far; we've overstretched the resilience of too many of the biological systems on which we rely.

The world is draining aquifers and pouring mining and industrial waste, pesticides, and fertilizers into rivers, streams, lakes, and bays, which become unsafe to drink, unusable for irrigation, and inhospitable to fish. Rains scour soil from deforested landscapes and played-out farms, degrading water quality and amplifying floods. As the process continues, it becomes much more difficult to restore either soils or waterways to productive use. Global warming may only exacerbate these processes. Low-lying parts of the world, for example, fear the loss of freshwater sources to saltwater infiltration as sea levels rise.[7]

Around the globe, people breathe killer air, wallow in their own waste, and can't obtain clean water. Food crops won't grow because the land is ruined and there is no water. And yet we rarely admit to these costs. Economists call them "externalities," aptly underlining the fact that we don't figure them into what we pay for goods and services.

This overview does not engage the enormous demands that global growth will place on nonrenewable resources, from oil and natural gas to the huge assortment of minerals that high-tech industry demands. It is difficult to estimate whether the world has indeed entered the claimed "peak oil" era because both private companies and energy-exporting nations tend to keep such data secret. And for most commodities, the size of the resource is elastic, dependent on how much is recycled, how fast technology comes on line, and how much consumers are willing to pay for extraction and refinement.[8] In the past few years, for example, America's claimed natural gas reserves have risen enormously not because of new discoveries but because new technologies and higher prices make exploitation of existing reserves financially viable. As the Deepwater Horizon disaster of 2010 reminded us, these new techniques come at greater risk to the environment—risks we plan for and account for too infrequently.

Ecologists have begun to see feedback loops: human actions that hasten environmental decline, which hastens the decline of natural resources we can't live without.[9] Discrete effects, such as air or water pollution, now interact with other environmental effects to feed a self-reinforcing cycle of environmental destruction that threatens us, as global warming does, with its diverse effects: from killing coral in the tropics to unleashing the devastating spruce budworm in northern forests.[10]

I am indebted to Michael Gallis, an urban strategist and city planner based in Charlotte, North Carolina, for connecting globalization, intensifying resource use, and its environmental consequences, which he dubs "Codevolution."[11]

Americans—and most of those who live in the developed world—are for now isolated from the most severe of these effects. By reducing pollution, preserving valued landscapes, and saving endangered species, the United States blunts the rapid environmental decline that does so much harm around the globe.[12] That does not mean that wealthy nations escape the consequences, however. Habitat losses and strained agriculture worldwide affect what wood we can buy, what foods we can import, and what we pay for these items. If we don't address ecosystem decline, the consequences will only restrict our options more as time goes on. We're also competing for nature's ability to support our needs, called *biocapacity*, along with everyone else.[13]

Are these vast challenges a recipe for fatalism or inaction? After all, how can we respond when so many threats come at us from all sides? We can no longer afford to consider our collective actions, which Gallis calls the human network, apart from their effect on natural systems. Growth and well-being will increasingly depend on restoring and creating resilience in nature rather than heedlessly exploiting it. This is not ecological altruism but a recognition that Co-devolutionary effects will only loom larger, cutting into economic growth, spurring resource-scarcity battles, exacting an ever higher price in ways we can't anticipate.

"We have long pretended that natural resources are cheap," explains Gallis. That has led to what he calls "low efficiency" use of those once abundant resources, with corresponding "high impact" on the natural environment. Scarcity economies have quickly developed for water, fish, many kinds of woods, and some agricultural products, Gallis argues, "because we've failed to recognize that we must reverse the equation. Our economy must build on the high-efficiency use of limited, increasingly expensive resources. Our actions must rebuild natural systems, if for no other reason than that we need those systems to keep producing resources for us."[14] Gallis was asked, how do you expect people, even those most devoted to doing good, to forgo their own interests in favor of the environment? The degree to which Co-devolution is damaging our economy and constricting our choices, Gallis responded, is forcing us to do good for the environment as we do well for ourselves.

Although *The Agile City* focuses overwhelmingly on climate change, I consider the issues it raises in these terms of what Gallis calls Co-Evolution: human-network actions that can systematically restore natural systems to health and resiliency.

The Agile City approaches these extraordinary challenges through an appeal to the heart and the head. Even though too many Americans struggle just to make ends meet, we rely on our hearts to set the nation's course to the future based on what kind of people we choose to be and what kind of legacy we want to leave behind for our children. So you'll find a deep look into our values and our culture; the book is not arguing on the basis of statistics alone. Still, we need to know how much we spend, how serious problems are, and whether solutions are scaled to solve the problems at hand, and I provide the most accurate figures I can find. Another reason the book does not barrage you with statistics is that too many are inaccurate either because the data is lacking (the United States does a poor job of collecting information on urban performance) or because a great number of assumptions that underlie the numbers add too much uncertainty, and partisans of one position or another often don't disclose key assumptions. (In speaking of urban performance, for example, it makes a difference whether people talk about New York as politically defined—population some eight million—or the New York City metropolitan area—population perhaps fifteen million, depending on how you count.) Lastly, the best news: green techniques and technologies are moving forward very quickly, in spite of a hostile economic and policy environment. So I've avoided setting out technologies we must adopt or goals (in terms of kilowatt hours or any other measures) that we should deem essential, because all of it is changing very rapidly.[15]

The challenges may be global, but *The Agile City* focuses primarily on the United States, where our cities can and must adapt at a scale and speed that is unprecedented. It is not the overwhelming task it might seem. The book helps readers take charge of their community's future by understanding the processes that make communities dynamic and adaptable. The future seems so challenging only because we've allowed our adaptive skills to atrophy. We've accepted the idea that communities grow, mature, stagnate, and decline by economic forces as immutable as the tides. In fact, most of the mechanisms that drive development and building design are artificial inventions of government and finance—unique to America, if not particularly well suited to what America has become. To the extent that they have a purpose (and are not simply habitual), they continue a simplistic, obsolete, one-size-fits-all method of city-making that is neither agile nor very adaptable.

Our collective job is not to assume a defensive crouch but to open our minds to possibilities, the many that are out there already and the multitude we need to encourage people to think up.

PART 1

The Land

1

CLIMATE CHANGE IN THE LANDSCAPES OF SPECULATION

On a visit to a traditional stepped-gable North Sea town in Holland's Delftlands called Scheveningen, I climbed with a group over a broad grassy dune that looked like the back of a four-story-high humped sea creature. A beach, among the widest I had ever seen, stretched out before us. We were being shown not works of nature but works of civil engineering. This massive dune and beach were created to shield the village from North Sea storms of growing violence. The Dutch are good at this sort of thing, having been forced to keep the sea out of their low-lying landscape for hundreds of years.[1]

The super dune and beach were an example of how seriously the Dutch take global warming effects, which they are already feeling, not just on the coast but in rainwater that fills drainage systems and in larger and more prolonged river flooding. (The Rhine River and many of its tributaries drain much of Europe through Holland.) The issue is especially urgent as much of the country is below sea level and weather changes threaten to overwhelm already elaborate protections.

I tried to imagine such beach fortification along low-lying American coasts. Would residents agree to hunker behind such a massive ridge of sand, one that would deprive them of their view and easy access? Who would pay the tens of millions of dollars per mile? (Similar protections were considered by America's dam and levee builders, the US Army Corps of Engineers, for the Katrina-battered coast of Mississippi, but they never gained favor.)

The Netherlands does what America can't yet do because its cultural and legal approach to land is profoundly different from America's. This is why a book about communities becomes a book about land. Cities do not happen without citizens making choices about how to divide and parcel land, and about what can get built where.

US senator Mary Landrieu is determined to bring the Dutch approach to flood protection, and its technical prowess, to America. She led the delegation that scaled the Scheveningen dune so that Lisa Jackson, head of the US Environmental Protection Agency and representatives of the Army Corps could see what was possible. Landrieu had become a convert to the Dutch approach as she looked for means to protect and restore the coastline of nineteen fast-eroding Louisiana parishes—about one-third of the state she represents. Coastal marshes that nurture fisheries and protect low-lying towns and cities have been shrinking alarmingly since well before Katrina (1,900 square miles lost since the 1930s[2]), but the storm dramatically weakened coastal defenses. She had a plan, but it could cost $50 billion and was going nowhere in Congress. The Netherlands, with a population the size of Florida's, commits between 5 billion and 7 billion euros annually to water management (which equals up to $9 billion). By contrast, "I can't even find a couple of hundred million," said Landrieu on the tour. "I'm pushing to the point where I'm aggravating people in Congress. But they need to understand how much we need to do." With hurricane season approaching as we spoke, she added, "people are living in abject fear."

No hurricane pummeled Louisiana that summer, but the fate of two flat, grassy lots on the ocean near Charleston, South Carolina, show what Senator Landrieu's campaign was up against—and it wasn't just the money.

WHOSE PROPERTY RIGHTS?

David Lucas, a developer, expected to build and sell oceanfront homes on two lots, homes much like those all up and down the beach in the Wild Dunes development on the idyllic-sounding Isle of Palms. Lucas had not reckoned with South Carolina's Beachfront Management Act, which prohibited building on the lots because the shoreline was unstable.[3] Houses so close to the ocean were also at risk for destruction by the high winds and storm-surge waves of hurricanes.

Lucas took the state to court, arguing that the act created what in legal terms is called a "taking" by the government, because it deprived his land of its value. The Constitution's Fifth Amendment requires the government to pay compensation to landowners if it takes private property for public use. Though the clause is intended to assure owners compensation in the case of outright appropriation of land (condemnation for use as a highway, for example), Lucas's attorneys argued that the Beachfront Management Act constituted a *regulatory* taking, in which the government needed to compensate Lucas because the law caused his property to lose value. When you consider that his lots were surrounded by lots already developed, it is easy to sympathize. The law seemed to single him out.

The state's law, however, was designed to prevent well-documented perils of heedless coastal development. Up and down the East Coast, the federal government had been throwing billions of dollars into projects that dumped dredged sand on beaches to protect properties, most of them owned by affluent people. At times, millions of dollars have been spent rebuilding a beach that washed away in a single season.

Lucas's case went to the US Supreme Court, which stopped short of ruling that he had suffered a taking but ordered the state to take another look at his claim. South Carolina got the message and eventually allowed Lucas to build. It and other states have either loosened shoreline regulations or quietly stopped enforcing them. The Lucas case did not prove to be the landmark that property rights activists had hoped it would be; subsequent decisions by the Supreme Court, if anything, have further muddled the question of just what the government "owes" landowners when a regulation limits their development options.

In the meantime, hurricanes validated the regulations. In 1992, Hurricane Andrew, in Florida, wrought more than four times as much damage as Hugo, just a few years earlier. In 2004, Hurricanes Ivan and Frances slammed both the Atlantic and Gulf Coasts of Florida, killing 108 and leaving $50 billion in wreckage.[4] The year 2005 brought Wilma and Rita, but they have been all but forgotten because Hurricane Katrina, moving slowly and deliberately, flattened most of the Mississippi coast and relentlessly probed New Orleans's levees until it found vulnerabilities. It was the first hurricane to bring a major American city to its knees.

The rush to build in harm's way may seem senseless, but it goes on even as the effects of climate change—higher floodwaters, more severe storms—raise well-known risks higher. In the Lucas decision, Justice Antonin Scalia was skeptical of South Carolina's reasons for protecting the shoreline (and, of course, the property abutting it) and proposed that the state may have deprived Lucas of the entire value of his land in pursuit of mainly esthetic objectives. The Lucas decision meant a great deal to many people because it struck a blow for individualism, freedom from intrusion by government, and the entrepreneurial spirit. Yet those sentiments neither restore storm-ravaged communities nor make whole those who have lost houses to ubiquitously relentless beach erosion.

Agility, in urban terms, will mean that we can't mount the property owners' desires on a pedestal untouchable by wider community concerns. We will have to act in concert in all kinds of ways. We can't be mindlessly coercive; nor must everyone cede power over their lives to a central authority. But slowing climate change and dealing with its effects will challenge us to rethink our values and ask ourselves how we meet the challenges of the future in a way that retains what's truly fundamental to each of us.

Senator Landrieu has bought into a level of spending on flood control America has not attempted, but she has also embraced a Dutch culture of land use in which, comparatively, the desires of the individual landowner count for little. Over hundreds of years, Holland could never have kept the sea out, nor diked and drained vast tracts to build new land, if they had to do it one farmer and land parcel at a time. They needed to do it on a bigger scale and cooperatively. The result has been to create a culture of consensus, where the overarching need to keep everyone dry, through the power of government, takes precedence over the desires of the individual.

This small nation can afford to so elaborately protect Scheveningen because it is a town that government has shaped into compact form to efficiently use the land so laboriously reclaimed. The town does not string along the beach for miles, in the pattern of American shorefront development. The super dune wraps the oceanfront and sides of the village, yet it is in total less than about a mile in length.

It is unlikely that Louisiana and the United States will adopt the Dutch model wholesale. But we will have to learn from the Dutch and others, simply because the future will require us to renegotiate not only our rules and spending priorities but also our values and culture of land use—and these run deep.

URBAN REALITY TRUMPS AGRARIAN VISION

The United States became a nation of individual landowners as an alternative to hierarchical organizations of church and aristocracy in Europe that restricted political participation to the powerful few owners of land and kept the vast majority of people in some form of indentured servitude. In an overwhelmingly agricultural America, founding fathers James Madison and Thomas Jefferson could plausibly regard land itself as wealth, and therefore the key to each American's independence. As Joseph Ellis, a historian of the era, puts it, the Revolution's "core principal" of individual liberty, which "views any subordination of personal freedom to governmental discipline as dangerous," came into conflict with what developed in the Constitution's ratification debate "as the sensible surrender of personal, state, and sectional interests to the larger purposes of nationhood."[5]

The agrarian-centered vision conflicted with Alexander Hamilton's view that a powerful, centralized state was necessary to survive in a world that even then featured growing cities, global powers, emerging large-scale industry, and an international banking system that could exert great power from across oceans over an economically weak and fragmented young nation. His Federalist vision didn't resonate, writes Ellis: "At the nub of the argument the colonist had used to discredit the authority of Parliament and the British monarchy was a profound distrust of any central authority that issued directives from a great distance."

The Hamiltonian views and the Jeffersonian views were left unresolved by the founding fathers, argues Ellis: "Both sides speak for the deepest impulses of the American revolution." Yet Jefferson's bucolic vision of the landowning agricultural America won people's hearts (figure 1.1). Hamilton's more pragmatic outlook anticipated the enormous growth and concentration of financial power that occurred over ensuing decades and the parallel rise of cities of unimagined size as centers of wealth creation. The city sophisticate fleecing the honest yeoman has long been a staple of American literature—cementing in people's minds a perpetual suspicion of cities and city "slickers."

Madison—and to an even greater extent, Jefferson—famously thought economic success lay in getting government out of the way to allow natural economic laws of growth to proceed. This sentiment has largely governed the American attitude toward land use ever since. The idea that government should not actively organize, promote, and control land use and development, however, is almost unique in the world.[6]

The Jeffersonian reluctance to constrict owners in their use of land remains deep-seated in the American consciousness even as our society and economy have transformed themselves well beyond any state imaginable by the founding generation. As the nation grew and moved from its agrarian roots to become a "Hamiltonian" industrialized powerhouse with an increasingly urban and fi-

Figure 1.1 Monticello, the home of Thomas Jefferson, in Charlottesville, Virginia. Jefferson lived away from America's early cities and built his house to face the seemingly endless wildness of nature, reflecting his belief that a nation of landowning farmers would truly be free. Credit: James S. Russell

nance-dependent economy, an individualist ethos alone would guide the way land was turned to urban use.

It's a model of growth that got established early. William Penn laid out Philadelphia in 1681 with the idealistic vision that the chaotic, disease-ridden city of the Old World could be supplanted by a rationally organized, spacious, and green city carved out of the New World's wilderness. He drew tree-lined, generously scaled blocks, lined with large houses entwined by gardens. Green public squares interrupted the grid of streets. It was beautiful—and doomed. Speculators quickly drove narrow alleys through the spacious blocks and filled the back gardens with fetid tenements.

The making of cities through speculation has been the story of American growth ever since. The approach is taken for granted to such an extent that it's hard to imagine any other way of doing things, though, in fact, growth through privatized land development is a relatively recent phenomenon in the history of cities. (Historically, religions and empires, both political and mercantile, had largely guided city growth.) Funded by ever more sophisticated private finance and energized by the great wealth generated by the Industrial Revolution, colonial villages became fast-growing privatized cities, such as New York and Philadelphia. They made good on the promise of opportunity that was at the root of the American idea, and they rewarded hard work, even though they were also degrading, criminal, immoral, and exploitative. While the dream of America drew millions from the crushing serfdoms of Europe, the vast majority ended up not on the character-building farms or installed amid pure wilderness but in the cities, with their opportunities, exploitations, and temptations.

A primacy of landowners' rights governed even as villages became metropo - lises and a farm might suddenly find a smoke-belching, mile-long steel plant as its neighbor. With the growth of industry and the gathering of people in cities, land became less a source of personal sustenance and more a potential source of monetary wealth. Privatism remains the reigning American city-making model: we try to accommodate any entrepreneur anywhere.[7] Our Jeffersonian reluctance to tell landowners what they can do works well—until we hear of plans to run a new beltway past our backyard. Then we take to the streets and airwaves.

Speculators act; the rest of us react. It's a clumsy and often growth-strangling way to reconcile the diverse values we hold as both citizens and owners. In an era that must respond to unprecedented environmental challenges, it's not good enough.

In January 2006, I visited New Orleans, ravaged four months earlier by Hurricane Katrina. In small sections of the city, contractors clogged the streets with pickups and piles of new siding and roofing, but it was hard to see the old city springing to life. At that time, I toured the worst areas with local architect Allen Eskew, who was in favor of what was then called a "shrinking footprint" to rebuild New Orleans. That was post-Katrina lingo for consolidating rebuilding effort in areas that are the highest above sea level.[8]

At the time of my visit, about eighty thousand residents had come back to the city, about one-sixth of the prehurricane population. A Rand Corporation study thought that only about half the population would return.[9] "We can't maintain our old infrastructure with such a diminished population and such limited resources," Eskew observed as we drove around the city. The "shrinking footprint" idea was first proposed by the Urban Land Institute think tank. When planners published maps suggesting that immediate reinvestment be funneled to high-ground areas, people noticed that the left-behind tracts, whether in poor Central City and the Lower Ninth Ward or in affluent eastern New Orleans, were predominantly black.[10]

Rebuilding in risk-prone areas may defy rationality, but returning to the same house on the same lot, in the same street and neighborhood, was almost a primordial desire for many New Orleans residents. Rebuilding on high ground seemed a rational position when the Army Corps could not guarantee flood resistance if a Category 5 storm hit the city (Katrina was a slow-moving Category 3). As residents of the very lowest swaths of the city stared at the muddy waterlines left behind by the flood, they asked themselves who would buy their property. How would they move? What kind of place would the city be without the old streets, and the seemingly unchanging neighborhoods lined with modest houses of curlicue carpentry and colorful paint?

What if people didn't want to move? Would the government force them out of their homes and into some neighborhood they might not want to be in? Must they accept whatever money the government offered and see their houses and streets bulldozed for parks or drainage canals? The planners had not even begun to engage those questions before the idea of "shrinking the city's footprint" was abandoned, made poisonous by the city's long history of decision making by and for whites and the powerful.

Desperate to get back into their own homes and rebuild their lives, New Orleanians were not ready for a drastically different way of thinking about land, about ownership, about a dramatically reconfigured city, and about a wholly different role for government in the city's restoration. If the city did not find a way to rebuild in a more compact form, some experts warned, New Orleans would be pocked with "jack 'o lantern" blocks, where only one or two fixed-up houses would sit lonely in the midst of weed-strangled blocks.

By Katrina's fifth anniversary, many more people had returned than Rand had predicted, about 355,000. That's still 100,000 fewer than pre-Katrina numbers, and many of those jack 'o lantern streets can now be found.[11] With the city's budget stretched beyond the breaking point, New Orleanians, in numerous conversations with me in 2010, talked of the need to physically consolidate more neighborhoods to kindle greater revitalization. But no one yet knew how to make that happen.

CONSEQUENCES OF A TRANSACTIONAL LANDSCAPE

Though Katrina placed disaster-rebuilding dilemmas in huge and frightening light, it is comforting to think that such a disaster could happen in the United

States only once every two or three generations. But climate change and other environmental challenges may raise the same questions more often, perhaps in slower motion, and over even larger vulnerable landscapes.

Land development and construction are usually thought of as little more than economic transactions, but they have unique consequences for a community. If a business fails, its assets can be transferred to creditors and its employees can find new jobs. Although a wrenching process, the damage rarely lasts. The consequences of a building, far more often than not, are permanent: the rusting hulks of abandoned factories that blight vast tracts of midwestern cities and ooze pollutants into rivers for decades after they have been shuttered; the big-box discounter that floods local streets with traffic then later lies abandoned behind a vast empty parking lot.

Citymaking through speculative development offers an important efficiency: developers succeed when they give people what they want. On the other hand, consigning the urban future entirely to the vagaries of the real estate market has its limitations. Communities rise up when the rules of the market fail to encourage forms of development that residents find compatible. The market is not driven to help cities create long-term value. The failures, excesses, and insults on the landscape of wrong-headed or simply outdated speculative development are visible everywhere and have long been decried: the unsanitary tenements of the nineteenth century that crammed families into buildings deprived of sunlight and fresh air; the jury-rigged, opportunistic industrial districts of the early twentieth century that belched lung-scorching smoke into the air and poured offal into once-pristine rivers; the fast-food polyps that metastasize then die along the eight-lane arterials of modern suburbia.

A building, even if shoddily made for short-term gain, almost invariably alters the landscape forever. Americans have long tolerated the notion that corporate goals or common accounting practice may generate a useful life of only a few years. But should we continue to accept the making of throwaway places, when these private decisions have such profound public consequences?

HOW ATTITUDES TOWARD LAND EVOLVE

The way Americans think about land and property rights can seem immutable, but attitudes have changed with the times. Just as America has made a tenuous peace between Jeffersonian and Hamiltonian visions of the nation, conflicts between the rights of individual landowners and the larger public welfare have frequently landed in court. Old questions are becoming new again in a climate-change era that calls on us not only to do less harm to the environment but to restore natural functions on local, regional, and ecosystem scales.

An owner's cash-gushing strip shopping center is her neighbor's value-depriving eyesore. This truism is a simplistic way of illustrating the conflicts endemic to land use, which are as old as jurisprudence. Does ownership of the quarter acre my tract house sits on extend "upward, even to heaven," as Sir Edward Coke put it more than 350 years ago?[12] Or can your high-rise hotel block light to the pool deck of my low-rise one? Can a coal company drill a mine underneath my house even if it causes my house to subside? Am I to be denied the proceeds of the tannery I want to erect even if the smell stings my neighbors' eyes and the offal pollutes the river we share?[13] A nation that at its founding equated landownership with freedom would predictably be vexed in sorting out whose interests should prevail.

An enormous percentage of American land-use disputes center on a debate that was first philosophically engaged in England in the decades preceding the founding of the United States. Jeremy Bentham argued that the welfare of the community must take precedence over individual concerns. Adam Smith felt that the social interest was best served through individual enterprise. It was Smith's view that prevailed when the nation was young.[14] It is most powerfully embodied in the clause of the Fifth Amendment cited by Lucas when he made his "taking" claim.

But the special status that was accorded to private ownership of land evolved as technological advances and the ever-larger scale of economic systems conferred on landowners and developers enormous power to change the landscape—and to create conflicts with neighbors.

As early as 1851, Chief Justice Lemuel Shaw articulated the notion that the free use of land by owners did not include the unlimited right to create nuisances for others.[15] When the Constitution was written, however, it was not conceivable that an oil refinery might pop up next to your nice subdivision. Not surprisingly, in balancing public and private interests, courts saw the stakes rising as pristine rivers became sewers, thanks to urbanization, and the air over vast areas was befouled, thanks to industrial processes.

Over decades, the courts increasingly sided with the government's use of its "police power" (the power to regulate). It seemed obvious that landowners' activities that physically or literally injured neighbors (creating a "nuisance") could be regulated. But judges also began to permit regulation of activity that injured or impaired only the economic use or value of others' land. It was not always an easy call to make: does a junkyard so reduce a neighbor's land value as to constitute a nuisance, calling for interference by government? As land's transactional value in a capitalist economy trumped its colonial role as a bulwark against serfdom, courts increasingly said yes.

In the twentieth century, courts legitimized an increasing array of regulations as long as they furthered "public welfare"—which gave the government yet more power over landowners. Yet this narrowing of landowner rights has been essential to economic growth and to resolving knotty issues presented by the vast scale and power of modern economic endeavor.

On the one hand, the idea that government could regulate in the welfare interests of all the public allowed officials to prohibit houses of prostitution and other uses that were thought to imperil the public's morals. On the other, it gave a legal basis to zoning, which represented a vast expansion of the government's power to restrict what landowners could do, to the point of telling them how large a building could be erected on a site and what kinds of uses it could house. America's earliest zoning ordinance, the one enacted in New York City in 1916, even dictated the shape of buildings to ensure daylight for all, giving the city's high-rise core a wedding-cake profile—a zigzag skyline that still says "New York" to people the world over.

One reason that a wide swath of the public welcomed an ever more complex range of regulations was that many rules (such as separating noxious industry from genteel residential neighborhoods) had the effect of maintaining or improving the property values of many while aggrieving only a few. Tensions remained between those who benefited from the Benthamesque "public welfare" regulators, while others wished to return to a purer Adam Smith/Jeffersonian idea that government should get out of the way.

Neither view has definitively prevailed. We're taught to think that one's house is one's castle—not to be violated by neighbors or unwarranted government intrusion. But the border between our homes and the outside world is far more pervious today than the image of moat and high walls suggests. You can't pull up the drawbridge when you rely on utilities and roads, school systems, and shopping for the vital needs of everyday life.

We live in a nation that commonly regards ownership as a pure and essential state, with a substantial bundle of rights that goes along with it. Because those rights are so powerful, the only way a community can control its destiny is to push back with an equally powerful and intrusive pile of regulations. One environmental rule may demand that you maintain natural shrubs and trees because they shelter a threatened species of bird. Another may require you to remove the beautiful specimen trees that shade your house because they provide fuel for wildfires. Some people voluntarily agree to even more constraints by signing deed restrictions in planned communities. These demand that residents hew to preselected architectural styles should they choose to remodel.

Today, in other words, your home is your castle as long as its tower does not extend above the thirty-foot height limit, the color and form of its crenellations are consistent with community-design standards, and you do not intend to park an RV on the drawbridge. Property-rights activists, who are motivated by passion, emotion, and righteousness as much as by sober legal analysis, want to hack back that thicket of land-use regulations to restore the owner's exercise of free will in the use and development of land. But such absolutism, while perhaps delivering a win here or there, is ultimately doomed when our urban lives are so intimately entangled—as Oregonians learned in a pair of ballot battles over the state's strict division between urban and rural.

OREGON DRAWS A LINE IN THE SAND

On a characteristically misty Pacific Northwest day, I cruised some streets in Hillsboro, a suburb west of Portland, where new town houses huddled cheek by jowl on one side while farm fields stretched into the tree-studded, gently rolling distance on the other. In the normal American scheme of things, the next subdivision might have plowed up the peaceful fields. But that has not been possible at the edge of Hillsboro. In Oregon, you'll rarely find the isolated rural subdivisions, golf communities, farmettes, and highway-hugging outlet malls that pock the exurban outskirts of metropolitan areas.

That's because Oregon has had a land-use regime since 1973 that strictly bounds cities, preserving close-in farmlands and forests by drawing urban growth boundaries around every city, town, and forest hamlet, which forces developers to look for opportunity in leftover urban and suburban tracts inside the line rather than bulldozing a rural farm field and hoping a beltway comes along to connect it to everything else (figure 1.2).[16]

In a global warming era, Oregon's strict division between urban and natural realms is attracting attention. In environmental terms, the contained urban bor-

Figure 1.2 Oregon's urban growth boundary draws a clear line between urban, suburban, and town growth zones and agricultural and forestry zones, which permit very little urban-style development. Credit: © Alex Maclean/Landslides

ders mean less disruption of natural systems by development, fewer roads, more efficient use of infrastructure investments, and urban areas dense enough to efficiently support transit. In spite of the ubiquitous misty rains, Portland has become the capital of cycling obsession. In the future, a more compact form for cities would mean fewer linear feet of riverfront and beachfront that require protection from flooding and erosion, and more flexibility to address those that need protection. More forest acres would store carbon, and fewer forest developments would require government protection from fires. More acres of intact natural environment are innately more resilient to the forces of change than are areas fragmented by diffused urban development.

Earlier than in most places, Portland investors figured out that not everyone likes to live in subdivisions, and so its downtown is famously lively while its older neighborhoods and suburbs don't suffer as much of the creeping stagnation that afflicts older neighborhoods in cities such as Phoenix or Houston—places where it's easier to move on than to reinvest, and where you see patches of worn housing or strip development alternating with swaths of weed-grown land unlikely to attract investors. The urban growth boundary is a tool that works at a scale big enough to make a real difference. A recent Brookings Institute report put Portland's carbon footprint at the third lowest in the nation, smaller than Seattle's and San Francisco's, which share such local carbon-saving qualities as a mild climate and reliance on hydropower.[17]

The division between urban and rural enjoys wide support and has created palpable benefits. But it has also attracted vociferous opposition precisely because Oregonians did something almost unique in America: they took their land-use future into their own hands.

The abrupt edge between urban and rural drives some people crazy. After all, land values on the urban side of the growth boundary, where you might be able to build upward of a half dozen houses every acre, may be many times those on the rural side, where sometimes only one house is permitted per eighty acres. Such disparities in value, determined by government fiat, seem unfair and arbitrary to some, especially to property-rights activists, who have fought unsuccessfully to overturn Oregon's urban/rural divide since it was enacted.

In 2004, this simmering anger found its voice in Dorothy English, a ninety-two-year-old woman who hoped to subdivide some property northwest of Portland so that her grandchildren could live next door. She was tantalizingly near the edge of the growth boundary, but because she fell outside it, her application was denied. In TV ads, she urged support of Ballot Measure 37, which would require the state to waive property regulations that caused a loss in value—or else to compensate her for that loss. Few could resist the hardworking grandmother who was not, after all, seeking to build a retirement city in precious wilderness. Measure 37 passed overwhelmingly.

The goal of Measure 37, and other property-rights legislation that has found its way onto ballots in dozens of states, was to broaden the reach of the "takings" clause of the Fifth Amendment. The argument, as in the Lucas oceanfront lots case, was that regulations could be considered a government seizure of private land as surely as condemnation and forced purchase would be. Measure 37, sold to the electorate as releasing owners from regulatory inflexibility, substituted a different kind of arbitrariness. Owners were able to make claims for compensation according to whether their land had been zoned for urban development when they bought it. "A lot of land, some of which I'm farming, could be developed into two-acre or five-acre housing tracts—anything allowed prior to 1973," explained David Vanasche, a farmer I visited whose neatly trimmed grass-seed fields, just a short distance from Hillsboro's high-tech office parks,

Figure 1.3 Had Oregon ballot measure 37 gone forward, the land to the right of the street sign, long protected farmland, could have been rezoned for homes, while the land to the left would have remained protected. Credit: James S. Russell

are part of a farming zone that seems to stretch on infinitely. "That will make it very difficult to farm here." He pointed out a barely visible furrow that marked the line between his property and the otherwise identical parcel his neighbor farmed (figure 1.3). Vanasche's neighbor filed a claim asking for compensation or a waiver. He had owned the property long enough that rules permitting a house per acre had once applied.[18] The ultimate result of Measure 37 would have been to pock one of America's most productive agricultural landscapes with blobs and striplets of houses, dictated solely by the rules that had applied when the land was purchased.

More than seventy-five hundred claims were eventually filed statewide, many for tracts covering tens of thousands of acres.[19] Nor did everyone understand what undoing regulations freed property owners to do: one claim demanded a waiver to dig a pumice mine that would deface the Newberry Crater National Monument.[20]

The contradictions built into Measure 37 went little discussed in Oregon prior to passage. With the "remedies" for aggrieved property owners of either compensation for their "losses" or waiving the regulatory restrictions that applied, officials universally opted for waivers. Claims climbed to an estimated $20 *billion*, but the cost to localities of assessing, litigating, and making the payments was also prohibitive.[21] Of course, the loss of value, which in many cases would have to be calculated across decades, was purely guesswork. Faced with the law's fiscal consequences and vast impact on forests and farmland, the legislature crafted Measure 49, which made the 1973 development restrictions slightly less strict. Measure 49 passed as overwhelmingly as Measure 37 had.

Measure 37 should have been seen as nonsensical, but reconciling private interests and public welfare in terms of land has vexed the nation since its founding. Understanding what's at stake in this long-running debate is key to dynamically adapting to an unpredictable urban future. Property-rights expert Harvey M. Jacobs, a University of Wisconsin-Madison professor, succinctly explained the roots of this conflict in a presentation at the Lincoln Institute of Land Policy, in Cambridge, Massachusetts.[22] He cited James Madison as an early advocate for a unique status for private property in American laws and culture: "Government is instituted no less for the protection of property than of the persons of individuals." Jacobs set that view against Benjamin Franklin's demurral: "Private property is a creature of society, and is subject to the calls of the society whenever its necessities require it, even to the last farthing." The founders tilted toward Franklin by omission: the Constitution promises "life, liberty and the pursuit of happiness," not "life, liberty and property," as Thomas Jefferson preferred.

Elevating the status of property as akin to life and liberty wasn't unreasonable when land was about the only way to create and preserve wealth. But as cities grew, land values increasingly depended on such external factors as access to infrastructure and proximity to customers, and that meant that the needs of all would inevitably come into more frequent conflict with the desires of individual owners. A piece of farmland may increase ten times or one hundred times in value when it fronts a brand-new freeway interchange. If some landowners are entitled to such a benefit, aren't all landowners? Litigation erupts when government decides not to extend water and sewer services to rural tracts. (You need water and sewer to achieve urban densities and, hence, land values.) The owner feels entitled to the services others enjoy. By contrast, the larger public interest may be served by controlling urban growth and by reducing the cost to taxpayers of forcing the expansion of roads and sewers at the whim of speculators. In some cases, developers have persuaded courts to require towns to extend urban services, in effect coercing taxpayers to subsidize urban growth that may harm their interests, to put money in an owner's pocket.[23]

In such a confusing mélange of public and private interests, the idea of landownership as the individual's bulwark against the incursion of government seems quaint indeed. We blur the line between private and public ownership rights all the time, making legal agreements that place owners in partnership with government, and giving up some rights to gain a government-approved advantage, such as taking payment for granting an easement that allows a utility company to string power lines across our tract. We accept a payment to transfer the right to build subdivisions from our valued farm onto another piece of property that offers a more conducive setting for development. We accept zoning restrictions that do not allow us to cover all of our lot with a revenue-generating building. A community may want to protect historic structures or maintain key wild habitat, so it permits an owner to develop another portion of a site to a higher intensity in compensation for permitting protection of the resource the community values.

Though the property-rights absolutists would like to return to what they view as the Constitution's first principals, there's nothing wrong with all the ways we've altered notions of ownership. We realize ourselves, pursue our interests, and create wealth in this way.

Dozens of court cases have failed to draw a clear line between public and private interests in landownership; nor has Oregon's civics lesson in property rights, waged over years through costly election campaigns and lawsuits, done so. Said Jacobs in a later interview about the state's ballot issues: "The property-rights movement was quite successful at getting out its message, which was to focus on the point at which the government asks too much of the individual in terms of regulations." As for rules aimed at cutting carbon emissions: "There is tremendous potential for fundamental conflict between what appears to be necessary for the greater good of neighborhoods, cities, and regions and what individuals think of as their property rights and the protections the constitution affords them."[24]

Oregon's aggressive goals for carbon emissions were not prominent in the debates on Measures 37 or 49, but the same battles may be rejoined. "Land-use planning plays an important role in reaching the greenhouse-gas-reduction goals the state has set," Eric Stachon, communication director of the environmental group 1,000 Friends of Oregon, told me at the time.[25] Property-rights activists promise to push back.[26] These deeply held views cannot be idly dismissed as we seek solutions to problems that must transcend property lines. On the other hand, neither history nor the courts supports an uncritical deference to the primacy of ownership rights.

The demonizing of regulation has created widespread sympathy for property rights. But communities react—slapping a regulation on something they don't like—because they do not take the making of communities into their own hands. We let speculators do it, then try and contain their worst excesses, which makes rule making rampant. The trouble with trying to control our urban destiny almost entirely through regulation is that this is not effective in reducing the most egregious sins of urban growth. Alone, regulations cannot tame traffic. Environmental rules have barely stemmed the loss of key wild lands.

Many of the most onerous, costly, and difficult-to-enforce regulations attempt to preserve land that has cultural, ecological, or historic value to the public. The community can preserve such values by buying land outright or by condemning it, but the costs of either method are so prohibitive that these tools can only be successfully used in a limited way. We must learn to be proactive.

TOWARD AGILE OWNERSHIP

The hard, straight lines we draw to mark off the parcels we own have little to do with the ecosystems they are drawn over: watersheds that may stretch for dozens of miles in either direction; wildlife-movement corridors, slopes, streams and bay edges that aren't static but, unlike property lines, move. A climate-change era demands we pay closer attention to those natural systems that flow within and beyond our tidy land divisions. Can we find a similarly fluid idea of ownership that helps us realize our aspirations yet is mindful of the natural world we all share?

That means yet again rearranging the owner's relationship with the public's welfare—a task that makes many Americans uncomfortable. In most of the world, it is taken for granted that government will hold significant power over land use and will wield these powers to advance the greater public good. Armando Carbonell, chair of the Department of Planning and Urban Form at the Lincoln Institute of Land Policy, describes "a spectrum of approaches" worldwide to private-property rights. Clear ownership rights are essential in capitalist countries, but in much of the world, he said in a telephone conversation, "there is no sacredness of private development rights." In the United Kingdom, for example, any development must seek planning permission: "There is no 'right' to develop," Carbonell explained. "The northern European model is that government largely decides where you do what with your land."[27] Holland's elaborate flood defenses come from centralized decision making because without government intervention to keep out the North Sea in this low-lying country, no development at all is possible. This has translated into a culture of intensively planned and organized development that is neat, orderly, convenient, and relatively low cost. Dutch people also appreciate, as one acquaintance put it, "knowing exactly what will be next door."

In most other countries, some kind of local planning authority is supposed to defuse land-use disputes by laying out master plans for growth. The plans put housing to the west, along the commuter-rail line, and shopping and offices near the central station. Such agencies typically control infrastructure-construction purse strings as well. You can't put your office park on any piece of land outside town, because the authority will not build a road to it and can refuse to issue building permission in any event. You'll have to put it on land near the train line, so workers can commute without driving.

This is not to say that we need to adopt a Dutch or Nordic model. These models illustrate that people happily live and realize their dreams in places with very different approaches to ownership and government involvement in land development—and where costly land disputes do not endlessly tie up courts.

The concept of such strong planning powers is unassailable: the planner will synthesize expert opinion and the people's will, giving the community a proactive voice in the way it grows and revitalizes. The United States, with its historic distrust of government, has never had much faith in city planning or in master plans assembled by experts, and it has tended to abandon planning with teeth in the face of failure—as in the massive "slum clearances" of the 1950s and 1960s—rather than trying to plan more fairly and effectively.

Critics have long said that planning agencies lacked the expertise, the acumen, and the private sector's profit motive and therefore should not be betting the public's money on a speculative future. So most US cities react, throwing money at an industry that promises to move in and create jobs, or building the latest urban bauble (aquarium, sports stadium, museum) that is thought to confer (inevitably) a "world-class" edge. The one-offs rarely pay. Regulations, not to mention subsidies, targeted tax benefits, and other government actions, are also bets on the future, entailing exactly the same risks as planning. As in business, some succeed and some fail. Communities really have no choice but to bet on the future in some way.

The excesses of the past are not a reason to fear planning but a reason to do it better. Planners today are brought in to do little more than fix things, or to veneer the product of crude political horse trading with a gloss of "community input." Most of the regulations that protect us and annoy us are drafted by planners, because they have few other tools to keep the last development outrage everyone's mad about from being repeated. America need not adopt Oregon's growth boundaries or any existing city-planning model—indeed, many well-established planning regimes, in and outside America, are not yet tuned to the challenges of the future. Planning, for the purposes of this book, simply means leaving behind our overreliance on reactive regulation in favor of a proactive approach that anticipates what the future is bringing us and prepares for it.

It's becoming evident that planning must go on at different scales than we are used to—at the scale of a watershed, forest, or other ecosystem, in ways that recognize large-scale economic relationships and regional mobility and infrastructures. These scales do not comfortably fit within the political categories we use today—local, state, federal—which are already dysfunctional in both urban and natural system terms (as part 2 of this book illustrates). Indeed, political boundaries and natural system boundaries usually match only by coincidence. In truth, America has barely engaged the idea of robust planning and certainly has no systematic approach to revitalization; think tanks and university urban centers are artisans of ideas they hope others will pick up.

Rather than spell out a prescription for planning, chapter 2 sketches a new land ethos that can inform it. The epilogue describes techniques that involve both citizens and leaders in planning proactively together.

When a Katrina or a World Trade Center disaster hits, we realize that we're not prepared. Yet even a messy emergency response is comparatively easy. It's when you rebuild that the really tough questions intrude. What and how do you rebuild? In American cities, we not only don't know, but we don't know how to find out.

2

A New Land Ethos

From the head of the Snoqualmie Valley, the Snoqualmie River plunges over a spectacular 270-foot-high falls, then wends peacefully forty-three miles north through flat farmland between fir-covered ridges. The valley appears at first to be one of those unspoiled, "have it all" rural locales. As the crow flies, it's only about twenty miles east of downtown Seattle, but long lakes and high ridges form a topographic barrier. A lack of direct access by modern highways puts most of the valley an hour or more from urban destinations. Nurseries serving the outer suburbs alternate with dairies and pastures. Some truck farms flourish, planted with boutique vegetables selected for their ability to tingle urban palates.

Residents, farmers, foresters, and officials are working out a new land ethos here, forging a new relationship to nature as we live within it—not just cordoning it off in preserves. Officials have asked farmers to erect fences and maintain forested buffers as deep as three hundred feet along rivers and streams. It's part of a very ambitious effort by King County and Washington State to restore rapidly declining wild salmon stocks.

The effort was spurred by the listing of nine salmon species as endangered by the federal government. The elaborate procedures for protecting streams and spawning beds have become a huge public-works effort that may cost more than $3 billion, with some elements of recovery taking as long as fifty years.[1] The presence of wild salmon, which still can be hooked occasionally only a few hundred yards from the skyscraper-lined shoreline of Seattle's Elliott Bay, has remained deeply embedded in the identity of the Pacific Northwest. Salmon have remained iconic long after the dwindling of a Native American culture that lionized them.

The salmon have not had an easy time with urban growth, however. The difficulty of the state's task has to do with the fish's life cycle: though they spend most of their life in the ocean, they require quite specific spawning conditions in freshwater streams, rivers, and lakes. To make more streams salmon friendly, crews in urban neighborhoods "daylight" waterways long ago confined to pipes. Specialists plant stream-shading shrubbery and silt-filtering grasses. Where once storm water roared in a muddy torrent down concrete culverts, contractors dig meandering watercourses braided by ridges of gravel, and tip downed trees into streams to create quiet eddies friendly to persnickety egg-laden females.

In urbanized areas, salmon-habitat restoration has stymied a mall developer hoping to expand over a buried stream. It stopped a golf course owner who sought irrigation water from a salmon-critical source. But a great deal of the effort—and the controversy—is focused on the rural Snoqualmie Valley, because its environment is less degraded and more readily restorable.

Some years ago, I asked Tim Trohimovich, the planning director of 1000 Friends of Washington (an environmental advocacy group now renamed FutureWise) to explain the extraordinary measures that King County has undertaken in the valley. A stream's quality has to do with conditions far beyond its banks, he explained, and it is compromised when "more than 10 percent of a river basin is covered in impervious surface [roads, parking lots, buildings] and more than 65 percent of the forest cover is gone." The cities and suburbs can't be restored to these conditions, but the valley can be.

Although the state and county are spending to naturalize river edges and remove levees so that seasonal floodwaters will flow safely into low-lying bottomland, the burdens of salmon preservation have fallen hard on farmers. The stream buffer strips can significantly reduce usable pastureland and must be managed to avoid manure pollution and erosion. Those measures cost money and reduce revenue.

As you drive the valley, you see fast-growing cottonwoods sprouting from fields that once supported herds of dairy cows. While dairy farming nationwide has been declining, the last straw for many farmers in the valley has been the struggle to accommodate the preservation of salmon runs. Farmers feel whipsawed because the scientific consensus is in flux on just how much forest must be kept and how deep the buffers must be. Do you want farmers, goes the refrain, or salmon?

The county is trying to have both. A separate effort has aggressively attempted to help farmers prosper. The Farmlink program draws young ur-

Figure 2.1 The urban growth boundary in King County encourages higher-density development in established Snoqualmie Valley towns, such as Duvall (shown here), to preserve valuable farmland (seen beyond). Credit: James S. Russell

banites to farming, boosted by rapidly growing demand for locally produced food. Hmong farmers, originally from Cambodia, sell Snoqualmie Valley flowers in Seattle's famed Pike Place Market. Thanks to "Puget Sound Fresh," a marketing campaign, valley farmers can sell direct to consumers in an expanding network of almost forty public markets countywide.[2]

The Snoqualmie Valley is the kind of place where the subdivisions would move in as the farmers sold out, but the county uses an Oregon-style growth boundary to funnel limited urban growth and development into the valley's rural towns. Another growth boundary keeps suburbia, now just a ridgeline or two away, from invading the valley. Drive into Duvall, a small farm town that had languished largely forgotten for decades, and you see its once desultory main street, Highway 203, lined with substantial new houses, apartment complexes, sidewalks, and a strip center sporting an appliqué of bungalow-style crisscrossing beams (figure 2.1).

By focusing development into compact form and paying close attention to how much land is forested (and therefore permeable to water), King County does much more than save salmon. It reduces demand for storm water and domestic sewage infrastructure and for road miles. Farming need not compete with subdivision-development pressures (where it would lose). Fewer roads crisscross the forests and valley, and fewer development blobs interrupt wildlife movement and dump runoff from acres of asphalt into streams. Compact development reduces the number of miles people have to drive and reduces costs to provide auto alternatives, such as transit. More kids can walk or bike to school.

The salmon-saving regime was not undertaken in response to climate change (it's unclear how much global warming is implicated in collapsing salmon runs), but it is analogous to an agile city approach because of its comprehensiveness. The state and county have organized salmon recovery at the scale of watersheds—the drainage systems of streams and rivers—because salmon may swim into the mouth of a wide river with their goal the quiet headwaters of a tiny tributary tens or hundreds of miles inland.[3] (Indeed, the largest efforts, and the greatest controversy, have to do with tributaries of the Columbia River in eastern Washington, and whether taking down dams that aid irrigation and shipping is necessary to restore once-enormous runs.)

Improving watershed quality doesn't make sense only in salmon streams. Restoring streams to a natural state can aid flood control (the threat has been increasing), improve air quality (with more tree cover), and improve water quality (by reducing sources of both pollution and eroded soil). Stream systems act as corridors for wildlife migration, and they offer a variety of habitats as they merge with upland meadows or forests—a diversity that offers greater natural resilience in the face of climate change. Salmon recovery, compact development, and farmland preservation looked some years ago as if they were undertaken as discrete efforts to solve singular problems. Especially as global warming has asserted its prominence, however, officials have integrated these programs. Agricultural flood-control measures promoted by King County in the Snoqualmie Valley, for example, include measures to protect salmon streams. A review of urban growth boundaries in four Puget Sound counties has been integrated into an action plan to meet climate-change goals.[4]

King County has done much in the Snoqualmie Valley that advocates of rural values and lifestyle would like to see. Like so many other precious places, the valley retains a look of tradition, wildness, and authenticity. But it is a look that can be sustained only through a complex regulatory structure and a governmental engineering of the rural economy that may not prove sustainable. The ambitious goal to preserve 65 percent of the forest cover doesn't mesh with golf course development or supermarket-style parking lots. Even a home-owner's addition of a barn and driveway can involve hairsplitting by biologists and ichthyologists over whether a stopped-up ditch must be deemed a wetland of potential interest to a browsing maternal salmon. After years of effort, sal - mon recovery is slow.[5]

The invasiveness of the regulations has led to strife, with rural residents ac-cusing urban elected officials of dumping the greatest burdens on them. (A court case overturned the 65 percent tree-cover requirement in 2009.[6]) For the foreseeable future, the delicate balance among fish, farming, residents' aspira-tions, and the pressures of urban growth can be maintained only by perpetual negotiation.

King County's policies have been tough on those who expected to farm the way they used to, or to sell their underused forest or pastureland to sub-dividers. But these expectations have begun to give way to new ones in which the benefits become more evident. If the county government does not keep its promise to help built-up parts of the county gracefully absorb development, voters may lose faith in the growth boundary.

King County's imperfect efforts show that we can adapt landscapes and live within them in a more agile way. Moving ahead, we'll have to find ways to do more in a less onerous way: with better science on what's truly necessary to pre-serve salmon, leading to a simpler, less micromanaging approach; with greater participation in salmon preservation by wealthier, developed parts of the county; and with a fair balancing of burdens and benefits.

CONSERVING WHILE DEVELOPING

So often, land-use debates turn on a simplistic duality. We insist on pure pres-ervation, in which the hand of man is all but eliminated (represented by the federal wilderness system). Or we defer to, accommodate, or encourage what-ever private owners choose to do. America too infrequently considers the vast spectrum of possibilities between these two extremes. That spectrum is rich with opportunities for many more of us to live and create wealth in a graceful relationship with the natural world.

Clark Stevens, whose New West Land Company is based in Los Angeles, is among a new breed of environmentalists, planners, developers, and investors who cross the divide between traditional environmentalism and one-size-fits-all development to create profit-making projects that conserve and restore damaged landscapes.

If one of Stevens's clients, the Pace family, longtime owners of an eleven-thousand-acre tract on the big island of Hawaii, had sought the greatest and quickest economic return, they could have sold off their land in twenty-acre "ranchettes."[7] Instead, Stevens devised an ambitious plan, called Hokukano Preserve, that would subdivide only a thousand acres. Sandalwood and ohia forests that stretch from the edge of the town of Kealakekua up the island's western slopes toward the peak of Mauna Loa would be protected and extended through reforestation of the parcel's ranchlands. An adjacent nine-thousand-acre tract would become part of the Federal Forest Legacy Program (which grants cash while legally obliterating any right to develop the land), so the outcome was to be a very large chunk of land restored to nature with a relatively small investment by both government and private owners.

Stevens marked out building sites on the lowest elevations, nearest Kealakekua, by pacing the land and finding spots that offered breathtaking views of the ocean and the peak without extending existing ranch roads. "We have devised incentives for residents to reforest their land," explained Stevens at an early stage, which means that the forest would actually expand most rapidly on the portions of the site developed for homes. At least three-quarters of each twenty-acre parcel would remain in agricultural use or conservation. At Hokukano, fences would not mark property lines. Rather, they would define wildlife corridors and defend native forest and understory from the depredations of nonnative wild pigs.

Parts of the vast site would continue to support coffee growing (tucked into remnant forests) and the ranching of bison and cattle (rotated to inspire forest growth yet keep too much fire-inducing deadwood from accumulating).

The agricultural uses may seem surprising in a development devoted to conservation, but mixing conservation, development, and ranching or forestry represents an evolution in the way humans can be present in precious landscapes. Human activities, clustered or otherwise limited, offer income to offset the profits owners forgo when they give up the right to cut forests or build vacation homes. But the reasons run deeper: "Retiring land from human use is more complex than it appears," says Stevens. Natural systems, he explains, adapt themselves to long-term human use, creating a different kind of environmental diversity than would occur otherwise. Stevens is also concerned that "removing people from the land disengages them from it." The people who work a forest or farm know it most deeply. When they leave it behind, they take their understanding and emotional connection with them. Like-minded conservationists, he finds, seek "to move beyond a conventional environmentalism that separates humans from the land."

As of this writing, the plan had fallen victim to the collapse of the resort-home market and tight credit, though the Paces did put the planned acreage into the Forest Legacy Program. Stevens expects a new plan to be viable, perhaps tying forest conservation to carbon credits. Hokukano shows what enormous promise conservation-sensitive development holds as well as underlines the considerable—but hardly insurmountable—challenges of this unfamiliar way of investing for conservation.

An increasing number of public-spirited institutional and private investors seek to marry enterprise and environmentalism. These pioneers are trying out new ways to sensitively nurture a vibrant economy in some of the nation's most naturally gorgeous places. They are redefining land-use regulations and real estate finance. They're broadening the conservation ethos, rethinking the human presence in the natural landscape.

On a small scale, cluster developments and conservation subdivisions have existed for years. A dozen houses occupying a fraction of a tract that is otherwise preserved is laudable if the ponds, forests, or farms they seek to save are not isolated from contiguous natural or farmed areas. Too many of these subdivisions fail to aid ecological resilience because they further fragment natural systems with roads and parking. By scaling up efforts, or uniting small projects into large parcels, conservation development can bring back entire watersheds, valleys, forests, and species habitats—a scale that's become increasingly important. Such investments have drawn attention from the largest financial institutions as these large firms seek to hedge conventional investments with a variety of forays into the emerging "green" economy.

Large-scale conservation development got its impetus in the Rocky Mountain West, where investors snapped up ranchland. Much of it was cheap because it had been severely overgrazed in a desperate attempt by small American ranches to compete with the rise of globalized meat production. (Steaks on American dinner plates can come from cattle raised on huge tracts in South America.) Conservation-oriented buyers brought in specialists to restore grasslands for hunting and sustainable grazing. The new owners stopped erosion and returned streams to their clear natural state, and they now support fishing, horseback riding, and recreational wildlife-watching. The assembled tracts can be vast: cable-television entrepreneur Ted Turner, who owns two million acres in seven states and Argentina, has bought entire mountain valleys. He has put wild-roaming bison on American menus. Many of the wealthiest owners hold lands for family use or for what might be deemed gentleman ranching. But they sketch a future for non-elite ranching that may help it survive by diversifying income streams while restoring resiliency to the environment.

"Coming out of the downturn, developers are saying that green has got to be part of the equation," says Kendra Briechle, who manages the Center for Conservation and Development at the Conservation Fund, in Arlington, Virginia. "Green building is part of it, but there is increasing interest in the landscape and the benefits that can come from improving the ecological function of landscape." The Fund, partnering with the US Army, among others, is helping assemble a 532-acre community-owned forest in Hoke County, South Carolina, near Fort Bragg. The forest will be managed to retain homes for red-cockaded woodpeckers, to continue timber and pine-straw harvests, to create new recreational opportunities, and to host a minimal-footprint affordable-housing development.

"More urbanized areas have held their value," continues Breichle, "which means that compact urban form in exurban locations has the potential for meeting the conservative financing approach developers are now interested in."[8] Carl Palmer, a cofounder with Robert Keith of Beartooth Capital, one of the few conservation-oriented real estate investment funds, agrees. "Between traditional conservation and traditional development there is great potential in blending conservation and development."[9] He's proudest of the work Beartooth has done with a 1,200-acre ranch tract in the Pahsimeroi Valley of Idaho, where big game again roam grasslands and where salmon and steelhead have moved rapidly into spawning areas created by stream restoration.

If conservation development is to grow larger in scale, and move beyond dedicated nonprofits and a few boutique investors, making the financial risk understandable will be essential, pioneers in the field say. As lenders stick to known investment types, "We're still struggling to document results for these new kinds of developments," says Briechle. Adds Palmer: "For the most part, conservationists don't understand private investment tools, and traditional developers don't have environmental credibility; they don't understand how to work with environmental goals. We're going to see a lot of growth in startups that blend those skill-sets to fill that gap." Beartooth, operating in four western states out of Bozeman, Montana, uses its expertise to analyze ecological values that can be nurtured along with sustainable agriculture and forestry. Chapter 3 offers more detail about some of the financial tools Beartooth and others use.

Many environmentalists fear conservation development, seeing it as a smoke screen for bringing overdevelopment to pristine landscapes. But it has its greatest potential as a means to repair damaged landscapes, which, like overgrazed ranches, are abundant. As more such developments prove their value (and tax, regulatory, and land-use policies shift to enable them), conservation development could soon draw substantial mainstream investment. It has the potential to restore natural environments that are enriched by the hand of man.

RESCUING THE RISKIEST PLACES

American communities already struggle with wildfires, atrophied bays, beach erosion, and cliffs that slump into rivers. Climate-change effects, such as gyrating weather, more severe droughts and floods, and rising seas, are almost certainly a factor in these problems, and these places will become more vulnerable quickly. Shorelines, where the clash between private owners' interests and public welfare has vexed generations of policymakers and jurists—witness the Lucas case (in chapter 1)—are a good place to look for a new kind of reconciliation. The nation has known for decades that building too close to shoreline bluffs or at the edge of beaches was a recipe for disaster.[10] On undisturbed natural beaches, winter storms rip away the sand and gentle summer currents quietly restore it. Most natural shorelines move both inland and shoreward in cycles over years or decades, fed or eroded by changing streams of sand.

Many local governments that should have known better chose to let opportunistic developers erect fixed structures over shifting shorelines in zones of known danger. They now find owners clamoring for protection as storm waves slop into the swimming pool or as the sundeck tips into the sea. Owners on eroding shores want to build high bulkheads, which save their homes (at least temporarily) at the price of the beach. Bulkheads, jetties, and other "armoring" gambits cut off the natural flow of replenishing sand, which guarantees that the beaches will only recede (figure 2.2). Long-bulkheaded communities lose their value as beaches shrink and bulkheads rise to prison-wall heights. Worse, beach "hardening" spurs a kind of arms race against the sea as owners build

Figure 2.2 High walls have long protected the beach town of Sea Bright, New Jersey, because development too close to the shore prevented the beach from replenishing itself. Repeated replenishment with offshore-dredged sand prevents the beach from narrowing. Credit: James S. Russell

bulkheads higher and the shore recedes further, leaving their properties even more stranded and infuriating adjacent property owners as their beach disappears too. (A group of wealthy homeowners on a 2.7-acre, high-risk spit of land worth some $1.2 billion sought to secede from Southampton, New York, to avoid a local prohibition on bulkhead building. They did not succeed.[11])

Local governments may fight the bulkheads because they preserve individual owners' investments at the cost of the beach resource shared by all. On the other hand, it's very difficult for any of us to watch waves gnaw at someone's home. So government funds assist rebuilding and fix storm-shattered roads and utilities—and the bulkhead builders often ultimately get their way, while the community loses the war of rising seas.

This is a classic case in which America's deference to the individual landowner has proven very costly indeed. Regulators step gingerly along the beachfront, thanks to the Lucas case, and yet the problems are too big for landowners to fix themselves. For a couple of generations, the federal government has papered over these disputes by sending money. Billions have been spent pumping sand onto eroded beaches. These beach nourishments are not as damaging as bulkheads, but they require new doses of sand as often as every two or three years, at millions of dollars per mile.

The federal government also underwrites flood insurance for vulnerable communities, since the private market deems the insurance risks too high. This in turn has encouraged owners to upgrade old beach shacks to full-fledged luxury homes, since the flood insurance backs their investment. Premiums are supposed to pay for the program, but it has repeatedly had to borrow billions from taxpayers in bad flood years. Premiums have risen, the number of properties (and thus premiums paid) have expanded rapidly, and the program strictly limits losses it will cover (limitations hundreds of thousands of homeowners discover too late), but the program still had to borrow $17 billion for the *annus horribilis* of 2005, which it is unlikely ever to pay back.[12]

The costs of protecting communities built in river floodplains, on landslide-prone bluffs, and in fire-vulnerable forests are also growing rapidly. Federal generosity cannot continue in this way as needs explode over time. Consider that one hundred thousand people in California's San Mateo and Orange Counties alone may need to be protected from the effects of sea-level rise, according to a report by the Pacific Institute.[13] Along America's thousands of miles of coastline, major airports, roads, schools, hospitals, and sewage and power plants may all require relocation.

Many environmental advocates demand an end to beach-nourishment and flood-insurance programs, correctly pointing out that they are a costly subsidy to those building precisely where they shouldn't. Because urban development lines almost all the Atlantic Coast, much of the Gulf Coast, and major stretches of the West Coast, that tactic alone may cause chaos along the beaches. Making up the insurance program's losses will create prohibitive insurance premiums for perhaps millions of owners. That would reduce the value of many vulnerable properties, making many of them unsellable, especially if the federal government cuts beach-restoration programs.

Still, no one is entitled to have the government protect their investment, and it is time to wean owners from these programs as we prudently assess future risks and take cooperative action to avoid them, rather than passively awaiting the worst, which is pretty much what communities do now. The costly status quo neither fully protects property owners from natural events of growing intensity nor preserves natural and community values.

RETHINKING PROPERTY RIGHTS

Let's try on a few solutions that rely less on engineering but require legal and political innovation. (Yes, "political innovation" sounds like an oxymoron, but it's almost certainly less expensive.) Experts speak of "managed retreat," for example. The idea here is to leave an eroding beach alone and move the structures it threatens. The advantages are manifold: the beach resource (both its economic and ecological value) is maintained without constant infusions of cash and construction. The disadvantages are knotty: How do you get people to give up their homes and their memories? And who will pay the cost? It's no surprise that few communities have even considered the possibility.

In a California case, it took $2.2 million to purchase two homes and some surrounding land. The city hauled off the homes, as well as concrete, rubble, asphalt-reinforcing steel, and old tires. However, the retreat was less expensive than armoring a creek front and a beach.[14] Clearly, buying out every owner along vulnerable shorelines will never be affordable. If managed retreat can ever be scaled up to help entire towns or beach regions cope with rising seas, everyone along the beach must agree to move to keep the place from looking like a gap-toothed grin. It can be done. After a devastating Mississippi River flood in 1993, the nine hundred-person town of Valmeyer, Illinois, decided to move in its entirety out of the vulnerable floodplain and up onto a cliff overlooking the river.[15]

It may not be entirely possible to both save built-up beaches that are disappearing (thereby protecting inland landowners) and make oceanfront owners whole, but tools we use for other purposes suggest some possibilities.

Land Trusts

A community or group of owners could set up a land trust to take collective ownership of a threatened community's land. The trust would exercise its control of the land when eroding beaches make the home unsafe or unusable. In the meantime, owners would have the right to use the house as long as the beachfront is intact.

The trust would remove endangered buildings to save the beach and let it rebuild itself as storm cycles and currents permit. The trust could then resell or redevelop the property for a more adaptive and compatible kind of development, with the trust owners sharing in the proceeds. Though no threatened beachfront community has created such a trust as far as I know, there are parallels in the common use of conservation land trusts to save precious landscapes. In these cases, a group like The Nature Conservancy purchases development rights from an owner (say, the difference in the land's value as a farm and its sale value to a developer for a residential subdivision). The trust arrangement reduces the taxes so the farmer can afford to keep farming, and the larger community benefits from the natural value of the preserved land.

Land trusts also buy *development rights*—the right to build the square footage on a given lot permitted by zoning—to preserve wild lands. The trust owns the development rights in perpetuity, which it prevents from ever being used, thus preserving the land's natural function. The owner retains compatible rights of use, such as farming. Some states and counties use dedicated taxes or a bond issue to raise money to purchase development rights at large scale. Similarly, governments can encourage people to move from vulnerable locations by allowing *transfer* of the development rights from the beachfront land to a nearby location that is less vulnerable. In this way, owners can retain some or all of the value of the land they are giving up, and coasts will retain their resiliency.[16]

Mitigation Banks

A community can consider buying land for the future out of harm's way. If there is space behind a line of threatened beachfront houses, for example, a town or homeowner's association might purchase land in case it's needed, so that houses could move out of danger in tandem, preserving a coherent, appealing form for the town and preserving property values and natural values at once. The precedent is what the wonks call "mitigation banks." These banks don't have loan officers or ATMs. They were developed as a tool to preserve wetlands (which are the "deposits" in the bank), but the currency of a mitigation bank can be any environmentally valuable commodity. Here is how they are used now. Your highway department needs to run a road through a marsh, but regulations require the department to make up that wetland loss, so the department pays to renovate sick but valuable wetlands nearby (usually on the order of three times the area damaged) or pays to construct new wetlands. (There is an industry now that knows how to build natural-acting wetlands.)

Through a combination of regulations and tax advantages, government could make coastal land banks appealing. It would be a less adversarial and less costly means to manage retreat than to have government buy beach land out-right by condemnation and less costly for individual owners who otherwise end up spending endless amounts in a vain effort to permanently protect their investment.

Land Readjustment

A community threatened by rising waters or crumbling bluffs might want to manage retreat by heading to an urban-planning chiropractor for some land readjustment.[17] Everyone throws their property into a pool, dissolving all the property lines. Then the land is reallocated, with the zone that is vulnerable to landslides or flooding held by the community as a safety buffer. Everyone gets a new lot configuration that is proportionally the same value as before. The street layout can be redesigned to create more value, reconfiguring land that had little value to make it more appealing, fixing access problems, and so on. The idea is that the rearranged community would be safer and more valuable, with greater development opportunity.

Land readjustment is used in many crowded countries—Japan, Korea, Germany, Spain, the Netherlands, among others. In Japan, it has been a way to unite many tiny properties at the urban edge to make urban growth possible. A private corporation, Solidere, rebuilt the war-torn center of Beirut with the contribution of some 1,650 lots. The substantial proceeds were distributed to the owners. In Holland, two-thirds of the land area has been readjusted since the 1950s. It has been used to amalgamate tiny farms to create much larger, more efficient ones. But it has also been used to create large enough par-cels to efficiently make "polders"—drained or filled areas that can be farmed or can accommodate new neighborhoods. If a consensus-driven process like land readjustment did not exist in Holland—a nation where almost every square inch is protected from the sea by dikes and drainage systems—it could not exist as a developed-world state. Readjustment tends to work best when the land values after the process is completed are much higher than those before.

Land reallocation is not systematically used in the United States, though consensual deals are often made by owners to cooperatively amalgamate prop-erties to attract a developer. It can be a government-led process, as it is in Israel, to convert agricultural land into room for urban growth. Or it can be initiated by the owners themselves who become the equivalent of voting stockholders in a company dedicated to redevelopment. After the new master plan has been made and property lines reestablished, the readjustment entity dissolves.

A less scary approach may be to leave property lines in place but to use an adjustment process to reallocate development rights such as zoning density, uses, and building form. To avoid lining an eroding beachfront with condos, a community could cooperatively choose to transfer high-density development rights from the beachfront to a commercial boulevard that's at a safe distance. The new value created along the boulevard could subsidize the loss of development rights along the beach.

A land readjustment scheme is clearly not an effort for the faint of heart. Every place that uses land readjustment offers some kind of track for those who disagree with the plan or hold out, usually involving eminent domain. Disputes tend to arise when owners are not persuaded that new plots are as valuable as old ones. The process may not be simple or fast, but by building trust and consensus, it can run smoother than a redevelopment scheme that relies substantially on condemnation. Readjustment has fallen out of favor when government abuses its land-taking prerogatives, as it has in Japan and China.

Borrowing Rather than Buying

A low-cost, low-impact way of living in a precious landscape is to consider yourself a visitor, even if a long-term one, rather than a resident. You build only structures that are adaptable, removable, temporary. The time-honored beach shack comes to mind. Its low cost reflected the vulnerability of its oceanfront location. If a storm or flood sweeps away a shack, no one is much the worse because no one had invested much or expected the structure to last forever. Using modular-home construction, you can make a "shack" that's readily movable.

A further step is to consider leasing a special parcel of land rather than owning it. This is already a fact of life for weekend-cabin developments within national forests. You lease the cabin and land for a long term, which makes investments in maintenance and modest upgrades prudent. The terms of the lease are the mechanism by which the government owner can maintain the natural resource of which it is a part, and can convert the property to another use should that be necessary. You are secure knowing that the beauty that attracted you to the place will remain forever and that the cost may well be modest because you have given up ownership rights.

This idea of private parties leasing use of public land is widespread. It's how we arrange extraction of oil and gas from under the public oceans and minerals from under public land. We have not been creative about the division of public and private rights in precious landscapes, but it could be a key to cooperatively maintaining what all of us value while permitting continued private use.

The advantage of temporary structures, land trusts, or some other cooperative arrangement is that they are voluntary and proactive. They create an opportunity to plan an orderly transition as the future demands, the kind of transition New Orleans could not make because it did not imagine a world in which swaths of the city might become uninhabitable.

AN ETHOS OF STEWARDSHIP

There's not much of this thinking going on in threatened communities these days because we've gotten locked into a mind-set symbolized by the Lucas decision: we can only see land as either publicly owned or privately held. We don't need to, however. Cooperatively rearranging selected ownership rights between private owners and the larger community is a less strife-prone means to benefit all. If we don't adapt our attitudes to property, we're left with today's all-or-nothing choices.

When each owner can only act alone, as they must today, the only option is to armor one's own property in what may be a vain attempt to hold back nature. Along Katrina-bashed coastal Mississippi, some homeowners have created storm-resistant fortresses along streets otherwise abandoned by owners. In New Orleans, you see houses rebuilt on stilts at levels varying substantially even from next-door neighbors. It's because no one knows what the real risk is. The sight is amusing until you think of them as the shot-in-the-dark bets against disaster that they are.

King County, in Washington State, is not the only place that encourages urban families to farm or forest. All over the country, people have come to see living in precious landscape not just as a view from a picture window but as a privilege that involves an obligation to nurture the place. It can be a more rewarding way to live, anyway. Water costs may force you to rip out your water-sucking lawn in the desert, but that hassle creates an opportunity to nurture plants that offer pleasures unique to the locale: delicate flowers that open amid the spiky branches, a breeze suddenly tinged by mesquite. You begin to realize that that scrap of New England, nurtured at great cost amid the plump cacti, was never much like the real thing.

All over the United States, local volunteer groups plant trees and remove invasive nonnative weeds and vines so that forests grow stronger and lake edges provide food for fish and nesting places for migratory waterfowl. They clean up beaches, seed oysters in shallow bays, and put up nesting boxes to attract song-birds. The pleasure derives from nurturing a place, bringing out its specificity. It develops its own genius loci and is no longer engineered to reproduce, for example, France in Massachusetts. Localness, discussed in greater detail in chapter 10, has become an ethos, too.

CROSSING BOUNDARIES

Witnessing the struggle in New Orleans to figure out how to consolidate a block or a neighborhood on high ground, it may seem too daunting to co-operatively attack problems that don't recognize property lines and political boundaries. Unfortunately, litigation in the West over the Colorado River is not producing one more drop of water. A long-term pact among six states, Washington, DC, and the federal government that began in the 1970s has not been able to restore the heavily urbanized Chesapeake Bay to health, in large part because the main sources of pollution come largely from diverse, hard-to-control sources: agricultural fertilizers and manure from factory farms as well as runoff from roads and parking lots.[18] Yet large, shallow estuaries like the Chesapeake are among the world's most treasured, productive, and most threatened natural systems.

In casting about for metaphors for reweaving the human-made and the natural at that scale, I sought out Frank and Deborah Popper. He is an urban planner and she a geographer who in 1987 proposed the Buffalo Commons, an environmental-restoration vision that they hoped would lead to a brighter future for the depopulating Great Plains.[19] Though the plains are rarely central to the American conversation these days, they cover an enormous chunk of the continent, stretching across parts of three Canadian provinces, ten American states (from North Dakota south into Texas and running west roughly from Interstate 35 to Interstate 25), and into Mexico. This vast area is a bioregion sharing many characteristics: it is essentially flat, semiarid prairie with few or no trees.

"As urban people, we were struck by the population losses in the plains," explained Deborah Popper. "We wandered through small towns with empty storefronts and we could not figure out how counties that had seven thousand people a few years ago could get by when they're down to seven hundred." Their idea was to unfence vast territories, replant native prairies, and reintroduce herds of wild buffalo and athletic pronghorns. They felt that a healthier landscape might be more appealing, which would inspire people to live and create businesses in proximity to the beauty, romance, and vastness of the now-vanished primordial Great Plains.

They had proposed that the federal government take on the task of braiding parklike swaths through the farms and ranchlands. "The reaction was, 'over our dead bodies,'" said Frank Popper. The region is conservative, suspicious of governments that send directives from capitals located outside the plains, and of business interests that control their destinies from distant cities.

More than two decades after it was proposed, the Buffalo Commons seemed a romantic notion going nowhere. Not so, said the couple in a telephone interview from their home in New Jersey. They no longer advocate a federal role, or any kind of overarching governmental role, but instead see the Buffalo Commons as an idea that emerges as individuals make choices and see that, as Deborah put it, "trying the same old things doesn't work." Herds of wild buffalo don't thunder across the plains yet, but ranchers have discovered a market for buffalo meat. Others are turning to raising grass-fed cattle and protecting stream quality by allowing native species to regrow. Grassroots conservation advocacy organizations have sprung up, including the Grassland Foundation, the American Prairie Foundation, and the Great Plains Restoration Foundation.

The Buffalo Commons exists primarily as "a metaphor," says Frank Popper. There's no plan or set of principals, no recommended step forward, no label certifying Buffalo Commons places or products. "People in the plains are entrepreneurial and anti-planning," says Deborah, adding that if people see advantages in restoring habitats, "they will make changes on their own." In so strongly individualistic a region, few look to make common cause. "Native tribes, individual farmers, megaranchers like Ted Turner [who owns more than a dozen buffalo ranges on the plains], and conservation-oriented nonprofits all pursue different paths," observed Frank, "and no one can know yet what will work and what will fail."

The plains may pay a high price for failing to come together to forge a common future. Widening federal deficits may require a paring back of agricultural subsidies heavily used in the plains. Subsidized corn for ethanol fuel, which some in the plains see as a boost, may prove a bust, as the full environmental impact of biofuels sinks in. Aquifers, such as the Ogallala in Kansas, are drying up.[20] People still leave.

An ambitious prairie restoration in northeastern Montana is sketching a future of large-scale conservation coexisting with agriculture. The American Prairie Foundation hopes to assemble a 3.5-million-acre reserve near Malta, Montana, linking private purchases of land to the 1.1-million-acre Charles M. Russell Wildlife Refuge. It has purchased 100,000 acres to date, on which it runs one hundred bison. The effort, which has tapped a nationwide funding base through such partners as the World Wildlife Fund, the Conservation Fund, and National Geographic, has inspired local ranchers to adopt wildlife-friendly practices that in effect extend the "reserve" without taking land out of ranching. They have mixed grasses differently, changed grazing practices, and replaced the lowest fence tier with barbless wire to permit safe passage of wildlife.[21]

"Pure" reserves that restore the plains to wilderness status in key locations linked by wildlife corridors may be essential. (The even larger, 2,000-mile Yellowstone to Yukon corridor is another bioregion-scale effort that has moved slowly as advocates and skeptics sort out how people live with its ambitious ecosystem conservation goals.) But if innovative farm practices can achieve almost the same goals, then the value of restoration (both in environmental and economic-diversification terms) can be almost infinitely extended in tandem with agriculture. That would take the Buffalo Commons from metaphor to very compelling reality.

"I wish to speak a word for Nature," Henry David Thoreau wrote, "for absolute freedom and wildness." This sentiment goes to the heart of what Americans identify with in land, even as most of us settle for what Thoreau would, at best, call "the merely civil." There is no clear road map here, nor is there a necessity to accept a duality of overregulation versus anything-goes libertarianism. If we focus on why it seems so hard to knit together the natural and the human landscapes, the path ahead becomes clear. Yes, we need the urban economy that for many people equals "making it," but we can link it to a natural world that is useful for more than providing a pleasant backdrop to our lives or for the "ecosystem services" we can document. However driven our lives, we can bring into them the country's "unbroken horizon, the monotony of an endless road, of vast uniform plains, of distant mountains," as Ralph Waldo Emerson wrote, "the eye invited ever to the horizon and the clouds."

PART 2

Repairing the Dysfunctional Growth Machine

Cities seem to grow and change according to immutable forces and mysterious flows of capital. But much about urban growth is actually under our control, if we're willing to dig deep into how urban economies work. I've appropriated the idea of the city as a "growth machine" from urban sociologist Harvey L. Molotch. His work has explored not only the way that business leaders, entrepreneurs, government officials, activists, and ordinary people unite around the idea of growth but also the way that the city itself is a field of growth and wealth creation. In most places, there is a sense that decisions related to growth lie in the hands of some kind of elite, whether it be "the developers," the "downtown interests," or a public-spirited combination of interests.[1]

Certainly, growth coalitions can do much. In part 2, I go beyond Molotch to consider four lifeblood drivers of growth that shape city form and largely define whether communities thrive or stagnate. These chapters show how the mechanics of the growth machine actually shape and steer the decisions speculators make. These drivers include regulations, the tax code, subsidies, ingrained habit, bureaucratic inertia, and the culture of development and finance. The way real estate is financed tells you what you can build affordably and where. In the United States, government determines which housing markets get served in the way it distributes subsidies (chapter 3). Where you are able to live and how you are able to get around is substantially determined by how the nation builds and pays for transportation (chapter 4). Clean water (chapter 5), once all but free and universally available, nowadays constrains growth as some cities face dwindling supplies and others face difficult decisions about flooding and drought. These powerful engines of growth apply nationwide. America has not been ready to cope with this fragmented, nonintegrated assortment of growth stimuli. Now it must.

The growth machine does not operate in a planned way. Its mechanisms weren't designed to do what they do; they were designed mainly for other purposes but have become extraordinarily important primarily because we haven't paid enough attention to how they work. Each is as rigid and change-averse as real estate. While each has a stimulative effect on the economy, and on growth, the benefits of all are becoming increasingly poorly distributed. The mechanisms that drive the growth machine stand squarely in the way of effectively reducing carbon emissions and coping with the effects of climate change.

The subsequent chapters in Part 2 show not only how these mechanisms make our communities but what *kinds* of places they make (because they "make" in both intended and unintended ways). The result is the mutant form of suburbia that I call megaburbs, the American dream 1950s suburb blown up to multicounty, sometimes bi-state metropolitan scale that acts urban but looks suburban, and inflicts an autos-only, one-size-fits-all scale of development on cities and countryside alike (chapter 6).

Do these mechanisms and their results nurture communities and the values we expect communities to represent? Will they help us meet the challenges of the future? Regrettably, the answer today is usually no. In these chapters, I propose ways to remake the growth machine. That's an essential task if we ever hope to cope with environmental challenges. It is no coincidence that many growth drivers long ago became obsolete. Redesigning them will diversify the kinds of communities they nurture, unleash innovation, and help create economic resilience along with environmental adaptiveness.

3

REAL ESTATE

Financing Agile Growth

L ooking like two small cottages stitched together, the Nguyen house in
Biloxi, Mississippi, doesn't look futuristic. The house was built over several
months in 2007 in a neighborhood scoured by Hurricane Katrina in 2005. It
was intended to use new wind- and flood-resistant standards in innovative and
affordable ways, and to employ green design and construction techniques that
could easily be replicated.

"It's hard to reconcile making a housing model for the future with what a
family needs that's still living in a FEMA trailer," reflected Michael Grote, in a
slightly apologetic tone. He was the young, beefy program manager with Architecture for Humanity, a disaster-relief organization, and we stood on the shady
porch of the handsome, nearly completed house for shrimp-boat mechanic
Cong Nguyen, his wife, Oanh Luong, and their four children. Grote had nothing to be apologetic about.

The house is elevated ten feet above the ground to rise above the kind of
flooding that smashed through the neighborhood, and it includes an upgraded
anchoring system to resist hurricane-force winds. The young Houston architects of MC2A Architects, who worked with the Nguyens, Chuong and Chung
Nguyen (no relation), offset the two cottage wings to make room for the generous decks the family wanted and to aid cross ventilation, which would reduce
the need for air-conditioning. Painted teal blue, trimmed in white, the house
looks better than many spec houses, even perched on stilts (figure 3.1).[1]

Figure 3.1 Architecture for Humanity project manager Michael Grote at the Nguyen house when it was under construction in Biloxi, Mississippi. Volunteers built homes high above potential future floodwaters using new wind-resisting tactics. Credit: James S. Russell

But its green aspirations largely fell by the wayside, and it is only affordable to the Nguyens because it was largely built by volunteer labor, supplemented by donations and public grants. Though the house was highly suitable for the Nguyens, it failed as a prototype that could set a new standard for housing after Hurricane Katrina. It became difficult to balance the architect's innovative design ideas with the engineering the coast now requires—and impossible to do on what the Nguyens could afford to pay.

"No one had tried this before and there were growing pains," Grote explained. Without intending to, Grote had made a damning statement. *No one* but his tiny nonprofit and a few other similarly idealistic organizations builds houses that are hurricane resistant, flood-safe, and low energy for low-income homeowners. America's huge home-building industry doesn't serve this market. Government tax benefits, incentives, and housing programs rarely go beyond lowest-common-denominator construction standards.

Was it naive of Architecture for Humanity to innovate in so many ways? Regrettably, given the hidebound way America builds, the answer is yes. The

nation's vast but fragmented building industry is little focused on affordability and resists innovation. American private and public building research is
miniscule—even on energy, where great strides can be made without investing
in pie-in-the-sky technology.

In New Orleans, I found the story much the same when I visited a small
house with stylishly sloped shed roofs that was built as a prototype in the Holy
Cross neighborhood by Global Green, an environmental education and advocacy group based in Santa Monica, California. The architect, Manhattan-based
Workshop/apd, had packed the compact volume of the house with tactics that
advance environmental sustainability, storm resistance, and flood safety.

Challenges? Just a few, said Beth Galante, Global Green's director. No one
locally knew how to install solar panels or geothermal wells. Building officials
wouldn't approve the dual-flush toilet or a filtration system that recycles water
from sinks because they had never seen these devices before. The Army Corps
of Engineers feared the geothermal-well cooling system might undermine the
nearby levee. These concerns slowed planning and added costs.

As the project continued, four more homes were built (figure 3.2), and
an eighteen-unit apartment complex and a community center were planned
that can become a place of refuge in the event of future floods. The project has
begun to change the construction economy of New Orleans. "You don't have to
special-order green products as you did before," Galante told me on a return
visit in 2010. "They are in Home Depot or the local hardware store, because
12,000 people toured our first Global Green house and saw what was possible.
With technical assistance from the Department of Energy, the city now knows
how to deal with solar panels."[2]

After I caught up with Galante, I drove just a few minutes to the Lower
Ninth Ward, where actor Brad Pitt had founded Make It Right to build houses
for people displaced by Katrina. (Pitt was also instrumental in getting Global
Green's beachhead in New Orleans established.) If you had seen Tennessee
Street after Katrina hit, the ordinary scene of people chatting with one another
from porch to porch seemed unbelievable. A wall of water burst through the
Industrial Canal levee, just west of Tennessee Street, and blasted four thousand
homes into kindling. A barge tumbled through the breach and lay at a crazy tilt
just yards away from where I walked.

By the fifth anniversary of the storm, close to 50 colorful houses with bat-
wing roofs and louver-trellised porches had been built or were in construction.
(The goal is to replace 150 destroyed homes.) Like Architecture for Humanity

Figure 3.2 By August 2010, Global Green had built five homes at its site in the Holy Cross neighborhood of New Orleans. The environmental group was able to introduce many energy-saving and other environmental features for the first time in New Orleans. Credit: James S. Russell

and Global Green, all of the architects have rethought traditional architectural elements to fit the city's post-Katrina reality: informal living accommodated at modest cost in houses that stand above possible floods yet are tied down tightly against hurricane winds. Make It Right has trained local subcontractors in green-building techniques and has planned to build a factory to make strong, low-cost, highly insulated prefabricated wall panels called SIPs (structural insulated panels). Though it has been able to apply some economies of scale, Make It Right has faced the same barriers to affordable innovation that Architecture for Humanity and Global Green did.

Where was the vast collective intelligence of the design, construction, real estate, and financial industries in the Gulf Coast's rebuilding process? Where was government, which might have seen this disaster as a critical opportunity to build smarter in a world likely to be afflicted more often by such events?

Nowhere. Sure, much conventional rebuilding has gone on, but almost none of it is truly responsive to the new realities of the hurricane belt. Conventional construction at best addresses minimum standards demanded by building codes and FEMA flood maps. But the new realities include not only flood and wind risk but affordability, storm drainage that's still inadequate, and punishing utility and insurance costs. Even if insured, many owners' homes were not worth what they would cost to replace. Tiny, underfunded nonprofits like Architecture for Humanity didn't worry about whether they could afford to be involved or whether they were taking on too much. They just leaped into the breach.

They probably didn't know they were entangling themselves in America's most hidebound industry: real estate development. Real estate is so important because it builds most of the United States. Many of the rules it follows profoundly affect the way cities grow, but many of them are not only destructive to the quality and longevity of communities but make it very difficult to adapt to a future that demands quick-turnaround innovation.

America's real estate industry will finance little that falls outside a very limited menu of largely obsolete residential and commercial building types. How can this be? The answer requires a look first at how our current real estate finance system came about, and then at why lenders love highway strips yet can't find a way to finance, say, the rebuilding of a once-vital neighborhood or an old industrial site with stunning potential.

UNDERWRITING THE BIGGEST BOX FOR THE BUCK

An American home-buying revolution began in 1933 that helped millions of people afford quality housing. That year, at the depth of the Great Depression, the government began to underwrite and insure self-amortizing mortgages, the kind that pay down interest and principal together.[3] Before that time, few people could afford to pay off mortgages in monthly payments, which meant they paid only interest all their lives or could buy only if they could save enough to pay cash. Government lending standards and insurance made offering such mortgages much less risky and cheaper for banks. Mortgage-interest and property-tax payments are also deductible from federal taxes.

After 1933, something extraordinary happened. Homeownership soared and America's middle class burgeoned. (Many housing experts credit the one with creating the other.) In the years after World War II, Veterans Administration (VA) and Federal Housing Administration (FHA) loans smoothed the way with low down payments. Most of the new homes in fast-growing suburbia tucked families of five or six in one-thousand-square-foot Cape Cods because low-cost mortgages came with strict income caps. You slid the Ford Fairlane into a one-car carport. For decades, the value embodied in the owned home has been a much more important means to build wealth for most families than has been savings, ownership of stock, or pensions.[4]

Much was wrong with this system, which in its early years shut out blacks and redlined city neighborhoods. It was for single-family houses only. Those restrictions were long ago lifted, but lending standards for the most desirable loans, along with developer preference, still favor new construction of single-family houses on undeveloped land at the suburban edge. It's easy to calculate the value added by turning a farm or forest into a housing tract. Plopping a house on the center of a lot is a relatively easy way to build. By contrast, redeveloping an inner-city neighborhood or a stagnating downtown is more complicated: land costs can be higher, and the advantage conferred by an infill project or redevelopment requires calculating more variables. A finance system built on the most simplistic home-building method triumphed over all others, meaning that change would be hard and innovation would be hard. The revival of cities over the last few decades happened almost entirely outside the conventional real estate finance system, which meant urban lending came at higher cost than that which served subdivision builders clearing land at the outer suburban edge.

Congress, in recent years, has fattened homeowner benefits considerably. It made interest on home-equity loans deductible, but owners need not use loan proceeds to remodel the kitchen or replace the roof. In the recent price run-up, people used those loans to turn paper equity into a cash machine—to pay bills, to go on a cruise, to buy a nicer car. Owners can deduct interest expenses and property taxes from vacation homes, so the old beach shack was bulked up with extra bedrooms, marble bathrooms, and big TVs. Capital gains realized from a home sale were freed from taxation for all but a fraction of owners. A couple could shelter up to $500,000 of a gain from taxes—easily costing the government $150,000 per sale. Enter the flipper who got a very generous tax incentive to ride (and pump up) the inflationary wave. Lower- and middle-class owners often can't benefit from the tax breaks because they don't earn enough to itemize taxes, so those benefits have skewed steadily to the more affluent.

The expanding menu of homeowner benefits—especially the forgiveness of capital gains—skewed the benefits of homeownership even more to the wealthy and to speculators. The higher your income, and the bigger your mortgage, the more you get to deduct. (Nowadays, Uncle Sam can be paying one-third or more of your mortgage and property tax thanks to the deductibility of these items. Owners can deduct all interest on mortgages as big as $1 million; there is no limitation to the property-tax deduction and only minor exceptions to the capital-gains benefit. Interest on up to $100,000 in home equity loans may be deducted.[5]) No other form of consumer debt (not for student loans, say, nor emergency loans to cover a catastrophic illness) offers such generous tax advantages.

Though climate-change concerns and a greater focus on environmental sustainability grew, these little-discussed tax-subsidy policies aided speculator fever, pushing the dramatic increase in house size, even as family size generally shrunk. (It hit 2,500 square feet on average at the peak—which does not capture the mammoths at 5,000 and 10,000 square feet that sprang up in high-net-worth communities from Los Angeles and Aspen to Sugarland in Texas and the leafy "wealth belt" of northern New Jersey.)

Buyers went for what one builder I met called the "biggest box for the buck" in outer-outer suburbs. Mom and pop builders morphed into nationwide giants, such as Toll Brothers and KB Home, by selling families of three or four on tile-roofed behemoths with whirlpool-tubbed master-bedroom suites as big as 1950s starter homes. Torrid price rises in hot markets let those owners move up to even bigger houses as complicit mortgage makers collected new fees on loans that tapped paper equity. "Funny money," a prescient architect called it a few years ago. No one's laughing now. Many builders would like nothing more than to return to that "normal." But the McMansion era was an aberration. It can come back only if the toxic policies that created it are not fixed.

The justification for all the tax goodies has been that homeownership is a social good that stabilizes communities. Tell that to the mayors who have had to shell out scarce cash to mow weedy lawns and nail broken doors shut so that squatters would not take over abandoned foreclosed homes in Riverside County, California, or along Florida's Gulf Coast. Ownership does have a genuine wealth-building effect, even when prices rise only modestly. When 1950s buyers in suburban subdivisions retired, the paid-off home, with its growth in value over time, became the basis for a comfortable retirement. In recent years, though, ownership became ideology, shamelessly advertised as the investment that never lost value (oops) and the surefire way first-time buyers could scramble into the middle class. VA and FHA loans—with understandable

Figure 3.3 An emblem of the hypergrowth era, this condominium tower, built away from established neighborhoods, was one of many victims of overbuilding in Las Vegas. Credit: James S. Russell

terms and modest down payments—lifted the wartime generation. Boom brokers, by contrast, pushed buyers struggling to clamber into the middle class into easy-to-get subprime loans at punishing rates. Those terms meant that few such buyers could ever realize ownership's economic benefits—even if the good times hadn't stopped rolling. By contrast, Canadians, the British, and Australians cannot deduct property taxes or interest, or be forgiven taxes on capital gains. But they enjoy the wealth effect of owning, and the percentage of people who own is comparable to that of the United States.[6]

To review: America has a hidebound housing finance and tax system that rewards risk-averse developers, affluent buyers, and the lowest form of speculators (figure 3.3). This system was costing the federal treasury $127 billion in 2008, vastly more than any other deductible item or tax credit. That cost has been rising steadily and is predicted to hit $185 billion in 2013. As the housing bubble burst in late 2008, a desperate federal government had to throw $780 billion into a bank bailout, another $6 billion to stabilize foreclosure-devastated neighborhoods, and $17 billion into a tax credit to encourage people to buy houses.[7] Think of the things the country could have done for itself with this river of cash. As of this writing, the system isn't fixed. Have we lost our minds?

HOW STRIP MALLS BECAME PORK BELLIES

In business, there are so-called commodity suppliers. They seek to sell at the lowest possible cost the most generic thing: flour, sand, plastic bags. Then there are people who seek an edge by delivering something special, new, innovative, intriguing—an iPhone. A vibrant economy makes room for both kinds of supplier. Real estate development, however, has become solely a commodity business, one in which a numbing rigor is applied to making each "product" as close as possible to whatever everyone else has been making for years.

The model seemed low risk until toxic mortgages tipped real estate into a readily predictable death spiral in the late 2000s. Some fraction of the square miles of empty houses in the outer reaches of Phoenix, for example, should be preserved as monuments to the lazy hubris of conventional real estate development and finance. Instead, they will be gotten off the books as soon as possible so that the same players can dust themselves off and start doing the same thing over again.

This benumbed real estate development economy prevented prototype builders in Biloxi and New Orleans from benefiting from the free-flowing house-building cash. Advocates of modular housing, who know that making houses in factories increases quality at lower cost and with greater energy efficiency, couldn't figure out why financing was so elusive either, and why America's manufactured home industry is so innovation resistant. "Smart growth" advocates have struggled for two decades to create denser conservation-oriented and transit-centered development in an urban-growth economy set up to do neither.

What is the real-estate industry good at? Have a look at a recently built commercial strip center. There is a national-chain supermarket at one end. Attached to the market, you'll find a string of smaller national-chain retailers— druggist, shoe store, "casual" restaurant, dress discounter. A fast-food cube will sit amid the parking in front. (The parking will always be in front.) The strip will be, as developers put it, on the "going-home" side of a big, suburban arterial. Drive around town and check out other similar strips. You will find they differ in no important detail. In fact, they will differ in no important detail whether they are in Miami or in Maine. It's why you can confuse an office park in Rochester, Minnesota, with one in Rochester, New York. It's why that brick-faced arch over the entrance of a tract house in Parsippany, New Jersey, is indistinguishable from the one in Plano, Texas.

What you will not find in growing communities today is uniqueness (or any recognition of the special qualities of a place), innovation (the means by which we find new ways to adapt places to evolving realities), or longevity (materials and construction methods that add lasting value in ways that keep communities beloved). These are all qualities that a competitive and diverse real estate development industry could offer, but they are qualities that have pretty much been driven out of the development calculation.

It wasn't always this way. Banks used to convey their fiscal substance through the heft of their dour columns and pediments. A downtown office building would once aspire to soar in carved limestone. A house would be made of substantial materials with details lathed and fitted by carpenters out of lumber stock destined to last.

Some years ago, I began a series of conversations with Christopher Leinberger, a real estate analyst turned developer who has probably dug deeper into the mysteries of real estate finance than anyone.[8] Leinberger is convinced that innovation and higher quality belong in the real estate development process and that they can be valued—but not under the real estate finance assumptions that apply today. The real difference between the era that built soaring limestone towers and now, he contends, is that investors then expected to reap their rewards over a very long time—and did.

He offers a unique perspective. From 1981 until he sold his stake in real estate consultant Robert Charles Lessor & Company at the end of the 1990s, Leinberger frequently advised clients to get out of declining downtowns and into shiny-windowed office parks on the outer beltways. ("The market was saying move out, and I was often quoted on that," he confessed ruefully.) Over the years, he found himself appalled at what he saw his clients build, and how his business-relocation services seemed to feed the most exploitative land-use patterns.

At the same time, he saw that such pioneering New Urbanist developments as Seaside, in Florida, became wildly successful by replacing the cookie-cutter cul-de-sac with the walkability, appealing architectural details, and higher density of early 1900s neighborhoods. Seaside "turned the Redneck Riviera into the Hamptons of the Southeast," as Leinberger put it.

Moved by such examples, Leinberger decided to involve himself deeper into development. But he discovered, as builders of places like Seaside had, that lenders didn't like higher densities, even though they were pedestrian friendly. They couldn't value the mix of housing-unit types, even though the idea was to make the community affordable to a wider range of people. (Seaside has been so successful, however, that even modest units have sold at premium prices.) And they could not reconcile the mixing of retail and residential uses that is key to these projects' character and their aspiration to reduce traffic and parking.

Determined to find out why what seemed to make good sense for communities seemed to make no sense to lenders, he set about categorizing the kinds of projects that could qualify for conventional financing. He found that they fell into only nineteen highly simplistic, rigidly proscribed real estate "products." These kinds of projects are easy to finance because real estate lenders have long thought they understood their risks and have been little inclined to look at how they affect the communities they are in.[9] Banks would lend for a strip mall plopped in the middle of a parking lot or a condo complex separated from everything else by a roaring torrent of traffic down an eight-lane arterial. But you could not conventionally finance a row of stores on a tree-lined sidewalk along a pleasingly intimate two-lane street and erect on top of it apartments with terraces and bay windows so that people could share in the street action and walk to shop.

The kinds of developments Leinberger wanted to do—oriented to transit, environmentally sustainable—didn't fit the formulas. "All but two of the nineteen products that lenders recognize create sprawl," Leinberger told me. "They are car oriented, rely on surface parking, are unrelated to surrounding environments, and they consume land wastefully."

The hardening of development standards into rigid formulas happened after the now-forgotten real estate scandals of the 1980s. That bubble and bust, a smaller-scale version of the meltdown of the late 2000s, wiped out most local savings and loans (the banks that then did most local real estate lending) in favor of commercial banks and mortgage brokers, all of which steadily consolidated into such national behemoths as the now-vanished Washington Mutual bank, which, fattened on mortgages tapping paper wealth, imploded in 2008 as the nation's second-largest financial failure ever, exceeded only by Lehman Brothers.[10]

The nationalized system of real estate lending increasingly focused on short-term returns, which meant that what was on paper a forty-year asset class had to generate its greatest returns in one or two seven-year cycles.[11] It has naturally followed that the primary way to ensure high short-term returns is to reduce both "hard" construction costs (by using cheaper materials that wear out quicker and lower-quality craftsmanship) and "soft" development costs, which means fees paid to architects and other consultants. The result is that no one who works on a project can afford to innovate or design something unique or long-lasting even if it doesn't cost more to build.

Projects were not underwritten on their individual merits, says Leinberger. "They became graded and commodified—just like pork bellies." That's why real estate development has differed in no important way anywhere in the country. It is the reason that stores are made of cinder blocks plopped on vast acreages of asphalt, condo developments must rely on a few tack-on gables for "curb appeal"—and why tuning the design of a store to fit an existing neighborhood is a costly, boutique operation, and building on the site of a torn-down factory is a rarity. As Leinberger points out, when you are building a commodity, the only way to make money is to reduce the quality of the commodity and sell it for the same or more.

THE URBAN MARKET GOES MISSING

Developers working in older cities have long chafed at the rigidity of conventional underwriting because all the recognized types are suburban. You could put a new supermarket along a narrow street lined with pleasing small-scale established stores, but only if you are willing to blow up quite a few of them to make room for the standard box surrounded by parking. "If you want something different," Leinberger explained, "it will take a whole lot longer and the price of money will be much higher, so the developer faces a much higher hurdle before it gets its money back."

Real estate had become so rigid that it almost missed the market that seeks urban living in walkable neighborhoods.[12] Since the 1970s, artists have built studios in abandoned industrial lofts, gay couples have fixed up old houses in old neighborhoods, students have started colonizing neighborhoods left for dead, and the historic preservation movement has began to pump life into abandoned Main Streets. The rush of residents to downtowns and central-city neighborhoods is one of the big stories of the past few years. Developers with big-city savvy started following artists and historic preservation aficionados from SoHo in Manhattan to the Lower East Side, and from Brooklyn Heights to Park Slope Clinton and the once-feared, neglected beauty of Bedford-Stuyvesant. Chicago has transformed itself to an even greater extent, with gentrification moving rapidly west from the lakefront and south from the Loop into neighborhoods many in the 1990s would have deemed irredeemable.

People have not moved only into the traditionally appealing old cities such as San Francisco or Boston. Central neighborhoods in Miami, Dallas, Houston, and Atlanta—distinctly unquaint high-rise and parking-lot landscapes home to few residents historically—have become new residential magnets. Even in Detroit's downtown, where trees grew from the cornices of long-abandoned skyscrapers, lights blinked on in thousands of new downtown apartments brought to market before SUV obsession took the American auto industry down.

Estimates now are that the "walkability" market is about one-third of the total market. Leinberger says that singles will form about two-thirds of households over the next twenty years, and about 80 percent of households will be singles and childless couples (which includes retirees with grown children, who are living longer)—a profound change from the 1950s and 1960s, when households were about half singles and half couples. Households without children "tend to want more walkable urban locations where restaurants and other day-to-day services are nearby," Leinberger told me recently.[13] Even families sicken of endless commutes and seek lively, diverse neighborhoods, where strollers are more of a necessity than SUVs.

Old real estate habits die hard, though. The same risk-averse attitudes have strangled New Urbanist developments.[14] Too often, the loft look is cobbled together out of the same synthetic-stucco and vinyl-window ingredients as suburban condos. And if the parking lot brutalizes the scale of the old street, so be it. Because it's been financed the same old way, new lofts tend to be faux lofts.

WHY BEACH FOLLIES PAY

Leinberger didn't see a way to change such a juggernaut, so he went around it. In this way, he followed on the heels of his mentor Robert Davis, the developer of Seaside, Florida. Seaside, of course, is the storybook holiday village that was the first conspicuous success of the New Urbanism. Diminutive but assertive beach pavilions that bridge the ocean dunes are one of Seaside's most memorable features, and their distinctiveness helped the development succeed in its early years, in the 1980s. Even now, lenders and the many developers that have copied the look of Seaside fail to appreciate the value of "frills" such as the pavilions. After all, they don't generate revenue. Davis is mystified; for him, their value is obvious: "They paid off by creating a strong sense of place," he said in an interview.[15]

Davis told me he didn't talk to lenders about the pavilions and other grace notes he planned, because he feared they would compromise the financing. And he intentionally built Seaside slowly, even after its success was assured, so that he would not have to compromise his vision to get loans. "By being patient, I was able to capture the value we had created," he said. Davis is a rich man.

Placeness is not just about cashing in on what less insightful developers overlook. It's about looking for opportunities in problems. As we enter an era when we need to capture everything that's unique about a place in a way that reduces energy and carbon impact, Davis's kind of patience is a virtue. We can upgrade a fossil fuel–using appliance by buying a "green" one. Or we can take the time to find the tactic that avoids the use of that appliance altogether, like cutting the size of a home study or rec room in favor of a shady porch that captures breezes, beats the heat, and allows us to hail passing neighbors. We can't do any of these things if lenders won't or can't determine their value.

Leinberger formed Arcadia Land Company and made an Albuquerque development of housing, offices, restaurants, and a multiplex cinema a laboratory for a new finance methodology that could admit innovation, quality, and the creation of a unique sense of place by rewarding the patient investor. Two years after I first met him, he could point to $26 million of new commercial construction put in place. You could see how Leinberger's modest beginnings were seeding new residential and mixed-use projects by others—this in a downtown that had seen no new commercial construction in the previous fifteen years. At that time, he claimed $100 million of further development was in the pipeline.

He did it by a technique he calls "time tranching." What it does is return the long-term focus to real estate investment by involving investors willing to forgo short-term returns for better, but delayed, results. So the locally based McCune Foundation and the City of Albuquerque, which lent up-front money, committed to waiting twelve years for their returns to begin, but then should do much better than the short-term investors.

The time-tranching idea made low-cost capital available to cover higher-than-average initial construction costs. With a higher building budget, the design of the three-hundred-foot-long block fronts could be broken up to reflect the typical scale of historic downtown development. "We were able to change materials and window types along the block front," explained Bill Dennis, the architect with the local office of Moule & Polyzoides. "In conventional development, all the materials and all the windows would have been the same."

It doesn't sound like much. And in truth, it doesn't look like much—especially compared to the quality built into a merely average 1920s commercial structure. But by the diminished standards of recent years, Leinberger's approach was radical. One of his early partners actually bowed out because he could not understand how a project could make money that cost more than twice as much as the cinder-block box on asphalt he was used to. Once complete, the theater block leased at rents far higher than average for the area.

Time tranching may have even greater benefit for the kinds of conservation development described in chapter 2, because the investment benefits accrue once ruined forests have regrown and damaged streams have been restored—time horizons that are longer than conventional investment cycles. It has not caught on because the short-term investment mind-set is so deeply embedded in business-as-usual real estate finance. Short investment cycles and the rigid resistance to financing any but commodified developments mean many investments that make sense for agile communities won't pencil out.

REWARDING PATIENCE

There's nothing preordained about America's dumbed-down real estate development process. Other countries do things differently—very differently. At the edge of the Elbe River in Hamburg, Germany, I approached a seven-story building that looked like it was covered in bubble wrap stretched tight by cables and turnbuckles. All that yacht hardware is deployed in this building's race to the bottom—of energy use. It was one of several ways architect Stefan Behnisch, of Stuttgart-based Behnisch Architekten, replaced mechanical heating and cooling with natural ventilation for the headquarters for the German, Swiss, and Austrian operations of consumer-products company Unilever. Then he replaced electric lights with daylight. Doing that while maintaining modern business norms for comfort isn't easy, but it unleashes architectural creativity and technical innovation. The transparent wrapping is called ETFE, and the yacht hardware holds it in place about a meter outside the building's glass exterior. It cuts the chill North Sea winds so that occupants can open their windows for ventilation, rather than rely on air conditioning. It also protects external blinds that moderate warm-weather heat and glare.

Inside, the office spaces wrap a lively atrium crisscrossed by bridges and stairways. It is lined with balconies where marketers and product managers sip coffee as they plot world domination by Wisk. Big hula-hoop light fixtures are hardly needed in daytime because the whole thing is bathed in light from skylights overhead (figure 3.4). The atrium makes a big impression, but it is part of the low-energy scheme. As air warms from the heat of people and machines, it flows naturally from offices into the atrium and up through heat-recovery devices that harvest the warmth for parts of the building that need it. Almost everyone sits near a window, so I saw hardly an electric light on when I visited. People work at desks open to the river and atrium views—a far cry from the rows of airless cubicles found in conventional American buildings, most far from the dim, deeply tinted windows.

Unilever requires almost no conventional heating and cooling, which lowers what's called the primary energy use to one hundred kilowatt hours per square meter per year. Remember this mouthful, because it is fast becoming the new lingo of low-energy buildings. By comparison, an average American commercial building requires more than twice that amount.[16]

Unilever goes beyond Germany's stringent existing energy codes but was not expensive. At about four hundred thousand square feet, it cost less than $100 million. It achieved miserly energy use not by wholesale reinvention but by refinement of techniques used in Europe for years.

The double-layer curtain walls, external shading devices, and widespread use of daylight are long established in Germany and much of northern Europe but almost unknown in the United States because they don't pencil out in a real estate development culture of short-term investment horizons, fear of innovation, and the presumption that energy will always be cheap.

How could Germans afford what seems too expensive to Americans? Part of it is culture. Germans believe buildings should be sturdy and last a long time. "Buildings are expected to last sixty to one hundred years," Alex Hinterthan, head of project management at KfW, a German development bank, told me. That long time horizon justifies investments that can't pay back in the seven-to-fifteen-year investment cycles Americans are used to. "Historically, building codes and industry standards strongly encourage the use of rather solid equipment and fittings," added Tajo Friedemann, a consultant at the Frankfurt offices

Figure 3.4 Daylight floods the atrium of the Unilever headquarters for Germany, Austria, and Switzerland, in Hamburg, Germany. Stuttgart firm Behnisch Architekten designed the atrium as a meeting place for the company. The atrium also insulates the offices that line it while providing them with daylight so that electric lights can be turned off. Credit: © Adam Mørk, courtesy Behnisch Architekten

of the international real-estate services firm Jones Lang Lasalle. Which is why extremely sturdy windows, even triple-glazed ones (seen very rarely even in extreme US climates), are found in everyday construction. "These are standard product qualities and are taken for granted," Friedemann explained.[17]

Friedemann explained why Germany has so consistently built to standards that in the United States are thought to be too costly. Political unrest in the Middle East and elsewhere over decades has meant that Germany lost key gas and oil supplies, or was threatened with their loss. (The nation has almost no fossil fuels of its own to exploit.) Forests dying from acid rain and the fallout from the Chernobyl nuclear reactor meltdown drove Germans to embrace a green national agenda, he added. So the country has steadily tightened energy regulations, and early recognized the real threat global warming poses.

Berlin, almost a decade before *An Inconvenient Truth,* defined its future as green, most prominently in the rebuilding of the Reichstag, in which its clear glass cupola daylights the parliamentary chamber below and recycles its waste heat.[18]

In Germany, owners and landlords are now required to get an audit of their energy use (an idea floated in the United States as "cash for caulkers") and provide a certificate to buyers or renters that compares actual consumption to averages for conventional construction and for new construction compliant with stricter codes. (It's much like the energy guides Americans use to compare appliances.) Germany has pledged to reduce greenhouse gas emissions by 40 percent by 2020 (from 1990 levels)—a much more aggressive standard than America has contemplated.[19]

Germans do not look at energy tactics in isolation (as Americans so often do). A variety of forces unite to create the much higher performance of buildings, Friedemann said, from building codes to workplace design. This last is key because professionals tend to have far greater say about the quality of the workplace environment than do Americans. So Germans generally expect to work near a window, for daylight and a view. And that window needs to open, so that people have individual control over temperature and ventilation. Those expectations, and the ability to integrate them into a low-energy regime, are what drive much about the design of commercial buildings, including Unilever. Friedemann applauds these techniques to the extent that they improve productivity (as many do), because a modest improvement in productivity delivers a great deal more cash to the bottom line than even advanced energy-saving tactics, simply because salaries are by far the largest expense for almost every company. They dwarf energy costs even in Germany, where energy is relatively expensive.

DUMBING REAL ESTATE DOWN

Germany is not the only place you can find a quality and inventiveness of design and construction almost unknown in the United States. You find it in much of Europe, frequently in Asia (even now in China), and increasingly in Canada. You can see garden-suburb housing in Holland that experiments with new living arrangements that better fit shrinking households. In vast docklands abandoned by industry in Amsterdam, Rotterdam, Mälmo, and Dusseldorf, new neighborhoods rise that compete to be greener than the last. (Unilever was built as part of Hamburg's green HafenCity redevelopment, discussed in more detail in chapter 8.)

These structures were not more expensive than comparable-quality buildings in the United States (when such can be found). They commonly require the kind of up-front pollution cleanups and infrastructure investments that are enormously difficult to finance in the product-driven real estate culture of America. Since a high level of construction quality is standard in much of Europe, contractors have learned to build in high performance for far less than it would cost in the United States.

By contrast, the urgency of sustainability and the advantages of innovation and adaptation barely registered in American real estate development during the go-go years. I would come back from places where change is ingrained in the growth and development systems and tour American corporate campuses or spec office towers that were identically lumpy and anonymous, clad in shiny thin curtain walling that had the sense of durability and the visual appeal of Mylar wrapping paper. American companies constantly tout their agility in adapting to business conditions and their embrace of emerging technology, but that commitment generally does not extend to the office parks they lease or build, where you find new buildings that differ in no essential way from those built when fax machines were technology's cutting edge. I wasn't the only one who noticed that the United States was supposedly getting richer while building poorer. I hear from all kinds of people who visit foreign places and come back dispirited by the yawning difference in quality.

GROWING OLDER UNGRACEFULLY

When you wrap up the unintended consequences of America's rigid lending system, what you get is a very big penalty for aging. I'm talking about communities, not people. When tax, regulatory, and development finance line up to achieve the quickest profits by plowing up farmland at the urban edge for houses and shopping centers that value low first cost over the preservation of long-term value, you've got a system that offers little to mature communities. Think about it this way. Your neighbor recently bought her house and pays $2,400 in monthly interest, principal, and taxes. You rent but pay the same amount. After she takes tax deductions available to owners, your neighbor (depending on her circumstances) will actually be out of pocket probably $1,600. As a renter, you don't receive any of those tax advantages; you pay full price. She has $800 in monthly spending power that you don't.[20]

Now multiply your neighbor's advantage by many thousands of households, and you understand why new communities at the urban edge see the shopping malls and discount centers rising as quickly as the new tract houses are roofed. Growth, fueled by government benefits, drives more growth, and this pumps up highway demand (since urban-edge communities can almost never be efficiently served by transit), and local officials are only too happy to tap state and federal coffers for those roads—if some new beltway has not already made the development possible. (There's no federal or state aid for communities forward-looking enough to build transit—or the potential for transit—ahead of growth.)

Since the private, for-sale market for new houses reaches very few people who earn less than median income, that tax benefit–fueled growth advances the fortunes mainly of high-end subdivisions.[21] (Median income is useful because in most places it is an income level that should place you comfortably in the middle class. Half the earners are below and half are above median.) In the most expensive metropolitan areas, market-rate housing fails to serve families with incomes well above the median.

You rarely find the urban-edge building frenzy even in solid mature suburbs or in older cities. The homeowner's government benefits are worth less as people pay down their mortgages. There are more renters, receiving no benefits at all. This is why a great number of older suburbs, older towns, and older cities don't look as if they are attracting new investment even when they are stable and well maintained.

Lower-income earners, shut out of the high-growth belt, settle in older communities that tend to have poorer access to jobs, substandard schools, and lower-quality housing. The housing finance system has few tools to spur reinvestment in such communities. Investment actually tends to flow out of mature neighborhoods, because there are few owners with excess cash to plow back into their communities in the form of spending. Instead, people who can afford to leave are going to those newer precincts where government benefits lower costs while spurring jobs and growth. And there's no penalty for affluent communities that zone out lower-earning families by prohibiting apartment houses and small houses on small lots.

Worse, government support programs for people who are burdened by housing costs have declined steadily and precipitously for more than twenty years, leaving lower-income communities at greater disadvantage.[22] As a result, the percentage of people who are "distressed" (in governmentese) because they must pay too much for housing rose at the same time that the percentage of households that own (qualifying for generous government tax benefits) moved up. At the peak of the housing bubble, more than a third of households were either "cost burdened," as the government defines it, or "severely cost burdened": those who pay more than 50 percent of their income for housing.

This is a trend that has been growing for more than twenty years, too, even as home values, homeownership, and poverty levels have fluctuated up and down.[23] Families struggling with housing costs must often sacrifice other necessities—health care, car repairs, job training, school supplies for children. These are the people whose lives could be transformed by ready government housing assistance or a private sector focused on affordability. Massive foreclosures on subprime mortgages in low-income communities added legions to the underhoused.

I was once called a Nazi by a letter writer for daring to propose a reduction in bloated homeowner tax benefits. The ideology of home owning—and the tax goodies that go with it—are so deeply embedded in America's psyche that tampering with it is like tearing out the heart of the American dream. It isn't. The supposed moral goodness of home owning blinded buyers, mortgage makers, officials, and bankers to the abuses that led to the collapse of the housing market. That might be forgivable if we hadn't been blinded to similar savings and loan shenanigans in the 1980s, which cost a million people their homes in Texas alone, or the dot-com boom and bust of the late 1990s.[24]

REIMAGINING REAL ESTATE

We cannot adapt to the future if we continue to throw away so many wasteful billions exactly the same way we always have. We need to redesign the way real estate finance works so that it builds (and reinvigorates) environmentally responsible and economically vibrant communities, not just strip malls.

Tax advantages and other forms of subsidy for housing must focus on communities and families that need them, rather than just piling on subsidy gimmicks for subdividers.

The enormous pain of the housing crash demands that we rein in the most abused of the tax goodies for homeowners. In general, the United States should not forgive capital gains taxes on the sale of a home. Eliminating that subsidy will dampen harmful price inflation and encourage people to think of their houses as homes rather than investment vehicles. Deducting interest on home-equity loans should be permitted only when the loan proceeds go to fixing up a house—especially to make it more energy efficient or otherwise adapt it to meet environmental challenges. That will put a stop to the habit of using paper equity for ready cash.

Tax benefits and direct subsidies to homeowners should encourage builder and designer innovation and should reward homes that are smaller, more efficient, and sited to shore up existing communities and repair environmental damage. Put financing of multifamily projects on the same playing field as single-family housing, for example. There's a traditional bias against condos in a downturn, a prophecy often self-fulfilled by corner-cutting multifamily builders. High fuel prices and changing demographics (more childless adults of all ages with interests broader than lawn care) should at last trump habit, rewarding well-designed apartment buildings close to jobs and transit. Apartments are by nature more efficient because of shared walls and floors, and encouraging them is a painless way to cut housing costs and carbon emissions significantly.

Agility, though, means confronting some God-and-country stuff: phase out deductions for mortgage interest on vacation homes. When America is not adequately housing people with severe needs, it cannot afford to underwrite luxe digs on beaches and in mountains. Such a move would reward modest getaways—which is what a low-impact/high-efficiency lifestyle and economy demand.

Finally, we need to curtail the mortgage-interest and property-tax deductions, even for primary homes. This is the most incendiary change, of course. A cap would recognize that taxpayers should not be underwriting home-building profligacy, and it would dampen price inflation. (The years of double-digit price rises felt good to those who already owned, but they erected real barriers for those trying to own for the first time, which would have kept millions out of the housing market but for subprime and other mortgage exotica delaying the inevitable.)

Agile communities and an agile economy demand that we do a better job supporting the rental housing economy. Renting makes sense in a volatile economy, especially for young people starting out. And renting makes sense for older people, who are living longer and who want to live on the wealth created by owning and scale down their lives. Not all renters need subsidy. Strategically targeted aid could bring great benefit at low cost. Subsidizing low-cost housing close to workplace hubs is a high-efficiency tactic that offers a career boost to people starting out and delivers an economical workforce to business. Both municipalities and business groups have long been concerned that lengthening commutes between low-cost communities and job-dense business centers lowers the quality of the workforce. You can't hire janitors, security guards, and secretaries for jobs that require driving forty-five minutes each way in a wheezing econobox. Punishing commutes drive away well-educated and experienced talent, too. Today's vast distances between affordable communities and job-rich ones is, of course, environmentally wasteful.[25]

The scandalous "system" of financing affordable housing also needs to become less complex. If you want to build fifty apartment units targeting people earning 40 percent of median income, for example, you must assemble a phalanx of lenders and tap into a tax credit that relies on wealthy businesses needing tax shelters. Why shouldn't organizations seeking to house the underhoused go to the head of the financing line instead of the end of it? Projects that attempt to restore streams or forests *and* house lower-income people *and* create neighborhood amenity deserve white-glove treatment by financiers.

I'd like the industry to have a look at the work of the prototype builders in New Orleans and Biloxi. Developers need to ask, what would it take to make that kind of innovation safe for investors? These are the kinds of projects that could benefit from lower-cost loans offered by a development bank like KfW in Germany. KfW was established by the United States to reconstruct Germany after World War II. Now it lends to fund green projects in Germany and worldwide. The bank evaluates the viability of proposed projects forwarded by local banks. If they meet its criteria, KfW can lower borrowing costs because of its government backing. (The private mortgage-purchasing agencies known as Fannie Mae and Freddie Mac took on the same task in the United States, but in a far less direct and transparent way, and ended up abetting the mortgage meltdown.) KfW makes green projects affordable and stimulates green innovation. In lending 7.5 billion euros for German projects, some as small as single-family homes, KfW has generated 54 billion euros of new construction and redevelopment.[26] That's one place innovation would come from.

"Green accounting," as Leinberger calls it, can unite investors with tattered natural systems so that we can move quickly toward a high-efficiency/low-impact future by making it profitable. Financial acumen could "look at externalities—the impacts on the environment—and monetize them," Leinberger adds, "which may change the decisions that are made."

"A lot of investors are saying we've got to invest in LEED-certified buildings," Leinberger added, because their performance is measurable and comparable."That could become a prerequisite, just as back in the 1960s investors collectively decided not to buy buildings that were not air conditioned. If LEED becomes such a prerequisite, buildings that are not certified become the equivalent of a buggy whip, an obsolete investment."[27] Such an attitude adjustment would put us in the class of Germany and other cultures that build with long time horizons in mind.

Real estate professionals could offer specialized expertise to analyze the new kinds of development opportunities in the emerging green economy. According to Carl Palmer, Beartooth Capital (introduced in chapter 2) "works at a small scale but we imagine it up. When we buy and restore and protect a property, it creates tangible benefits for adjacent lands, whether public or private." Continues Palmer: "The land downstream has more fish, higher quality water, and less sediment that must be cleaned out of ditches. Traditionally these have been thought of as externalities. What we do is try to capture those benefits for our investors, not that we don't want others to benefit too. Buying a whole watershed and managing it ecologically appropriately—putting in financial capital to get the natural capital—should yield much larger benefits. If you do it at a landscape scale, you should be able to harvest that value in a wide variety of ways: improved agricultural production, fishing and hunting, better water quality, lower operating costs for property—a litany of improvements."[28] Markets like that, he is quick to note, are neither workable yet nor free of risk, but there are ways to make his kind of innovation safer, so that he and others can try them out, learn from them, and make them work better. Others are looking at forests not just as a timber source but as instruments that can be tuned—according to the timing of planting and harvesting—to sequester carbon now and release it when it would be less harmful. Global Green's Beth Galante told me that some experts are looking at a payment scheme that would finance the restoration of Louisiana's receding coastal marshes because they have the potential to absorb vast amounts of carbon.

Can short-term subsidies or R&D investment bring down the cost of solar panels or geothermal heating and cooling? Would some carefully tailored tax benefits quickly bring to market energy-efficient and sustainably sourced modular, factory-built housing, which has the potential to hugely reduce the costs of mass-producing housing adapted to storms, floods, and minimized energy use? Can conventional financing be tweaked to shorten the payback time of energy-conservation tactics or to make high-performance construction techniques affordable to people of modest means? We don't know the answers to these questions because they have yet to be asked in any systematic way.

LEAVING THE CHECKLISTS BEHIND

Checklist lending won't do for an agile development era, though it's not clear that the severely damaged real estate finance industry has gotten the message. It should be possible to analyze the financial performance of projects that engage with difference, localness, and innovation. It's what innovation-driven segments of any business do.

It's time to reduce the age penalty. The simplicity of the investment should not triumph over all other values. Rejiggering the tax code and regulations can bring externalities (like the cost of new infrastructure) into the greenfield-development formula so developers and buyers pay the true costs. We can also include the benefits of revitalizing mature communities: increasing the supply of appealing housing, for example, so that people don't have to migrate to the urban edge to find an affordable place to live.

People fear that shifting direct subsidies, rewriting regulations, and changing tax policies to nurture more environmentally responsible development may be expensive, but that is not necessarily the case. After all, building in existing communities takes advantage of investments that have already been made—in roads, sewers, and so on. New family housing helps fill schools long built and paid for. And as builders and developers learn to work in such communities, they find unexpected opportunities and new kinds of niches—like Gary Reddick, an architect I met in Portland, Oregon, who convinced a developer that he could make money building apartments over a supermarket parking lot.

You can see how opportunities grow rather than shrink when we start filling in existing communities. When Denver built a new airport, the site of its old Stapleton airport, close to the center of town, went from a single use that induced enormous traffic and noise to a ten-thousand-resident mixed-use community that's bikable and walkable and that added 30 percent to the city's park space.[29] Aside from the energy and global warming advantages, of course, rebuilding stagnant or declining communities offers enormous other benefits: reducing poverty and crime and shoring up communities to contribute human energy and economic wealth instead of leaving communities to decline, sapping human and economic capital.

The biggest enemy of real estate agility is inertia—many are happy just as things are, or they fear change. We cannot forget what the mortgage meltdown revealed: that the old rules weren't actually prudent, simply formulaic, encouraging lazy lending practices.

Even if climate change and large-scale environmental degradation were not issues, housing finance is broken, and regarding a mini-storage mall as among the most worthy real estate investments properly should be seen as ridiculous. The challenge for real estate is to find ways to expand the menu of what can be financed. Enough nonsuburban, non-single-family markets have developed in established urban places that lenders should be figuring out why they work and should expand such opportunity. From there, developing the means to fund adaptive, innovative, do-no-harm kinds of development isn't much of a challenge.

4

RE-ENGINEERING
TRANSPORTATION

In what sounds like a throwback to the epic freeway boondoggles of the 1960s, Seattle will brutalize one of America's great urban lakes with a $4.65 billion plan to replace the earthquake-vulnerable Evergreen Point Bridge. The existing bridge never won beauty contests, but its planned replacement is more than twice as wide, running well above the mountain-ringed Lake Washington on much larger, obtrusive pontoons (figure 4.1). It then broadens to the width of an airport runway as it hacks through the arboretum, a crown-jewel park, and paves over a hunk of Portage Bay, a beloved inlet that provides a watery setting for the University of Washington. As it dumps more cars on the overburdened city streets that serve the forty-one-thousand-student university, the plan bowdlerizes a gracefully arching street bridge with a second replica span. The Evergreen bridge, a key link between Seattle and Eastside suburbs, will pour more traffic onto Seattle's gridlocked I-5 backbone and the Eastside's jammed I-405 beltway.

There's more. State coffers also are opening to replace an elevated highway along the downtown waterfront that's another seismic accident waiting to happen. A two-mile, $3.4 billion tunnel has been deemed the answer, even though it provides less access to downtown—which is what the elevated highway has chiefly served. (More ramps would have cost more millions.) An ongoing expansion to the perennially congested I-405 suburban beltway could ultimately come in at $10 billion—if funds can be raised.[1] The total price tag for this mess cannot actually be calculated because billions worth of work will have to be

83

Figure 4.1 Seattle plans to double the width of the Evergreen Point Bridge, even though it is simultaneously building light rail in lower-demand corridors. Credit: Washington State Department of Transportation

done to deal with the traffic that the Evergreen bridge will add to I-405 and I-5, which has not been admitted to, let alone priced.[2]

Though Washington State voters upped the gas tax a whopping 14.5 cents per gallon, the Evergreen bridge project is still short almost $2 billion. The downtown waterfront road tunnel may need tolls as high as $5 per trip. By comparison, America's most extravagant highway project—the Big Dig, in Boston—doesn't seem quite so eye-popping even though it cost $14 billion. And what will all Seattle's dollars do? Rearrange the traffic jams.

This boondoggle is a colossal embarrassment to a city that touts its eco-friendliness. Like much of the United States, Seattle has started building light rail, but it does not seem to trust transit as an auto alternative.

I took a ride on Sound Transit's first light-rail line, completed in 2009. Because it was sited to suit neighborhood politics rather than transportation needs, it does not beeline from downtown along a heavily congested corridor to the airport, as it ought to. It departs every eight to fifteen minutes, wanders fourteen miles in a great U, runs leisurely through several neighborhoods, and finally arrives at the airport almost forty minutes after departure, about twice as long as it ought to take. After spending $2.7 billion, the line attracts fewer than twenty thousand riders a day.[3]

At about the same time, Vancouver, British Columbia, finished a $2 billion (Canadian dollars) twelve-mile light-rail line from the airport to downtown. The Canada Line is separated from surface streets for its entire length and runs in a more or less straight line, so the trip takes twenty-six minutes and trains arrive every four to six minutes. Within weeks of its opening, ridership had risen to more than one hundred thousand daily, far ahead of projections.[4]

As Seattle's light-rail line neared completion, area voters passed an $18 billion, fifteen-year bond issue that patches together a larger bus and light-rail system. The stage would seem to have been set for an integrated solution to the area's worst congestion, one in which transit and roads would share the burden along high-traffic corridors. Unfortunately, light rail remains relegated to second-class status. It follows slow, wayward routes. That keeps costs low (less than one-sixth the per-mile cost of the highway projects) and pleases noisy local constituencies as the route wobbles to take in each neighborhood. What Seattle needs, as most cities do, is high-speed, high-capacity lines because they can take people out of cars on the busiest, most car-clogged freeway corridors. The Canada Line, for example, serves a very busy corridor even though a freeway had never been built along it. Similarly, Route 520, the Evergreen bridge freeway, is the perfect candidate for fast, high-capacity rail because it links four of the metropolitan area's most activity-intense centers (two large suburbs, the university, and downtown Seattle).

A Vancouver-style transit line could double Route 520's current 115,000 daily vehicle capacity with just one track going each way. (The current road plan adds a bus lane and so achieves much lower and slower capacity. The state claims rail could be added later.) A less-blighting Evergreen bridge design is then possible, and the light rail could affordably tunnel its way from the Evergreen bridge to a conveniently located stop at the university, intersecting an already planned rail line from downtown Seattle. It would avoid the need to wreck the lake and clog the university with more cars.

Seattle's kind of muddle produces America's national land transportation system—if one dares call such a jury-rigged contrivance a system. Remaking transportation is perhaps the biggest untapped opportunity that is least discussed in the global warming debate. After all, transportation is responsible for 28 percent of US greenhouse gas emissions.[5] Fixing our haphazard way of

moving people around offers such profound economic and livability benefits that the great potential it has for reducing carbon emissions can seem
incidental—though, of course, it's not.

Transportation priorities have a profound and long-documented effect on
urban settlement patterns. Building the Erie Canal ensured New York's preemi-
nence over Philadelphia in the early nineteenth century. Great cities arose at rail
crossings—St. Louis, Kansas City, Chicago—while capitals of the age of sail
shriveled. In the era after World War II, freeway cities and jet-airplane hubs,
such as Los Angeles, Atlanta, and Dallas, blossomed, while rail cities foundered.

No such transformational movement technology is in the offing. Instead,
we need to deploy transportation modes to suit the settlement patterns we
need. This sounds reasonable, but the United States has never attempted to
grow in this way before.

WHY YOU CAN'T GET THERE

To get a sense of how we've limited our options, start with a street in a conventional cul-de-sac. The least polluting and most fuel-efficient mode of transportation is by foot. Many subdivisions don't even have sidewalks, and walking
in the street can be uninviting even when there's little traffic. Walk ten minutes,
about a third of a mile, and you may meet neighbors but chances are you won't
get as far as a school, church, supermarket, or drugstore. Or, if you do, you are
likely to confront a massive, dark, noisy, unsafe freeway overpass along the way.
Or you'll have to cross a busy arterial, one unlikely to have crosswalks or
pedestrian signals. You wouldn't want small children to tackle it alone.

A bicycle, maybe? After all, you can cover three miles in that same ten minutes. You can run a lot of errands in three miles—get to school, maybe even to
a job. But you will have to cross the same arterial, or ride along it, with drivers
passing inches away at 45 miles per hour. Wherever you go, you'll be competing with cars—in parking lots, at intersections. And you'll feel vulnerable: Does
he see me? Where did that pothole come from? Can't let the kids ride to
school—too much traffic.

Jump on the bus that stops a half mile from home, runs every forty-five
minutes, and takes twenty minutes to get to a destination five minutes away?
Please. Ride a streetcar? Take a train? Such systems serve a tiny fraction of
urban America today.

So whether you are commuting across town or running everyday errands locally, chances are you are climbing into a car. In the great scheme of things, chauffering kids around, meeting buddies at a basketball court, and picking up a couple of things at the drugstore does not sound like much. It adds up, though, not just in miles but in the forms our communities take. Those arterials lacing the subdivisions have been made four and six lanes wide to accommodate the daily errand running, not just the rush-hour commutes. Parking lots are twice the size of stores because retailers must make space for the shopper picking up two items as well as the customer filling a shopping cart. The freeways jammed much of the day are sized for people hopping on one exit and off two exits later to pick up the kids at ballet lessons. There's not enough space to accommodate that kind of driving along with the hordes of trucks hauling everything we make and everything we buy.

The same story applies as we widen our view to the scale of cities. A modest-size suburban commercial center containing five million square feet of office space must be served by two four-lane freeways in order to avoid major backups. But since those freeways need to serve a variety of other destinations and needs at the same time, they probably need to be twice the size.

Transit is not just a nicety that avoids pumping a few tons of carbon dioxide into the air; it's a mobility solution that has very powerful economic consequences as well. But Seattle is not the only place that doesn't match the transportation mode to the problem. It's how the United States wastefully spends transportation dollars.

TYING GROWTH TO TRANSPORTATION

To make any substantive change to the way we move involves overhauling the nation's habitual—and increasingly senseless—means of supplying transportation.

Though the nation spends a lot of money on buses and rails, we really have a one-size-fits-all transportation priority: the auto. Road supply is why Merrill Lynch was able some years ago to bulldoze a farm field at the rural fringe of Mercer County, New Jersey, and build on it an office park that they hoped would one day reach 5.5 million square feet—about the size of five downtown skyscrapers.[6] Many people who work at the complex drive a great distance to it, and they might not have been able to make this choice if federal policy was not so generous to drivers. That's because federal subsidies (copycatted by states) for driving long meant that Merrill Lynch (which was absorbed by Bank of America in 2008) didn't really have to consider whether it made sense to build a huge facility far from population centers and existing highways. It didn't have to worry about the costs to staff of the long commutes to bedroom communities. It didn't have to consider the costs vendors might assume in traveling the enormous distance from established centers to service the company. For a long time, it could depend on the state to step in and improve roads that became jammed due to the traffic generated by its development. After all, the state had plenty of money to spend on widening once-sleepy byways, thanks to federal largesse. Of course, the same policy also assists the transformation of what for neighbors might have been a rural idyll into yet another arterial strip lined with discounters and fast-food stores as well as office parks.

History may not be kind to the bet Merrill made. Steadily rising gas prices have made the cost of those long commutes a real consideration. New Jersey can no longer afford to keep widening the highways. (It has fought over any number of schemes for raising cash, including huge toll hikes.[7]) The planet cannot afford the business-location calculus Merrill Lynch used.

Is it realistic to significantly reduce America's car dependence? The answer is yes, but that answer comes not from inventing some supercar (though that would help), or creating a vast science-fiction system of personal transit (a panacea that pops up with regularity), but from methodically and systematically putting in place some prosaic auto alternatives that a great number of people can use. Bike lanes and rationalized local bus routes can replace some of the endless suburban errand running (figure 4.2). Rail lines and frequent express buses (called bus rapid transit, or BRT) can link high-activity destinations. Upgraded freight rail can remove hordes of trucks from highways. Bullet-train service replaces short-haul flights from overcrowded big-city airports, while high-speed rail links smaller cities to global hubs.

We can't efficiently diversify the way we get around except by tying land use and development more closely to transportation strategy. Instead of applying a Band-Aid of new highway lanes to any place that's congested, the idea is to build the kind of transportation that will most efficiently serve people's activities. Such an idea sounds perfectly sensible, but it is not what we do. A warehouse that employs few and moves a lot of freight needs to be near highways and freight railways. This is the kind of activity well served by the asphalt pouring we use to supply mobility today. A hospital, however, should be close to

Figure 4.2 So many people travel by rail and bike in Holland that a multilevel, five-thousand-bike garage was built at Amsterdam's central railroad station. Credit: James S. Russell

where its patients live yet draw from a wide area for its staff. If doctors' offices were clustered within walking distance of hospitals, rather than scattered in all directions over a five-mile radius, a nexus of activity would develop that transit as well as roads could conveniently and efficiently serve.

Such a nesting of transportation and high-density business and institutional centers almost never happens now. That's because a developer or government agency chooses a plot of cheap land; plops an office park, subdivision, or college on it; and then expects local government to put in new roads and widen existing ones to accommodate their decision. You understand why this gets expensive.

Modes other than the automobile can efficiently serve colleges, courthouses, city halls, shopping malls, airports, sports stadiums, convention centers, and business centers—in short, almost every key economic and civic urban institution—only if the constituent parts cluster in close proximity to one another in hubs along natural movement corridors. (Instead, extravagant boulevards and vast parking lots widely separate buildings in too many college campuses, business districts, and government centers. These layouts demand driving because they are unwalkable and too diffuse to collect people at a transit station.) It would take forty-five freeway lanes to deliver the same number of people at the rush-hour peak as New York's nearly one-hundred-year-old Pennsylvania Station handles.

Since government rarely insists that land use be coordinated with the way roads and rails are supplied, there is almost no opportunity to create bus or rail transportation capacity in any conventionally efficient way. It's why those rare suburban buses trundle so few passengers. It's why anywhere from one-third to two-thirds of urbanized space is paved for roads or parking, and much of that is empty much of the time. Not even the freeway web in most big metropolitan areas reflects an efficient idea about moving people. You find a tight and tangled web of highways in some places, a loose to nonexistent one in others—a diagram of the ad hoc, reactive, Band-Aid means in which we build these roads, etched in thousands of miles of concrete. Some parts of the network are always congested; others are clear, choked off by the clogged parts.

It's not just that auto-scaled, low-density urbanism puts too many people too distant from bus and rail lines. Most development today is flung down without any notion of connecting to related (possibly competing) activities. Strip malls, gas stations, and fast-food outlets dribble along endless miles of arterial. One subdivision curves east while the one across the arterial winds west so that they can't meet or connect together. It's why most suburban bus routes wander drunkenly rather than directly connect one point to another.

BANISH THE BELTWAYS

Beltways, though, are enemy number one. Those highway rings that wrap cities look tidy on engineers' drawings, but they are a costly and extraordinarily inefficient growth device posing as a traffic solution. The billions spent on beltways, outer beltways, and outer-outer beltways wrapping major cities would not be justified by local demand. There is little highway demand to be found when these behemoths ram their way through farms and forests. They're supposed to permit long-distance traffic to bypass the congested center, but that is not the kind of traffic that fills beltways. Instead, they induce huge amounts of new local traffic by shifting growth outward to cheap open land. (Since the interstate highway system was completed almost forty years ago, most new freeway construction has not linked cities to one another—which was the original reason for the federally funded highway system—but has cut outer-ring highways to open land for new urban growth.)

The beltway is an idea fixed in the road engineer's head rather than a solution that solves real problems on the ground. Cities and suburbs tend to grow outward in uneven wedges from the oldest centers along major transportation corridors, but beltways disregard this natural growth pattern by shooting a highway through a donut of mostly undeveloped land around the existing urbanized area.[8]

Beltways open vast amounts of space, often many times the size of the built-up metro—all of it poorly connected to existing communities. Local-road tendrils gradually grow out from the new intersections, feeding new office parks and subdivisions, all of which are miles from one another. (A fifty-mile highway ring will accommodate roughly twenty-five zones of new development opportunity—excuse me, exits.) A lot of open space remains but is fragmented, much of it of little value. New projects rise on the most accessible tracts, generating traffic that must use the beltway to get to any place useful. In this way, beltways rapidly fill, and jams quickly rival or exceed older through highways (figure 4.3).

Beltway settlement varies enormously in scale, density, and affluence, with corresponding variations in ability to affordably supply good schools and government services, as well as major infrastructure like power plants and water supply. Most important, urban growth organized by beltways is all but impossible to serve efficiently by any alternative to the automobile. Since beltways shape growth in most metropolitan areas, it is not surprising that transit patronage overall has stagnated or declined metrowide, even though urban systems and some suburban ones have seen substantial increases in ridership.

We would end up with much more compact and efficient communities just by allowing growth to extend around naturally occurring movement corridors and directly linking key activity centers with trunkline corridors of roads, buses, and rails.

FITTING BUSES, RAILS, AND STREETS TOGETHER

Transit, deemed in many cities suitable only for domestics and day laborers, becomes a useful part of anyone's daily life—even a pleasurable one—when

Figure 4.3 Beltways, promoted as bypass highways for long-haul traffic, instead ineffi-ciently open land for development at the urban edge, as in Las Vegas (shown here). Credit: James S. Russell

woven gracefully into the metropolitan fabric. On a local level, several cities are already building "green streets" (sometimes dubbed "complete streets," as if standard arterials are psychologically unbalanced, as perhaps they are). Green streets divide an arterial into separate carriageways for bikes, buses or light rail, and cars (figure 4.4). Widened, tree-lined sidewalks make walking more ap-pealing. Corner sidewalk bump-outs make pedestrian crossings less intimidat-ing. Trees and rain gardens replace the bleakness of arterial commercial strips with the shady scale of old-style boulevards (absorbing carbon in the process). In contrast to the signage cacophony of strips, they civilize their surroundings (raising property values) and attractively reduce the amount of rain dumped into sewers.

These streets can't move as many cars, but they move more people (this is the goal too often forgotten by transport engineers) by putting alternatives to the auto on a more even footing. Those buses and trams, with much higher ca-pacity per lane, move faster, becoming more attractive. Then it becomes afford-able to offer service at convenient speeds and intervals.

Figure 4.4 American cities are planning "green streets" like this one in Bilbao, Spain, which handsomely accommodates (from left to right) a separated bike lane, a sidewalk, two lanes for cars, and two streetcar tracks in a landscaped median. Credit: James S. Russell

The United States has tended to lurch from one transit panacea to another, when creating a truly useful system means layering several transportation modes. Light rail is the hot ticket these days, but a rail line that trundles along at thirty-five miles per hour and hits top speed of around fifty miles per hour is providing 1920s service, not twenty-first-century service.

Bus rapid transit enjoyed a vogue, and is successful in Los Angeles, but is slow to catch on elsewhere, even though it offers many benefits—reasonable speeds at a cost closer to conventional buses. BRT is an express service that speeds the ride by dedicating a special lane to buses. Riders prepay at waiting pavilions so they can step on the bus with no delay. Traffic signals may be tuned to favor buses. BRT works in spread-out suburbia, where destinations are so diffuse that the passenger potential does not justify rail investment. In such places, a well-planned BRT network sketches out a future high-speed rail network that can be put in place later as growth coalesces around well-served transit hubs. Streetcars are hot, but they rarely offer advantages over either well-designed bus routes or light rail. A recent line in downtown Portland, Oregon, though jammed, moves even more slowly than a bus.[9]

Vancouver's Skytrain system deserves emulation in US cities because it offers high-capacity, high-speed service competitive with drive times yet its cost is not budget busting. Frequent, fast, and cost-efficient should be the holy grail of transit design but is not. Getting across today's large metro expanses requires design speeds on key lines competitive with free-flowing freeways—on the order of eighty miles per hour—which today you find only on rare stretches of commuter rail built in the early 1900s.

Metro, which ties Maryland and Virginia to the District of Columbia, is the best-designed modern rail system in America. It is heavily used because it is fast, with five lines fanning out from the center of Washington in all directions. It is the most comprehensive modern rail system in America, even though it does not connect suburb to suburb and can't accommodate express trains (like New York City's ancient system does) until costly investment in additional tracks and tunnels are approved. Yet it has had real impact on the form of greater Washington. The greatest growth in office space in the Washington, DC, suburbs is in proximity to the Metro stations, according to Robert Lang, an expert in suburban growth at the Metropolitan Institute at Virginia Tech. Only New York and Chicago have more transit-oriented office space, he said in an interview.[10]

Truly integrated transportation planning is a dead art in America, so we'll have to rebuild our expertise. We have to layer services—local and express, buses and trains—just as systems one hundred years old do. Linking airports to downtowns and to hinterlands is desperately needed but involves making turf-guarding government agencies work together. Good rail service can avoid investments in new terminals (more than $1 billion each in crowded airports) and new runways (ditto the cost). A major new airport will run you $10 to $15 billion. Blistering-fast rail, like France's TGV and Japan's bullet trains, will pencil out in the United States when it lowers its cost by sharing its corridors with upgraded freight rail and speedy passenger service that accesses smaller hubs along the same corridor.

Freight rail is utterly unsexy, but it is many times less costly per mile (in both fuel and drivers) than trucks and emits only one-third the carbon emissions.[11] Rail fell by the wayside because the nation started subsidizing roads at the expense of rail, so railroads were consigned to moving commodities like gravel, timber, and chemicals—especially commodities that were low in value, heavy, dangerous, or otherwise unsuited to trucks. However, congested highways and spiking fuel costs have made even wobbly tracks and antique bridges a better bet for shipping goods that once went only by truck. Many rail corridors are busier than they have been for decades (with Amtrak trains and added commuter trains seeking growing access to tracks, too).

Ultimately a deal must be made to integrate the private rail system into a multimodal whole. Bringing rail more thoroughly into the transportation mix, tentatively begun under the Obama administration, offers such enormous benefits that it's worth renegotiating the public and private roles in rail— normally a political nonstarter. States, for example, may take on track ownership and maintenance (just as they do with roads) and collect rents from rail companies to operate on them, spurring competition.

RETROFITTING GRIDLOCKED SUBURBIA

Aren't today's cities too diffused and spread out to make transit work? Not necessarily. Las Vegas may not have an extravagant bus system but—as Steve van Gorp, deputy business development director at the City of Las Vegas, told me in 2005—it makes a profit, even at California-style density. That would make sense because the vast majority of the city's jobs are concentrated along the Las Vegas Boulevard strip rather than spread out all over the place. At a casual glance, Vancouver, British Columbia, has the same neighborhood scale as many American cities and suburbs, but the city has focused high-density development not just in its high-rise downtown but around stops on its three Skytrain rail lines (figure 4.5). That's part of the equation that makes the rail system run surpluses.[12] Note, also, that Vancouver is laced with very few freeway miles, and yet traffic moves in much of the metro area better than in the United States. There are road bottlenecks (on those few miles of freeway mainly), but not the epic beltway jams Americans have come to live with.

Can suburbia be retrofitted to reduce reliance on cars? A few areas have already done it. Traveling east from Seattle, the cluster of skyscrapers in Bellevue, once just a bedroom suburb, makes an impressive silhouette against the Cascade Mountains. The towers did not rise by accident but according to a concerted effort to focus development around a regional shopping center and bus-transit hub. Only a few years ago, Bellevue was like most so-called edge cities, blocks of parking lots dotted with mostly one-story buildings served by massive arterials. Today, with its parks, sidewalks, bikeways, museum, and library, it's a walk-to-work, walk-to-shop destination. Its downtown has grown

Figure 4.5 Surrey, British Columbia, a suburb of Vancouver, combined a renovated shopping center with university facilities and office space for an insurance company (Bing Thom Architects). The density and mix were possible thanks to its adjacency to a station of greater Vancouver's Skytrain rail transit. Credit: Nic Lehoux, courtesy Bing Thom Architects

enormously on a footprint little larger than it had in 1960, with the metro area's second-biggest transit hub. By contrast, car-centric Tysons Corner, outside Washington, DC, struggles to grow, because it can't fit more cars into its tangled web of super arterials. It hopes to benefit from an extension of the Metro.

Coordinating development to transportation is not rocket science to anyone in the business. It's conventional wisdom. Politically, though, tethering development to a planned approach to infrastructure is explosive because it's thought to mean ceding to government the landowners' opportunity to develop their land in just about any way they want. Of course, many landowners also expect taxpayers to bring roads and utilities *to* their land and to serve new subdivisions with schools, no matter how costly it is. Services can take the form of a rural-highway turnoff or that $100 million freeway interchange that transforms your weed-choked farm field into valises of cash borne by auto-mall developers.

A closer coordination of growth and transportation capacity is not the leap into command-and-control, Soviet-style central planning that it is depicted to be by land-use libertarians. We voluntarily subject ourselves and our communities to a wide variety of regulations that attempt to control tax expenditures, slow growth, or encourage desirable kinds of growth. The kinds of taxes we collect affect growth.

The question is simply the degree to which people will support an infrastructure growth and renewal process that explicitly furthers community goals—anticipating the future rather than reacting to the latest mall proposal after it has been made. Citizens have an interest in the provision of infrastructure not just because it encourages some kinds of growth and discourages others but because we largely pay for it through taxes.

Will rearranging the layout of communities and diversifying travel modes make enough of a difference in carbon-reduction terms? New and retrofitted communities that link dense development tightly to multiple transportation modes can cut per-person driving miles every year close to 30 percent, according to a research team led by Reid Ewing and Keith Bartholomew. The Vision California plan, which proposes an aggressive response to climate change by tying development and transportation together, could dramatically cut infrastructure costs, water use, building energy use, miles people must drive every year, fuel consumption, and greenhouse gas emissions.[13] If auto alternatives are convenient enough to allow a family to sell off one car, that family could save (conservatively) $10,000 a year.

Limping along with some semblance of old-style leapfrog development will actually induce so much growth in the miles we drive yearly that it will wipe out the advantage of the high-mileage auto fleet of smaller, thirty-five-mile-per-gallon cars and costly hybrids that's already mandated.[14] That's the key lesson: we can decrease fuel use by improving auto technology, but we can't really cut the miles we drive without rethinking the way we build communities. Economic efficiency and a global warming future (as well as a future of oscillating oil supplies) will demand we do both.

There are those who think a new generation of plug-in electric cars will save us. That's unlikely, though they'll make their contribution. Their cost, in the short term, will keep them a small percentage of the nation's auto fleet. Until battery technology improves, they'll be better for short-distance travel, which makes them a useful fit primarily in urban areas that become tighter and denser through more integrated planning of growth and transportation. In the longer term, their value will rely on the fuel source of the electricity they use. If they require a big boost in power-plant generating capacity and their electricity comes from dirty coal, we'll have gone in the wrong direction.[15]

CAN WE AFFORD TO KEEP SUBSIDIZING CARS?

Freeways and multilane arterials may be the lifeblood of suburbia today, but they have long represented a heavily subsidized prop to the kind of leapfrog, sprawling development that the Merrill Lynch project represents. Most people probably don't stop to think of the roads they rely on as subsidized. (*Subsidy* is, in the United States today, an evil social-welfare word.) After all, people pay 18 cents to the federal government on every gallon of gas they buy, with a wide range of local fees tacked onto that. The highway lobby portrays the federal highway-finance system as user supported, by which they mean that the tax you pay is really a fee that underwrites road building.

It's not just a difference of semantics. Unlike all but a few federal programs, highway funding largely rises and falls on those dedicated receipts and does not have to compete with other needs in annual budget battles. Not only do the fuel-pump taxes generate tens of billions annually, but they're available consistently, which hugely reduces the cost of road building because officials can borrow cheaply against future receipts.

Over the years, combined federal, state, and local user fees consistently covered only about 60 percent of highway building and renovation expenses, according to the Federal Highway Administration—but that percentage dropped to 50 percent in the late 2000s thanks to resistance to raising road taxes.[16] The rest of the cost comes out of an assortment of budgets paid by regular taxes (or, in the case of the federal contribution, the subsidy has been added to the deficit). What this means is that a significant percent of local taxes, the same taxes that pay for schools, fire protection, and other services, get diverted to subsidize drivers. The less you drive, the more you subsidize those who drive a lot.

This is the kind of argument that would belong in a policy paper on the fairness of various taxing methodologies (the main venues, unfortunately, for such debates) except that the subsidy powerfully influences important decisions people make about how and where they'll live, work, and play. It has had the power to make and break cities.

If it's cheap to drive, you don't really have to worry about choosing a work or home location that demands a great deal of driving. In the United States, gas has traditionally been cheap and people have been choosing to live farther away from daily destinations and choosing larger, less fuel-efficient vehicles. For decades, the miles we drive increased at about three times the pace of population growth. So we not only got office parks in the middle of nowhere, but we got the 100-mile chauffer-mom marathon and the 150-mile daily commute.

By contrast, bus and rail systems have not had a dedicated funding stream or consistent support from Congress and local government. So neighborhoods that are walkable in transit-dependent cities suffer diminishing service. Congestion and gyrating prices are slowing the growth in miles America drives; driving actually declined (almost for the first time) when fuel prices spiked while the economy was rapidly contracting.[17] We've let alternatives to the auto atrophy for so long, though, that leaving the car in the driveway is an option for few people. The most perverse effect of subsidizing auto dependency is that it makes traffic jams inescapable. There are still advocates who think we can build our way out of traffic jams, but they are fewer now. The trend in data is against them. From the 1920s to the 1990s, Los Angeles thought it could build enough lanes. Its huge expenditure has made it possible to find yourself stalled anywhere in the three-hundred-mile stretch between Santa Barbara and San Diego, or anywhere in the one hundred miles that the Los Angeles metropolitan area stretches east from the ocean to San Bernardino. Atlanta thought it could beat LA at the same game but has fallen victim to some of the nation's worst gridlock in spite of having more highway miles per capita than just about anywhere else.

No one knows how much money it would actually take to significantly reduce urban road congestion by adding capacity. It may not be an attainable goal, certainly as long as driving is subsidized. You can always find a parking place in central St. Louis, though, because there are few residents and little commercial activity to attract anyone. It's eerily convenient, but perhaps not the way we want to achieve easy mobility.

As road advocates note, the actual number of road miles built has not come anywhere near the growth in miles driven, even as some places have engaged in Herculean efforts to add road capacity, and even as record sums are now being spent. The nation has both thousands of miles of largely empty rural highways and enormous congestion problems because the most crowded roads, and the most expensive to expand, are the 20 percent of highways that serve 80 percent of traffic—the urban and suburban networks in the largest, fastest-growing, and most economically productive urban areas. It is precisely in such areas that expanding road capacity meets the highest barriers: astronomical land costs, construction-logistics nightmares, and battles with highly motivated communities over loss of open space, valuable environmental areas, or the severing of communities by roaring rivers of vehicles.

Few leaders, especially those seeking election, want to break the news that Americans, whether they want to remain as car dependent as they are or not, must ante up more in taxes, tolls, whatever—a great deal more. If we're serious about addressing climate change, we'll have to start spending big on transit, freight rail, and inter-city passenger rail as we discourage auto use. Fear not transportation sticker shock. We would just reverse the decades-long trend of spending a declining proportion of America's economic output on infrastructure as we stitch what the future demands largely into the streets, buildings, and systems we already possess.

So where do we start? How about a 25-cent rise in the gas tax, appropriately renamed a "mobility fee" because it would be sequestered for use only for moving us faster and more efficiently by whatever means. (In some states, this would mean removing a prohibition from using gas-tax proceeds for anything but highways. The shortsightedness of that limitation removes the most powerful anti-congestion weapon that exists.) By the standards of today's political debate, where adding a nickel to the current rate is deemed incendiary, this counts as a radical proposal. It is actually only a down payment on the problem, but a powerful one. Faced with higher costs and more traffic jams, drivers are already starting to take auto alternatives into their decision-making processes. That's why transit-served housing and business locations have seen the largest price rises in recent years.[18] After all, gas prices have bounced down—but mainly up—in increments of a dollar or more. Another 25 cents is almost meaningless. (For fifteen thousand miles driven in a car that gets twenty miles per gallon, you would pay less than $200 in a year.) More to the point, it would raise a great deal of money—$305 billion over ten years by one conservative estimate.[19]

That kind of cash would quickly buy a great deal of the multimodal infrastructure we need and let us put it in place rapidly. We've done that before. After a wrenching debate, President Eisenhower reluctantly signed into law the gas tax that underwrote construction of the interstate highway system. Though the system got built at the expense of all other travel modes, and in ignorance of the needs of dense cities, the result was an enormous leap in mobility for the nation, which directly translated into (at least initially) low-cost economic growth and vastly improved mobility. The system was largely completed in just fifteen years.[20]

We cannot get people out of cars, or reduce their need to drive substantially, until we put in place the alternative infrastructure that does not now exist. Combined with higher mileage standards for each vehicle, the benefits for the planet are extraordinary and quickly realized. Dedicating increased fuel-tax revenues to alternative mobility is both sensible and helps make such change politically palatable. Which causes me to underline a contention made at the beginning of this book, and amplified in examples throughout: an agile city doesn't simply impose new burdens but shifts incentives and disincentives (especially growth machine ones) that are more productive environmentally *and* economically. A California campaign to stop action on achieving carbon-emission goals, for example, contended that government "would tell you what to drive" and "where to live," but it is the incentives and disincentives built into today's growth machine that all but command people to live in single-family homes far from job centers and drive vehicles that get poor gas mileage long distances to do ordinary tasks.[21]

Since the United States uses more than one-fourth of the world's oil while totaling only 5 percent of its population, the potential of conservation is enormous and largely untapped. New infrastructure, as it comes on line, will permit us to further cut consumption, which not only reduces carbon emissions but puts downward pressure on prices, cleans the air, lets us build smaller roads and parking lots, and reduces congestion. Anti-taxers have plenty of ways of avoiding the fees by making choices about where to live, what to drive, and how much to drive. Such gas-fee avoidance is indeed patriotic, since it creates the very same benefits, lowering everyone's costs.

I call the 25 cents a mobility fee because a significant proportion of the cash raised needs to go to the bus, rail, and bike infrastructure that will get people out of cars. Many drivers, watching the steady rise of their gas bills, resist underwriting buses they don't use, but moving a lot of people off the roads is much more likely to reduce congestion than trying to build our way out of jams.

And we can only sort travel to the most efficient modes if we create a unified pot of money for urban transportation that flows predictably, not subject to legislator whim, and is allocated according to need and efficiency. It's another idea that makes sense even if you believe that carbon emissions will somehow balance themselves out naturally. Right now, local officials often make capital investments not according to need but according to how much of the cost will be covered by the federal government. If the subsidy for a transit project is half that of a less-useful road project, which do you think gets the local matching cash? This is why the fastest trains in America rattle over one-hundred-year-old bridges. If you want to get out of traffic by taking a train from downtown Los Angeles to Orange County, you'll find service frequency and track speeds little different from 1915 norms because that's how we allocate transportation funds. Of course, roads are now becoming so jammed that the antiquated train is often faster.

PAYING AS WE GO

Ultimately, we'll need to make driving truly "pay as you go." That would involve raising pump fees, adding tolls, or charging congestion fees to cover the direct costs that you incur by driving. If drivers paid for the environmental damage driving costs (which they now don't), the cost of driving would go much higher. The impact includes air pollution and the vast quantities of polluted water that run off of roads and parking lots, which is the largest source of wastewater that must be drained, piped, controlled, and dumped (much of it untreated) into rivers and streams. Estimates of how much driving should cost in taxes or tolls vary widely, ranging from less than $1 to as much as $4 or more per gallon. In other words, we'd pay what most of the developed world pays for gas—which, by the way, does not make them poor.

If auto transportation was truly pay-as-you-go, would a company like Merrill Lynch dare to locate a gigantic facility ten miles from the nearest freeway, fifteen miles from the nearest small city, twenty-five miles from the nearest business center, and an hour from the nearest major city? Would people live in places that demand a sixty-mile commute or the shuttling of children by car to every activity? Gas priced at the developed world norm (around $8 per gallon at this writing) needn't eliminate these kinds of choices, but people would have to think far more deeply about how important it is to live or work in a wooded enclave far from jobs.

A doubling of the price of gas is, to put it politely, politically incendiary. In almost every way—from our balance of payments to our individual health—we're likely to be better off. President Bush once described America as "addicted to oil." But what America is addicted to is the automobile. Dare we try and break the habit?

5
ENDING THE WATER WARS

Toward the end of 2007, houseboats began to settle onto the dry, cracked mud at the bottom of Lake Sidney Lanier in north Georgia. As tree stumps emerged that had not been seen since the reservoir was built, it seemed as if the lake's supply of freshwater neared depletion. But Lake Lanier is not just any reservoir. It supplies drinking water for five million people in and around Atlanta.

Winter rains barely averted a disaster. (A small town in nearby Tennessee actually did run out of water.) The city was lucky; it had not prepared for such an extended period without rain, even though lesser droughts had sent warnings. As the potential for dry faucets loomed, leaders dawdled, belatedly putting in place only basic water-use restrictions. After all, even in that extreme drought year, more than thirty inches of rain fell, three times the amount most of California receives.[1]

Atlanta has not had to work hard to develop water sources because freshwater had always seemed unlimited. "It's been develop first and ask questions later," Gil Rogers, a lawyer with the Southern Environmental Law Center, told the *New York Times*.[2] But now the region does not know where water for continued growth will come from.

HOW WATER PROMOTES GROWTH

Developers may have profited handsomely from Atlanta's hands-off approach to development, but they (like their counterparts nationwide) do not take water for granted. Raw land cannot be converted to any but low-profit, low-density uses without extending the water-supply and sewer systems. You can't build a one-million-square-foot office park on a timber lot you've bought for peanuts, nor can you construct the subdivisions, malls, office parks—the building blocks of modern city development—on wells and septic systems alone. For utilities, it is not cheap to keep adding new customers. The trunklines prove too small; the reservoirs and filtration plants need to be expanded. A big, new sewage-treatment plant can cost $1 billion or more.

The "system" we have in place today, however, doesn't encourage careful stewardship of water. Water is a tool the growth machine uses to pave over undeveloped land at the urban edge.

In most of the United States, even in the arid West, where supply has long been a concern (and has rapidly grown more costly), water has been considered endlessly abundant and all but free. Obtaining clean water is rapidly becoming more expensive as more of us compete for this essentially fixed resource—and those costs may quickly escalate as global warming effects bring likely oscillations between flood and drought. Costs to dispose of sewage and storm water are running much higher, too. As water becomes a more precious commodity, we will not be able to passively permit speculators to determine where sewers will go and how much freshwater we'll have to provide to accommodate urban growth.

Everyone pays for water and sewer through usage fees and assessments, so you would think that a prudent local government would look at the costs and benefits of each proposed extension and approve only those that are cost-effective, recognize future limits, and follow the broad growth goals of the community. Government's power over where and how such systems will grow is—theoretically, anyway—a powerful tool. It could be used to guide development away from flood-prone agricultural bottomland to areas within existing built-up areas or along corridors that are easy to serve with other urban services. It could reward users who are good stewards of water.

It usually doesn't work out that way.

Most communities see the power to extend water and sewer services as a growth-promotion tool. It's also politically easy because the costs are hidden, even if substantial. According to one estimate, it costs $50,000 to $60,000 to supply a new house on the outer fringes of Chicago with water, sewer, and other services, compared to $5,000 to $10,000 for a new house in an established suburb.[3] Developers of exurban subdivisions commonly build in "package" well-water and sewage-treatment systems, but these often fail within a decade or two. You can't leave neighborhoods with impure water or seeping septic systems, so the nearest water and sewer utility must take them in, like the rural water project that was supposed to replace failed wells at the astronomical cost to taxpayers of $146,000 per home.[4]

In most jurisdictions, everyone pays the same for water and sewer, so there has been little incentive historically to use the resource efficiently. As more water systems face more expensive supply and disposal problems, people have had to make buying decisions based on "real" costs, with punishing effects on rates—as in Atlanta, which is tripling water rates to pay for an overhaul of its antique water system.[5] Even communities that want to do right by themselves—focusing growth efficiently, prudently conserving resources—face a built-in conflict of interest. They may need the jobs and tax receipts that a new water-guzzling laboratory complex brings.

Should a community propose a moratorium on hookups or try to limit the area served by sewers and municipal water, the lawsuits (or threats of lawsuits) start flying. How dare the government act in such an "arbitrary and capricious" way by denying new service, the attorneys have argued. It's "discriminatory zoning."[6]

Taxpayers correctly object that developers are coercing them to supply government services, often below cost. Underwriting value created largely for the developer's benefit exacts a price that includes not only the rising cost to develop new water supplies and sewage treatment but now also the higher costs of more elaborate floodwater control and new measures that anticipate drought. The developer, on the other hand, argues that the community serves existing residents, so why should it not be required to serve all residents, even those who haven't moved in yet? And who will also pay taxes. Or, they'll argue, the community has granted developers hookups in the past, shouldn't they be able to develop their land similarly? These beefs can be legitimate—and expose genuine property-rights quandaries: limiting the growth of water and sewer services is the way some communities enforce growth control without admitting it. Cities can deflect legal problems when they make the reasons for restrictions on water-guzzling development explicit and spread costs fairly. Prudently expanding water and sewer capacity need not slow growth; jurisdictions can use rate structures and land-use regulations to steer growth to flood-safe areas, to underinvested areas, to areas with underutilized services, and to areas where transportation supply already exists. Then, strategic government infrastructure investments allow growth to happen safely, efficiently, and at lowest cost.

With water costs rising, taxpayers have already become much more involved in debating the wisdom of permitting water and sewer extensions wherever developers think they should go. Many communities have defined "urban-service" boundaries, which is plannerspeak for geographical limits on the extension of water supplies and sewers. It means that communities are no longer exposed to unlimited costs for new utility growth somewhere miles beyond existing built-up areas. More local governments now ask developers to assume more of the costs of providing these services. Builders complain loudly that hookup costs make the projects they build unaffordable. But if those costs are indeed too high, the economic message is clear: don't build this way in this location. As the wonks say, the builders can no longer "externalize" these costs—that is, place them on the shoulders of all taxpayers. And that will enforce needed prudence.

WATER WARS

For a long time, most people gave little thought to the water or sewer systems that serve their communities, because they rarely failed. But urban growth is already putting water on front pages across America. Georgia has fought a two-decade war with Alabama and Florida over water rights. The three states depend on Lake Lanier and six rivers that flow along the Alabama border into Mobile Bay in the Gulf of Mexico, and into Florida, where they feed oyster beds and precious estuarine environments in the Appalachicola Bay. The federal government has tried unsuccessfully to broker this dispute.[7] Even southern Florida, wetter even than most of the rest of the Southeast, has suffered both persistent drought and a lack of drinkable water.

Lacking new water sources, growing communities in the dry West have routed water to domestic systems that had been dedicated to agricultural use, but this "supply" is rapidly dwindling. Desert Nevada is considering tapping aquifers under much of the center of the state, supplies essential to agriculture and wildlife, now that it's using every drop to which it is entitled from the Colorado River.

From the 1960s through the 1970s, the nation spent big to develop sophisticated treatment systems and to separate storm-water systems from sewage systems. As a result, many rivers that once looked and smelled like open sewers are now sparkling, and the cities that line them are revitalizing.

Nowadays, most growing cities are having trouble sourcing new water and keeping clean the sources they have. Mining wastes pollute streams and infiltrate aquifers in Appalachia. Elsewhere, industrial waste and farm pesticides that seeped into the ground decades ago ruin water supplies today. Most established cities are looking for new ways to cope with severe storms that cause neighborhoods to flood and sewage systems to back up and overflow.[8]

Many of these problems have been quietly building as politicians avoid expenditures that could raise taxes. At the same time, adding to reservoir systems has become extremely expensive because even distant water sources lie in sites ripe for urban development—or are spoken for by agriculture, mining, and competing thirsty cities.

Even though many communities are spending lots to bring water from increasingly long distances, then spending more to treat it, climate change threatens to worsen water problems fast. Though the Army Corps of Engineers has beefed up levee-construction standards in the wake of Hurricane Katrina, cash for upgrades is scarce, and no American river city can say it is truly prepared for a more flood-prone future. By contrast, a recent report warned that the last few years of drought in the Southwest may signal a long cycle of water deprivation.[9]

In river-laced lowlands, like those around Sacramento, California, old levees aren't up to the task of more frequent drenching torrents. Rising ocean-water levels threaten coastal communities nationwide but especially in large, low-lying swaths of Louisiana, Florida, and Alaska. Even where these communities don't actually flood, salt water infiltrates water supplies that were once safely upland. Fast-growing cities of the west—Denver, Salt Lake City, Seattle, Reno, and Los Angeles—may not be able to depend on winter snowpacks in the mountains. Those frozen reservoirs are not only shrinking but also tending to melt much more quickly in spring, sending unplanned-for flood waves into valley cities. Indeed, few communities can yet weather the ups and downs climate change will likely bring. They'll lack freshwater or the ability to process storm water, or they will bump up against sewage-treatment capacity.

STARTING SMALL

A yoga retreat would seem an unlikely place to find next-generation sewage treatment. But at the Omega Center for Sustainable Living, a handsome, distressed-wood, shed-roofed structure wraps a classroom and workshop

Figure 5.1   At the Center for Sustainable Living at the Omega Institute for Holistic Studies, natural wetlands "polish" sewage that has already been treated by an "Eco Machine" using plants and naturally occurring organisms. Credit: James S. Russell

around a natural sewage-filtration system called an Eco Machine. It serves the 128 buildings of the Omega Institute for Holistic Studies, in Rhinebeck, New York, about a hundred miles north of New York City. It's a small project with big implications.

Skip Backus, Omega's CEO, describes the project in pragmatic terms: "Our septic system was living on borrowed time, and we decided to replace it in a way that was consistent with our values and educational mission." Instead of digesting tanks, chemicals, and pipe-tangled aeration basins, the heart of the treatment system is a long basin in a sunlit room planted with water-loving tropical plants that burbles reassuringly. Its plants, fungi, algae, bacteria, snails, and a variety of other organisms scrub sewage of sludge that's already been broken down by microorganisms in oxygen-free settling tanks and filtered by several natural-style wetlands planted in four basins outside the building, each about the size of a basketball court. After this processing, the nearly clean effluent is run through a "polishing stage" in a sand filter assisted by more microorganisms (figure 5.1). Since the system is mainly gravity fed, little power is required to do the job, and what is needed is supplied by a photovoltaic-panel array.[10]

These processes result in water clean enough to release into the Hudson River watershed. When I visited, Omega was in the process of raising money to use the scrubbed sewage to irrigate its landscape and flush its toilets. Ultimately, Omega plans to eliminate its "water footprint" entirely by handling its water supply and disposal needs entirely within its 195-acre site.

The Eco Machine approach is rare because it is neither compact nor cheap to build (at $3.5 million for Omega), but Backus explained that it's consistent with Omega's mission to connect personal issues with global issues—including water.

As keeping water clean becomes more challenging, credits of the kind governments offer to energy-saving retrofits might well help more Omegas build more facilities that take sewage "off the grid" of massive treatment plants.

Omega is a pioneer in the natural treatment of sewage, but the idea's potential grows with each drought event and flood-induced sewage treatment overflow. John Todd Ecological Design, of Woods Hole, Massachusetts, which makes the Eco Machine, has designed ponds in Hawaii that clean themselves and support fish and shrimp by recirculating water through native plant roots and a gravel bed. A walkway, lined with twelve thousand flowering native plants, scours a heavily polluted canal in Fuzhou, China. It's one of several systems that imitate the function of wetlands in their ability to clean water.[11]

At a much larger scale, wetlands have been constructed specifically to capture pollutants, say from mining or agricultural feedlot operations, and more often as a secondary or finishing treatment for conventionally treated sewage. They can be especially cost-effective, according to Wetlands Solutions, a company that builds them, when the outflow can fill parched waterways or restore wildlife habitat that development or agriculture has destroyed.[12]

FROM PARKING TO PRAIRIE

The office parks of Troy, a Detroit suburb, look much like office parks everywhere: low-slung buildings wrapped by parking lots about twice the size of each building. Amid the asphalt acres, songbirds twitter from a tiny fragment of prairie. This two acres of grassland, with a tiny duck-dotted pond, wraps the headquarters of the Kresge Foundation—and largely replaces an oversized parking lot. The plantings slow and largely absorb runoff. A *bioswale*—a shallow ditch planted with water-loving grasses—filters the water before it runs into the pond. The site delivers almost no storm water into Troy's drainage system, which saves enough money to largely pay back the up-front costs of the low-maintenance mini-prairie.

Most companies and most developers would not bother to do what Kresge did, because the savings don't add up to much in Troy. Kresge built its prairie as a demonstration of environmental stewardship. It's consistent with its mission to help nonprofits build needed facilities. But the value of Kresge's swaying grasses is rapidly rising as more extreme weather events place new, unanticipated burdens on storm-water and flood-control systems. I had never seen or heard of a bioswale before visiting Kresge in 2006. Within three years, they were popping up coast to coast. If the thousands of acres of parking all around Kresge could go green in a similar way, the savings could become invaluable in the next few years.[13]

Can Eco Machines cleanse the sewage of whole cities? Can fields of waving grasses replace square miles of asphalt parking? Right now, no. That's because we haven't asked what it would take to scale up these worthy ideas to match the scope of the challenges we face. As it becomes less possible to take clean water for granted, communities are starting to consider such questions and beginning to look at water systems in their entirety—from drinking sources to waste disposal. Many are keeping an eye on New York City, which has aggressively reduced water use while trying to preserve the high quality of its water sources tucked amid rocky ridges north of the city and west of the Hudson River.

New York City had the vision in the early twentieth century to create reservoirs and aqueducts as far as 125 miles from the city. The rocky topography of the Catskill Mountains and its gravelly soil do such a good job of scrubbing the 1.3 billion gallons the city uses daily for drinking water that New York is one of very few cities that is not required to filter its water. Keeping that water clean has gotten harder in recent years, and the city has undertaken an elaborate plan to avoid building water-filtration plants. It made a deal with the Environmental Protection Agency in 1997 to buy up land near the water sources, restore streams and wetlands, and enlist farmers in the creation of buffer zones and other measures that keep agricultural pollutants out of key streams. It has upgraded all the treatment plants that affect the water sources and has encouraged planning that minimizes roads and parking lots. All this has cost plenty and from time to time has raised ire in the communities that share the far-flung watersheds.

It has also made inroads in water use through conservation. The city has relentlessly tracked leaking mains and fixed them, and installed automated meter readers (where previously no metering at all was done). Residents and businesses have replaced millions of toilets and showerheads with low-flow versions. These and other tactics cut water use by two hundred million gallons per day, more than the entire city of Boston uses.[14] (It's hardly alone; with municipalities and the Environmental Protection Agency promoting the use of water-efficient appliances, conservation has turned out to be the easy way to save money and valuable freshwater.)

New York's effort to keep its water clean has largely succeeded, staving off the requirement to filter so far—except for the 10 percent of the system east of the Hudson, in heavily suburbanized Westchester County, and exurban Putnam County. The hilly, rocky topography that does such a good job of scrubbing and clarifying water makes an unholy mess when the subdivision and strip mall developers start sending streams of sand and gravel into waterways while carving out driveways, parking lots, and building platforms.

Because Westchester and Putnam Counties build the way suburban and exurban places everywhere build, water quality in reservoir systems more than 150 years old has steadily declined, and has presented New York City ratepayers with a big bill: the requirement to build a $3 billion treatment plant constructed ten stories underground at the edge of the Bronx. The landscaped roof attractively demonstrates the city's commitment by collecting and filtering all the rainwater that falls on it. Had a more sensitive development regime been put in place a decade or two ago, the filtration-plant cost (and its $100 million yearly operating cost) may well have been avoided.

If the city fails in its efforts to preserve the water quality in its Catskills system, the price will be much higher—$10 billion or more.[15] And the threats don't stop coming. In 2009, gas drillers sought to extract natural gas from shale deposits within the watershed.

Many of the tactics that New York uses could apply even in watersheds with far lower water quality. We're just not used to thinking that way. We default to simplistic formulas: take quantity of sewage, cost out treatment plant to handle it, build, and forget. (Or don't build because the cost is politically prohibitive until some regulator makes you build it, at which time it is even more unaffordable—see the discussion of Atlanta earlier.) As storms become more frequent and floods a regular event, that equation doesn't work anymore. You have to make that sewage plant much, much larger. Or you have to go much farther or spend much more money to obtain clean drinking water.

FORESTING PHILADELPHIA

The idea of an urban forest may seem unlikely as you stroll the streets of Philadelphia, where square miles of brick row-house blocks rise straight up from the sidewalk line, and even street trees can be few, bedraggled, and far between. Very large parks slice across the city, however, most notably the magnificent 4,100-acre core of Fairmount Park, which wraps the Schuylkill River and sends tendrils of greenery up the tributary creeks. It is from these large parks that the city plans to extend a carpet of trees all over the concrete desert, stitching its forest together from parking lots, playgrounds, schoolyards, vacant land, abandoned waterfronts, and underused utility rights-of-way (figure 5.2).

The agenda goes beyond Arbor Day esthetics. A canopy of trees linking streets and backyards will shade and cool people in the summer and make a city plagued by declining population and housing abandonment more appealing. The city also hopes to take the rain that drips from its new tree branches and runs off the roofs, streets, and parking lots, and let it percolate into the ground. So people are planting "green" roofs and hitching downspouts to rain barrels. The city is replacing paved areas and storm drains with rain gardens—shallow basins tucked into sidewalks, plazas, and parking lots that are planted with water-loving grasses and shrubs. It jackhammers concrete culverts and replants the sides of streams to slow their flow so wetland plants can filter the water.

These efforts, led by the city's Water Department, sound like ecological altruism but save money. Like many older cities, much of Philadelphia is served by a drainage system that combines storm-water runoff with regular sewage. Autos drip pollutants, and people pour chemicals, into street drains, and all of that pours into the same treatment plants that must sanitize household sewage—a more elaborate and expensive process than necessary. The real problem arises during heavy rains, when many times the normal quantity of water deluges treatment plants, overwhelming them. The plants overflow, dumping raw sewage into the Delaware and Schuylkill Rivers. Philadelphia could have built very large, very expensive new treatment plants because these pollution

Figure 5.2 Many cities have begun to turn underused sites into water-retaining land-scapes that also add value to neighborhoods, like this water-treatment plant in Hamden, Connecticut, where the planted roof blends seamlessly into the landscape (Steven Holl, architect, and Michael Van Valkenburgh, landscape architect). Credit: James S. Russell

events violate federal clean water standards. It has decided that a more benefi-cial solution is to take every opportunity to divert the rainwater from the sys-tem: by slowing it down, reusing it, or allowing it to percolate into the ground.[16]

Hired for a consulting project in Philadelphia, I spoke with Glen Abrams, the Sustainable Stormwater Program Manager in the Water Department's Office of Watersheds. I asked him to explain how this is done. "Our goal is to manage the first inch of water that falls during a storm," he said. That can be done with a planted retainage basin that absorbs some runoff and lets the rest trickle out. Instead of pipes and culverts that shoot water downhill at high speed, stream-side plantings and streambeds that twist and turn slow water down, allowing the sewage-treatment plants to catch up.[17]

Let's start counting up the advantages of this way of handling water. The city saves money by not building the treatment plant. The city pays less to sup-ply, filter, and sanitize water as people irrigate gardens and wash cars with water collected from rain barrels or cisterns. The tree cover can knock several

Figure 5.3 This new quarter in Amsterdam, called Ijberg, created a wildlife-rich water edge of vegetation, a model that can be used along streams to slow water flow and reduce flooding. Credit: James S. Russell

degrees off a hot day, which means air conditioners don't work so hard, which means those units are rejecting less heat into the atmosphere, which means the streets feel cooler, and so on. It sets up a virtuous cooling cycle that reduces the "heat island effect." That effect occurs when building and street surfaces absorb solar heat, then radiate it back, especially on summer evenings when people hope for relief. The heat island effect can boost air-conditioning loads from 5 to 10 percent.[18] Reversing the effect in turn helps the city reduce its emissions of greenhouse gases. On a house-by-house level, these differences can be meaningful, but cumulatively the impact can't be ignored, because the entire electric-power infrastructure must be sized for the hottest days.

Street trees and rain-catching swales are attractive, and they stabilize property values. Naturalized streams are better neighbors, adding value to adjacent sites. Reestablishing riparian habitats (the streamside ecological zone) helps clean water and air, nurtures ecosystem resilience, and holds stream banks in place (figure 5.3). Some advantages are intangible but real. Philadelphia children historically have had few encounters with nature. How does it affect city kids when suddenly a great blue heron wings majestically overhead or frogs from a nearby stream hop through their backyards?

Urged by the Water Department, residents themselves have begun planting trees and taking care of the streams that flow behind their homes, building a stake in the city's future. Schoolyards are now scheduled for Campus Parks projects, in which plantings for play and teaching replace bleak expanses of asphalt.

Managing the first inch of storm water turns out to be considerably less expensive than standard treatment. The many small actions the city is taking can be achieved incrementally, costing $1.6 billion over twenty years, often in combination with other necessary utility work.[19] By contrast, building the infrastructure to completely separate sewers to avoid overflows during storms would cost a staggering $16 billion.[20]

Other cities, including Portland, Seattle, and New York, have already begun to harvest similar benefits with a similar diversity of tactics to handle storm water. After all, Philadelphia's problems are not all that severe compared to places like Atlanta or Sacramento. The need to conserve water is acute in most of the arid West, where water-hogging lawns are fast disappearing. That's why rain gardens and tall grasses growing from sidewalk swales are quickly becoming common. But few cities yet comprehensively analyze the pluses and minuses of building a new sewage-treatment plant versus achieving the same goals by less heavily engineered means. They do not attempt to measure the multiple benefits of treatment-plant alternatives the way Philadelphia did.

Looking beyond compartmentalized ways of making decisions is essential for cities to be truly agile. The old question was, how large a plant do we build to process the quantity of water entering the sewage system? Philadelphia asked the question in a way that yielded richer, more efficient possibilities: how does the city manage the water that causes the overflows—that first inch of rain?

"FUTURE PROOFING" HOLLAND

The Netherlands would love to think only in terms of that first inch. Instead, more than half the population live below sea level, and almost 65 percent of its gross domestic product is at risk from climate change. The super dune in Scheveningen (discussed in chapter 1) is but one tactic in an arsenal of mea - sures the country is taking to adapt to climate-change threats, from storms to droughts, from Rhine River floods to rising sea levels, from fluctuating water levels in this canal-laced country to saltwater infiltrating from rising seas.

The country, with the same population as Florida and about the size of Maryland, has fought a seemingly quixotic battle to stay dry for centuries. After a catastrophic flood that killed some two thousand people in 1953, Holland undertook the world's most elaborate engineered defense against the sea. The commitment of resources over twenty years added two thousand miles of river and ocean levees as well as an intricate network of canals and pumps. The most impressive of this massive public works program was the Maslant barrier, a pair of gates hundreds of feet long that sweep into place to stop massive storm surges.

In the face of global warming effects, Holland has concluded that all the pumping technology and engineering expertise is no longer enough. "Sea levels continue to rise, the winters are wetter, extreme summer squalls are more frequent," explained Renske Peters, Holland's minister of water management and transport, in a presentation I witnessed on the nation's new approach.[21] "There's more water in the Rhine and Maas Rivers in the winter and a decrease in flow in the summer," she added. Much of central Europe drains to the sea through Holland.

Rather than simply pour more money into bigger dikes, the Dutch government united bureaucracies into what it calls a "triumvirate" of water management, climate-change adaptation, and urban stewardship. The idea, explained Han Vrijling, chairman of the Department of Hydraulic Engineering at the Technical University at Delft, was to "create benefits beyond protection." Coastal development is quite literally integrated into flood defense, with resort structures actually built into the land side of coastal dune projects, bracing them while they serve recreational use. Vrijling called it "making dikes habitable."[22]

Holland's adaptations to climate change have been under way for years, but you might not notice. Sunken canals, such as the historic Westersingel Canal in Rotterdam, are landscaped like parks, which disguises their water-retaining function (figure 5.4). When discreetly reconfigured, streets, squares, and even playgrounds become temporary water-storage areas in the event of heavy storms and floods.[23]

Dutch engineers have concluded that constantly raising levees along the Rhine and Maas Rivers won't work. Instead, they are making, as they call it, "Room for the River." Ideally, levee systems move away from the water to accommodate more volume. But in densely built Holland, that's a process both

Figure 5.4 The Westersingel Canal, in Rotterdam, is configured to retain excess water during storms and to release it when the water system is no longer overloaded. Credit: James S. Russell

controversial and costly. So water-management officials have commissioned a wide variety of projects that permit farms to live with controlled inundation. One of the projects creates a natural water-storage landscape out of the Noordwaard Polder, a two-hundred-hectare parcel of reclaimed land. Streams and wetlands will be braided among farm parcels to create islands, marshes, and eddies to slow storm-water flows and store water until the river returns to a safe level. The plan also augments agricultural income with recreational opportunities. Another project by the Hague landscape architecture firm Bosch Slabbers moves a levee line back from the main stem of the Maas River, leaving some farmland exposed to periodic floods. Barns, houses, and other structures would be raised on platforms, called *terps*, attached to the new levee. The levee keeps essential structures safe, and the terp helps strengthen the levee.[24] The Dutch have also updated their famous windmills so that, now, rows of wind turbines share space with rows of lettuce. They generate electricity and—inevitably— pump water.

The Netherlands does not depend only on this "soft path" approach to water. There is plenty of costly civil engineering in this effort, including more

Figure 5.5 This drainage canal in the Broadmoor neighborhood of New Orleans is so insensitively designed that it repels local investment rather than attracts it. Credit: James S. Russell

dams, levees, and floodgates. In Rotterdam, officials showed off a giant underground structure that parks cars and stores floodwaters—which struck me as an enormously costly way to accommodate both.

Nevertheless, the contrast with Louisiana, and therefore the rest of the United States, is startling, and it was pointed out again and again by Senator Mary Landrieu on the Dutch congressional tour I joined. In New Orleans, drainage canals are huge concrete eyesores or fetid ditches (figure 5.5). Massive earthen levees are capped by graffiti-attracting concrete walls. Entering New Orleans from its airport, the first sight you see is of a tangle of pipes, a pumping station, and an oozing drainage canal. Landrieu commented: "People don't want to live with these concrete walls and open ditches, and they shouldn't have to."

LEARNING TO BE A "WATER CITY"

New Orleans architect David Waggonner, of Waggonner & Ball Architects, agrees. He has spearheaded a series of conferences and sketch-design sessions

Figure 5.6 Bayou St. John, running along City Park in New Orleans, is a model of how to retain floodwaters and enhance values of the surrounding neighborhoods at the same time. Credit: James S. Russell

called Dutch Dialogues, which have brought Gulf Coast and Dutch expertise together. That's how I found myself staring into a fifteen-foot-deep drainage culvert where bourbon-tinted water gurgled darkly below. Architect Ramiro Diaz, who works for Waggonner, was trying to show me how that boxy drain could lead to a better future for New Orleans, at the disheveled edge of the Mid-City neighborhood.

Diaz had taken me along the Bayou St John, from its mouth at Lake Ponchartrain on the northern edge of the city, along the vast City Park. Graceful bridges arch their way across the serene waterway, which is overhung with bosques of trees (figure 5.6). The bayou wends its way gracefully through several neighborhoods until it ends abruptly near that dim culvert.

Waggonner, Diaz, and their Dutch collaborators would like to thread lushly landscaped waterways like Bayou St. John throughout the city—not just as a canoe-dotted amenity for battered neighborhoods but to retain water during the city's frequent deluges, in which you can take a wrong turn during a downpour and find your car stalled in several feet of water. "It's time for New Orleans to act like a delta city," Waggonner told me, "with water-sensitive design."

That humble box culvert is part of the plan. For more than a century, sailing ships skirted the laborious trip up the Mississippi by wafting into the city on Bayou St. John. They sailed along a wide 1.5-mile canal to unload at Basin Street, at the edge of the French Quarter. That canal was long ago filled in and the culvert, running in an overgrown, abandoned right-of-way, is all that remains. Waggoner wants to restore the canal as a first link in the water storage system. The idea makes sense economically as well as environmentally. People want to live in neighborhoods that line Bayou St. John. Investors ignore the Lafitte Corridor, as the space once occupied by the canal is now known.

The city still can't handle everyday floods, even though the Army Corps has been spending $14 billion to rampart the city against the next Hurricane Katrina with upgraded levees, floodwalls, pumping stations, and massive gates. Though augmented since Hurricane Katrina, the drainage canals and pumps can't work fast enough. The Army Corps wants to fix the problem by throwing more billions at higher floodwalls and deeper drainage canals.

Waggonner's Dutch-American team offered a different approach: use the city's abundant empty land for landscaped water storage connected in a circulating system of canals and human-made bayous edged with greenery. These would be sized to fill up with storm water and hold it while the drainage canals and pumping stations catch up. More water-retaining basins could be built in the medians of the city's many tree-shaded boulevards (called "neutral ground" in New Orleans). Sidewalks and backyards could host rain gardens. The city has long hoped to turn the Lafitte Corridor into a parklike bike trail, and the restoration of the canal would add more value, if it can be funded as an alternative to more pumps and concrete.

Corralling storm water for good use is immensely appealing in a city that's still dubious about leaving its destiny in the hands of the levee builders. Drainage structures designed to fit into neighborhoods could make the city infinitely more attractive, spurring investment. It's a system New Orleanians could take into their own hands, building it in manageable chunks. "I don't see this as a five-year plan," said Waggonner, "but a fifty-year one."

Though principles of the water-management idea are incorporated into the city's master plan, and Senator Landrieu supports it, Waggonner's vision could vaporize as so many post-Katrina plans have. Its unique power is the promise that New Orleanians need no longer cower in the shadows of the endless dispiriting levee walls. They could begin gracefully living with their age-old aquatic enemy.[25]

REDESIGNING THE MISSISSIPPI

Seen from the air, the lowest stretches of the Mississippi extend well beyond the coast of Louisiana and divide into several thin distributaries that form a "Bird's Foot" at the edge of the continental shelf. The lines of barges and ships that run down the river can only enter the Gulf of Mexico through the South Pass, which is maintained by the US Army Corps of Engineers.

Paul Harrison says the Bird's Foot is falling apart. He's the senior director for the Mississippi River at the Environmental Defense Fund. He arranged a boat trip for me down the river's lowest stretches with Paul Kemp, a vice president at the National Audubon Society in charge of Gulf Coast initiatives, and Ben Weber, a local representative of the National Wildlife Federation.

The river's fate and that of Louisiana's coastal marshes are intertwined.

Both are threatened (the marshes have long been receding alarmingly), but the staggering cost and complexity of fixing the river and the marshes have stymied progress. Coastal marshes miles from New Orleans might have formed the first line of defense against the massive surge of water that gathered in the Gulf when Hurricane Katrina barreled toward Louisiana. Natural flooding for millennia had deposited silt across the flat, low river delta—rich organic soils on which the marshes built and rebuilt themselves. The vast levee systems built to armor the length of the Mississippi River put an end to those deposits. Thousands of square miles of the marshes have disappeared and are no longer available to absorb storm-surge energy. Instead, the river sluices that valuable soil, collected over thousands of miles, into the river outlet deep in the Gulf. Also over decades, engineers had hacked canals through the marshes for navigation and to serve the oil and gas industry, further weakening coastal defenses as the canal banks collapsed, widening modest passages into marine superhighways.

Plans were made, both before and after Katrina, to stop the loss of the protective marshes. They were astonishingly ambitious: levee systems were to be entirely reengineered, with massive diversion works being created to spread silt over huge tracts. In many cases, getting sediment where it was needed meant somehow transporting it through settled communities, where people lived, farmed, and fished. Thousands of private-property claims would have to be adjudicated. Rip-rap erosion barriers would have to be erected along hundreds of coastal miles to prevent further erosion of beaches and bays. All of this would have to be carefully engineered to enhance fisheries rather than ruin them, to keep essential navigation channels functioning, and to keep salt water from seeping into freshwater sources.[26]

The catastrophic breaching of Louisiana's storm defenses by the hurricane spurred further studies. Researchers found that conditions were even more dire. From Lafayette and Lake Charles, at the western end of the state, to smashed St. Bernard Parish and Breton Sound to the east, hundreds of miles of erosion barriers, levees, and shoreline reinforcements would stretch like medieval ramparts across the marshes. The cost? "Tens of billions of dollars," one report said.[27]

There was one more complication, Harrison told me. The Army Corps of Engineers worried about diverting too much soil from the river to rebuild those marshes, because it would alter the configuration of the river bottom and its flow, both of which encourage an automatic scouring of the river bottom, thereby avoiding perpetual dredging. And yet, those marshes were what kept the Bird's Foot from melting away. Much of it is now barely protected. "We're thinking now about the delta as a design, architecture and infrastructure issue," Harrison explained. "Now you have the highly controlled river contrasting with the loss of land and the collapsing wetlands, but when you can build land, you can build vitality. We need to find a way that the delta can sustain itself, even with sea-level rise."[28]

Our trip began in Venice, which in no way resembles the Queen of the Adriatic. It seemed more a floating collection of oil-service equipment yards than a dryland town, and no roads penetrated the last miles of the delta. Our boat left shrimp-boat fleets and oil-service tugs and transporters behind as we pulled into the main channel of the Mississippi.

We slowed so Kemp and Weber could point out one artificial diversion that the Corps had cut in 2003. It had built little land but scoured the bottom deeply, as the river began to seek new ways to the Gulf. The Corps wanted to close it. I was struck by how little land separated river and gulf, a hundred yards in places, and how low-lying it was. The Corps could not let the South Pass navigation channel fall apart, though, because it would be impossible to maintain a deep enough pathway into the Gulf. As it is, the massive dredging barges we saw, anchored by high steel columns with pipe arms suspended like wings to either side, had to work constantly to maintain the pass.

The mouth of the river is utterly unmagnificent, just two thick inky lines of rock bulkheads with a fringe of marsh grasses, all looking ready to sink into the sea. Magnificent frigate birds, aptly named, roosted in the timber remains of bulkheads past. A windowless, heavily braced dormitory for river pilots posed bleakly atop massive, twenty-foot-high columns. The message: wind and water own this place. It would seem that sea-level rise of just inches would trump the bulkheads, the endless dredging, and the constant rebuilding of the channel banks.

Harrison finds the Corps losing its battle to keep the river flowing where it does not want to go. (If not for enormous dam and diversion structures, the river probably would have switched by now to the path of the Atchafalaya River, far to the west, possibly leaving New Orleans riverless. Unlike the Mississippi, the Atchafalaya still builds marshes.) The environmental groups, working with the Van Alen Institute in New York City (which promotes improved public architecture), were planning a design competition to find an entirely new way, using entirely new expertise, to keep the river navigable yet use the soils it carries to rebuild the coastal marshes and avoid dumping all that valuable soil off the edge of the continental shelf, where it forms a huge dead zone. The competing teams would have substantial sums to underwrite detailed engineering studies. The competition was announced as this book went to press, but whatever its outcome, it could show how new kinds of collaborations, taken deep enough, have the potential to remake enormous damaged landscapes.

Managing water rather than trying to confine it with massive engineering structures is a gigantic cultural change, one that communities worldwide face. Great Britain spent a billion pounds over decades to build the Thames gateway—an elaborate defense for London against storm-driven floods. Rising seawaters have made it obsolete. Because the Elbe River now regularly floods Hamburg, Europe's second-biggest port, massive flood-resistant doors now armor low-lying waterfront stores and restaurants. Pedestrian bridges lace streets in Hamburg's new HafenCity development to allow people to escape when waters rise (more about HafenCity in chapter 7). In much of low-lying America, building ever-higher levees with ever more elaborate pumps and gates may buy only a few years of protection at rapidly increasing cost. We'll need to make "room" in new ways for our rivers and coastlines.

From a cost perspective alone, the United States can no longer passively await the bill sent by rising seas, dwindling reservoirs, and water-sucking development that proceeds at the will of speculators. "We've got to replace our patch-and-pray approach," Senator Landrieu declared. "The Dutch told me that the problem in America is that you treat water like a drowning man. They know they have to live with it, that they're running a marathon."

6

MEGABURBS

The Unacknowledged Metropolis

D emographic data tell us that most of America lives in suburbs. But suburbia has quietly transformed itself into something the suburbanites of the 1920s or even the 1950s might find almost unrecognizable. The ingredients are the same, such as the leafy cul-de-sacs. The place names and political boundaries that once defined the small-scale, older bedroom suburbs may remain. Places like Petaluma and Cupertino, in California, may be dozens of miles apart, but growth or decline depends much more on the fate of the entire Bay Area than on actions each takes individually. In metro areas around the country, similarly once-separate communities have become mere components in an economically integrated, wealth-producing and wealth-consuming machine. I call it a megaburb.

Megaburbia is the altered reality that has emerged when three-quarters of a three-hundred-million-person nation lives in what we are used to calling suburbs. Suburbs—even the outlying satellite exurbs—are entwined with one another and with older central cities more than ever, homogenized by growth machine forces and united in a metropolitan economy (figure 6.1).

Populations within these far-flung urban landscapes have grown a hundred- or a thousand-fold over the past thirty years. The low-slung office-park zones have nurtured high technology, research, and advanced manufacturing, putting the mega in megaburbia. Overshadowing the central cities in terms of population and economic activity, places like California's Silicon Valley, the pharmaceutical belt in northern New Jersey, Chicago's western and northwest-

Figure 6.1 Large, mixed-use commercial landscapes, like this one outside Chicago, increasingly struggle to compete because their reliance on autos-only access limits their potential for growth. Credit: © Alex Maclean/Landslides

ern suburbs, and the crescent of Maryland and Virginia suburbs that wraps Washington, DC, have built economies comparable to entire nations.

For their residents, however, the suburbs have seemed to succeed as a patchwork of smallish towns and cities, many defining an identity in the pecking order of housing cost or schools' reputation. They may be surrounded by uncounted square miles of similar suburbia, but they have zealously guarded local control of zoning, taxes, and schools.

Coming to terms with climate change means coming to terms with megaburbia—the landscape that the growth machine has created. With big houses, megamalls, and long commutes, these are the communities that have locked in high energy and resource use. They've changed cities from entities that stretch across a few dozen square miles to ones a hundred miles across that flow across county and state lines, wrap estuarine bays, and leap across wooded ridges. As we watch these places unspool outside the car window over mile after mile—like one of those looped backgrounds of a children's cartoon—their endlessness conveys the "mega" character of modern suburbia, but it also seems hopelessly unadaptable. After all, isn't this kind of landscape essential to creating American wealth?

Megaburbia is more adaptable and potentially more agile than it looks, because the original suburban ideal of closeness to nature remains embedded in its DNA. For all the highways and parking lots, there are patches of farms, many miles of tree-buffered streams, and a great deal of leftover space—the raw material for reknitting natural systems within a prospering urban environment. I lay out the "mega" qualities of suburbia in this chapter because that's essential to reversing growth machine excesses and seizing the adaptive opportunities latent in these vast landscapes. Megaburbia also faces many challenges that aren't strictly environmental, and those have only become more urgent. Improving the environmental performance of megaburbia can address much else that's gone wrong with American dream suburbia.

SUBURBIA GOES VIRAL

Suburbia becomes megaburbia incrementally, as the subdivisions, the shopping centers, the office parks, and the local schools accumulate. You can overlook the way this opportunistic assembly of identical units of development can become under our noses something we hadn't expected: an urban entity that seems immeasurably large and inchoate rather than stable, predictable, and orderly.

More than two decades ago, Robert Fishman, a prominent historian of suburbia, wrote in his well-regarded 1987 book, *Bourgeois Utopias,* that the historic idea of the suburb had quietly morphed into something quite different from what it had promised to be over the preceding two hundred years: a residential refuge from the city.[1] The city was the place where business was done, but it was also capitalism's cauldron. It created wealth but in the process perpetually tore itself apart and rebuilt as it responded to the market's incessant demand and ever-changing whim. Living in the city meant contending with the chaos that was the inevitable by-product of a dynamic economy: congestion, pollution, crime, immorality. The city's promise of wealth and opportunity attracted every kind of person—especially the worst.

Suburbs, it was hoped, would banish both pickpockets and prostitutes. It was a place of shared values, of social rules enforced through an unspoken code understood by everyone. It was a way to live with people with whom one was comfortable and to avoid those who looked different, spoke differently, and adhered to different values.

The commuter-filled bedroom communities in the 1950s succeeded as clean, safe, stable refuges from the city for a massive new middle class. The railroad and streetcar suburbs that preceded them as far back as the 1880s worked similarly for an affluent elite. During the 1970s, however, American suburbia began to transform itself into a diverse and economically independent urban entity in its own right—a new kind of city that only looked suburban. Just pull out of the average subdivision driveway. Today, eight-lane arterials ring your residential neighborhood. Your commute may consume dozens of miles with lots of houses, lots of highway strips, and lots of warehouses or retail centers that look like warehouses slipping by. Your five-lane side of the freeway, broad as a jet-plane runway, may drop you into a suburban downtown of twenty-story mirror-glass towers.

Somehow the idea of the suburban home as a cozy refuge where one tends the garden on weekends morphed into the home as hub, where each occupant sleeps and briefly touches base for processed-food grazing between after-school activities, long workdays, night classes, the gym, the mall, and so on.

The debt-fueled growth in housing "wealth" in the 2000s simply delayed an inevitable reckoning with the contradictions of trying to live a suburban ideal in megaburbia. In the simplest terms, the "city"—at least in its identity as a dynamic, competitive, congested, factory-of-capitalism—had moved its disorder-inducing, opportunistic self unasked to the suburbs. You might think it sneakily took on sprawling, low-density, residential-looking form so as to disguise the full implications of this shift. You don't see too many smoke-belching factories in the megaburbs; more likely, it's the quiet hum of the office/warehouse. As you cruise the big arterials at forty-five miles per hour, you may not notice the tired, cracked-stucco, highway-strip apartment complex where kids play on the broken asphalt between sagging cars. This is the suburban equivalent of the industrial city's tenement slum. Poverty, like every other city ill, is growing in suburbs and manifests itself in the disheveled house on the chain-linked lot, where the lawn has largely succumbed to car parking because every family member must haul to work in paint-faded clunkers.[2]

What's becoming clear is that "the megaburban project," as academic jargon might put it—meaning the entire process by which it is created—must sprawl or the whole machine seizes up. First, you build the highways (or promise to build them) as far out as possible, opening as much land to development as possible. This ensures a surplus of buildable area (and buyer choice, such as it is), which keeps real estate costs from skyrocketing. Young families would traditionally "drive to qualify," hauling out to the urban edge to find a starter house that's affordable.

Opening huge territories to development also involves lots of jurisdictions, and they tend to compete for growth—especially commercial growth, because business picks up much of the tab for government services, especially schools, which are typically local government's biggest ticket item by far. Businesses benefit from inducements offered by officials: we'll reduce your taxes; we'll build the road you want; we'll offer job training—the list of goodies is lengthy.

This is the high-growth model of wealth creation that got assembled atop the Depression-era foundations of government-backed mortgages and ample federal highway money, amplified by fast-payback real estate development.

The mortgage meltdown, which hit outermost suburbs hardest, would seem to have put an end to the cycle of driving farther and farther for that affordable new starter home—the foundation of megaburban growth. Without a new growth model, though, growth can only resume in the old mode at the outer-outer edge, however robotically futile it seems. Meanwhile, the landscapes of disinvestment left behind in the inner suburbs (the price communities pay simply for aging; see chapter 3) grow larger, but the maturing trees idealistically planted by young families thirty, forty, or fifty years ago draw a veil over them. They're forgotten.

ENGINES OF MEGABURBAN WEALTH

Suburbs, the antidote to congested downtowns, had to invent their own places of commerce and work, and that growth coalesced around a strategic crossing of freeways, a new shortcut carved to the international airport, or the location of a major regional mall. The construction of I-90, for example, put Schaumberg, Illinois—incorporated as a 130-person village in 1956—thirty high-speed miles from Chicago's Loop. The development of O'Hare Airport—ten freeway miles east—as the metropolitan area's major global link made it even more strategic. When I-290, the north-south beltway connector, was extended to I-90, Schaumberg's status as a high-density node in the splotchy sprawl of the western suburbs was assured, certified by the opening of a 2.3-million-square-foot mall. By 1990, Schaumberg had grown to a sixty-nine-thousand-person accumulation of retail centers, office parks, and executive housing that employed fifty-five thousand.[3]

Places like Schaumberg can employ tens of thousands, and contain as much office space as a decent-sized downtown, but spread themselves over six times as much land. When such large-scale developments appear in an area still shot through with farm fields, budding suburbia morphs into what's called, in planner jargon, a suburban employment center (SEC). Actually *SEC*, coined by urban analyst Robert Cervero, is just one name. Historian Robert Fishman called these places "Technoburbs," and Joel Garreau most famously deemed them "Edge Cities."[4]

Like so many other aspects of megaburbia, these commercial centers are a bit hard to pin down. They don't look like centers or cities, for one thing, but stretch along a freeway frontage road or cluster along a wide arterial loop that shortcuts from one freeway to the next. Don't attempt to cross the largely sidewalk-free expanses of Tysons Corner, Virginia, the edge city that grew where the Dulles Airport tollway crosses Washington's Beltway. It strings office parks, massive malls, enormous planned residential developments, and the asphalt-entwined big and little boxes of generic suburbia along a tangle of intimidating arterials and freeways.

Consistent with the transformation of suburbia to megaburbia, these wealth-creating enclaves take on such amorphous form because they coalesce incrementally over time as each developer jockeys construction on each parcel. They don't do it to create a coherent business center or a pleasing composition, or to attract passersby, but to position their development in the most advantageous way along the arterials that feed the freeway network.

Whatever you call these commercial zones, they have become the mirror-glass economic engines of megaburbia, giving suburbanites a range of urban employment, housing, and recreational opportunities once available only in cities. Megaburbia has assumed the city's mercantile functions, too, and has reaped the benefits. It's able to offer diverse economic opportunity and generous government services. Many are so successful that they have become jobs magnets, employing far more people than they house. A classic edge-city scenario: you send your kids to great schools, but swarms of commuters from forty miles away hurtle by your condo.

The edge cities, with their tower clusters and megamalls, grew explosively in the 1980s. The phenomenon seemed so successful that Garreau could plausibly contend that "Americans today are once again inventing a brand-new future—the biggest change in a 100 years in how we build cities."[5]

Edge cities have turned out to be less a brand-new future than a fate to which suburbia has subjected itself. The small-scale ideal of village-centered and family-centered life that underpinned the American dream suburb does not take into account the steadily growing presence of American business in the suburbs. A modest-sized edge city ejects one hundred thousand autos onto the feeder highway system, requiring no less than a ten-lane freeway—more often two or three freeways. A megaburban commercial zone as big as Silicon Valley demands a web of freeways and expressway connectors on a two- to five-mile grid over an area twenty miles wide by thirty miles long, forming a multicounty landscape of start-and-stop driving.

Whether a commercial zone created with so little concern for its future will actually have one is now an open question. With the automobile as essentially the sole means of transportation, megaburban employment centers can adapt to changing business realities in only limited ways, because the density and proximity of uses is strictly limited by the need to accommodate vehicles. They are vulnerable to spiking fuel prices and lock in high carbon emissions.

A decade or so ago, the edge cities seemed a plausible alternative to downtown, but edge cities aren't sprouting like they used to.[6] Robert Lang, an urban analyst at Virginia Tech who has extensively studied megaburban transformation, posits a three-stage life cycle for edge cities. After an initiation and maturation phase, the third phase leads to possible stagnation as auto congestion steadily worsens. Neighboring communities begin to resist the continued commercial expansion, with its impacts on roads and its unstoppable appetite for land. The edge city can become denser, but then development costs and congestion rise. Lang writes that some of these commercial zones are now declining and haven't yet found ways to adapt to ever-changing business needs.[7] In the past two decades, for example, Schaumberg has actually lost population.

The megaburban metropolitan areas that grew rapidly from small cities to major population centers in the past forty years, such as Phoenix, Houston, Dallas/Fort Worth, Atlanta, Miami, and Orlando, have largely dispensed with the downtown-weighted model of older metro areas. Instead, they grew up as assemblages of subdivisions, office parks, malls, and highway strips into an almost undifferentiated carpet of urban development—a "Polynuclear Field," as architectural theorist Albert Pope calls it. This kind of megaburb may start out as a smallish regional trading center, as did Atlanta or Houston. But the small-town downtown loses its power once population leaps into the millions, downtown skyscrapers built atop twenty-story parking structures lose their allure, and the developed square miles multiply. "Phoenix" now encompasses Mesa, Scottsdale, Tempe, and innumerable small, once-separate towns that aspire to maintain a separate identity but which are indistinguishable to the casual observer and inextricably intertwined economically.

Most of us overlook the dissonance that has developed as the urban economy settled itself in suburbia's heart. Or we've accepted it as long as the place offered at least some of the amenities promised by the postwar American dream suburb. We've collectively willed a part of the landscape to fit that dream (primarily, the single-family house on a gardened lot), but we haven't wanted to give up the choices and opportunities that we can only secure within a dynamic, commercial urban landscape. In short, we try to live a culture of suburbia when what we've made is a city—that place that tears itself down and builds itself up, and that is noisy and chaotic in a manic chase to stay on the bucking bronco that is capitalism.

In failing to come to grips with the urban aspects of modern suburbia—its enormity and complexity, its impersonal nature and constant flux—many of us find ourselves resigned to an ever-shrinking part of it addressing our deepest aspirations.

Even absent the urgency of climate change, it's clear that the megaburbia we've been making is too expensive (with ever-rising tax and infrastructure demands), too simplistic (its jobs are too far from its residential areas; it can't accommodate any but auto-born densities), too dependent on low fuel prices. It can only intermittently deliver quiet, safe communities close to nature. Its predominance of single-family houses and its wasteful consumption of land are America's primary sources of both transportation- and building-related greenhouse gas emissions. Its settlement patterns fragment vast territories, obliterate valuable natural landscapes, sterilize waterways, and pour pollutants from square miles of paving into streams.

Many Americans wonder what happened to the barbeques and the kids wheeling their bikes around the quiet curving streets, the uncomplicated life promised by the American dream suburb. Now they have to wonder if coping with global warming means losing that dream forever.

The overwhelming consensus among planners and other students of cities is that the only way to fix megaburbia is for people to concentrate in older, denser, more walkable cities. There's an unwritten implication that conventional megaburbia will therefore vanish into a resurgent nature where Eden will return and engulf the strip malls and subdivisions. If only. After all, there are reasons that many, if not most, Americans still pursue a suburban American dream. Still, it's worth a look at what big-city density and diversity have to offer. Do those qualities—so long anathema in suburbs—make sense for megaburbia? Can the best of suburbia survive, even thrive, in a future that recognizes global urbanism's large scale and dynamism?

THE NEW ECONOMY OF THE CITY

In the months after the terror attacks of 9/11, major employers in Manhattan faced a tough decision: was it no longer prudent to house large groups of their people in skyscrapers vulnerable to attack? Were the risks too high when the concentration of talent and technology could be destroyed instantly by a bomb or a deadly gas detonation in the subway?

Urban experts predicted a greater dispersal of business deep into already-growing suburbs as executives concluded that both the risks and the costs were too high. The soul-searching was particularly intense in the financial business—the high-profit, high-profile mainstay of New York City's economy. In targeting the Twin Towers, after all, the terrorists had hoped to cripple the nerve center of American economic power.

That dispersal, however, did not occur. By 2006, Manhattan had more office skyscrapers in construction or nearing completion than any other city. Residential towers rose at rates unheard of for decades. The chief deterrent to more construction was high rents, rather than fear. (Ground Zero itself was an exception, where a bungled reconstruction dampened office-tenant interest, though not residential demand.)

Franz Fuerst researched business-location decisions for the Russell Sage Foundation a few years after the terror attacks and found that "financial firms have by and large decided to stay in Manhattan." Even Cantor Fitzgerald, the trading firm that lost two-thirds of its employees during the terror attacks, remained in the city.

In an e-mail exchange, Fuerst wrote that financial firms stayed because they recognize—more than almost any other business seems to—"the tremendous importance of access to sensitive knowledge through face-to-face interaction and a tightly woven network of personal relationships between industry professionals, clients, suppliers and other decision-makers." For these reasons, companies like to remain close together, within walking distance, just as they did in the early years of Wall Street's ascendance, when rents adjacent to the New York Stock Exchange could be forty times the rents of buildings just a few blocks distant. "The type of information needed to assemble highly complex financial deals and new products simply cannot be obtained via email or phone," Fuerst added.[8]

The big-city venues where such intelligence is shared do not confine themselves to formal meetings in wood-paneled conference rooms. Collaborating and deal making take place in restaurants, at health clubs, at charity functions, and even on street corners (where executive schmoozers tend to yak on the busiest sidewalks, as William H. Whyte documented some two decades ago—a sight you never encounter even in the most gorgeously landscaped beltway office parks).[9]

Interaction is the reason skyscraper downtowns exist. They put a lot of people in proximity to one another. After all, Wall Street is not just big rooms full of traders screaming into telephones; it is an ecosystem of deal makers, attorneys, accountants, and a constellation of analysts that value propositions and create new products. Urban experts use the regrettable term *agglomeration economies* to describe the efficiencies that develop in large markets: companies can access more customers and suppliers from fewer locations, and draw from vast pools of labor and expertise to bring in the most suitable people. Walkable downtowns at the nexus of a transportation network that includes buses and trains as well as cars can access talent from the city and most of its megaburban hinterlands. Because of growing auto congestion, no single suburban location can readily access more than a fraction of that talent. American business is becoming more reliant on interaction, not less, as bringing products and services to market becomes more complex, as supply chains globalize, and as companies must rapidly respond to online shopping trends that tend to reduce transaction values solely to price. In short, downtown is an agile environment, one in which business imperatives and reducing carbon emissions can be in synch.

Fuerst also examined the post-9/11 location choices of architects, who were highly concentrated in lower Manhattan—and who tend to be found downtown in most cities and rarely in freeway office parks. Even though few are large businesses and none have the deep pockets of banks, they, too, largely returned to their existing locations. From my firsthand knowledge, this is easy to explain and speaks to why technology encourages business concentration as well as diffusion (just as railroads, early in the twentieth century, begat both skyscraper downtowns and early suburbs). A few decades ago, architects could design a school working with just a structural engineer and a plumbing expert. Now, such projects entail a dozen or more consulting firms: experts in landscape architecture, engineering, lighting, acoustics, information technology, labs, sports facilities, and so on.

A great deal of collaboration can occur with the aid of e-mail and special intranet sites where the design team can work on documents simultaneously. But the intensity of teamwork today means that people meet more often to work out problems that no one even thought about a few years ago. The condominium architect does not simply sketch out luscious renderings but must have his or her work vetted by interior designers, apartment-layout specialists, real estate analysts, financial partners, marketing specialists, and attorneys who make deals for the land. The architect may need to meet with community groups and negotiate special zoning variances with city officials.

Clients often want to interview several architects before choosing one, and they often want to visit the firm's offices as a way to take its measure. In Manhattan or Chicago (where you can traverse America's second-biggest downtown on foot in twenty minutes), a client can visit half a dozen international-class firms in two days, which is why even architects headquartered in suburbs or smaller metro areas often maintain a presence in global-hub cities.

In real estate, all you hear about are the major companies that build million-square-foot office campuses or rent twenty floors of a skyscraper. But, the companies you've never heard of—many, many thousands of them—intertwine to make downtown's urban economic ecosystem. According to a New York brokerage firm, tenants using less than six thousand square feet (about one-fourth of a standard skyscraper floor) occupy 90 percent of all space in Manhattan—a percentage that hasn't shrunk much since the early twentieth century.[10]

The common thread among businesses that locate downtown is how highly each kind of business values interaction and collaboration, hallmarks of what economic-development expert Richard Florida has famously described as the "creative economy." He, too, recognizes the dispersing power of technology but also writes that "the tremendous productivity and creativity gains that spring from high density give shape to a powerful counterforce: geographic clustering and concentration." In the searingly competitive globalized marketplace, ideas can't be identified and turned to profitable products and services without deep talent pools of people who have both diverse and specialized experience.[11]

That is the reason the oil business has concentrated in Houston, when it used to be headquartered in Ohio, Pennsylvania, California, and New York as well as Texas. It has had to shed its wildcat past because it is now one of the most risky, complex, and technologically demanding industries. A concentrating of talent is necessary to design, develop, and operate the extremely expensive technology as well as to analyze huge risks that are affected by many variables. Modern oil wells, for example, are drilled fifteen thousand feet deep undersea, compared to one-tenth that depth just a few years ago.[12] Other places like Houston—such as Hollywood, Wall Street, Boston, and Silicon Valley—are "talent aggregators" for their dominant businesses, as Richard Florida puts it. That's why they succeed in spite of some of the highest costs, greatest congestion, and lots of regulations. They possess the depth and variety of expertise that wannabe regions can't assemble. In so many businesses, making the most of skilled people is the key competitive advantage.

The mythology of Silicon Valley, for example, may be based on college kids wiring together the next big idea out of a few microchips in an old garage. But no longer. Today, the valley still generates ideas and companies (most famously these days, Google) even though those garages have been replaced by McMansions, living costs are stratospheric, and traffic is impossible. The key advantage is the critical mass of talent ranged along that US 101 backbone.

Bio-pharm "startups" require great dollops of cash, specialized R&D facilities, and access to research universities operating at the outer edges of scientific inquiry. Cities all over the country came for years to David Clem's Boston-area office because his company, Lyme Properties, speculatively develops high-tech lab buildings. Officials offer him incentives to build biotech capacity in their towns, but he usually demurs. He told me that only half a dozen cities in the country possess the technical infrastructure and research depth to support even one speculative biotech lab.[13]

While outsourcing increasingly sophisticated business endeavors to far-flung shores has become controversial, a great number of companies outsource locally—for payroll or health care, and to undertake complex projects they are not good at, such as managing the construction of a once-a-generation building project or because they need specialized expertise to bring a new product to market. So many of these activities require such high levels of interaction and collaboration that it is impossible to send them to faraway places. Companies also insource expertise for the same reasons, bringing specialized talent in-house (like a management consultant or accountant) for a defined period. Being able to draw on specialized skills locally is a powerful advantage for both insourcing and outsourcing.

Downtowns can successfully access and mix up all this talent when they are at the nexus of the metropolitan transportation systems, and they can accommodate lots of people moving around by some means other than the auto. America has so starved transit that only a handful of downtowns can build the collaborative overlapping business, living, and recreational cultures that urban success increasingly demands—mainly, the older cities that still have functioning high-capacity rail transit. Elsewhere, people won't go downtown because traffic is terrible and they can't park. But if downtown is remade, as many have been, to accommodate all the cars, it is no longer a downtown but a plane of surface parking dotted with some tall buildings.

MEGABURBIA SEIZES UP

For decades, business-location analysts assumed that downtown was for finance and banking and that the suburbs, with their easy mobility, were for most every other kind of business. But highly interactive and highly collaborative ways of working have grown in tandem with the "distributive," supposedly suburb-friendly technologies that have matured in recent years, such as e-mail and the Internet. This has begun to change the game for megaburban business centers, which have depended on the ability to move quickly across very large landscapes by auto.

Have a look at what's happened to Hollywood—the industry, not the place. The movie and television (and, nowadays, computer game and animation) businesses grew within the greater Los Angeles basin everywhere but downtown, even though these are quintessentially creative and collaborative endeavors. You find studios north, in Burbank, or dozens of miles south, in Orange County, and scattered everywhere in between. For decades, it didn't matter that Burbank and Culver City were not close to each other, because freeways knitted them together. Today, traffic conditions require chauffeured producers to motor an hour from the coast to see bankers and attorneys downtown. Low-paid production assistants haul perhaps forty-five minutes from somewhere near USC to the San Fernando Valley. The stakes are too high in Hollywood, and the business too competitive, to afford to have so many people stuck in so much traffic. For now, though, that's the only possibility.

The realm that Hollywood occupies in metropolitan Los Angeles represents a tiny slice of its geographical extent—a reach that up to a few years ago was entirely accessible by car in under an hour. As the metropolitan area grows beyond a hundred miles in every direction, and "close-in" housing has gotten more expensive, the roads have congealed and greater Los Angeles has begun to divide itself into separate spheres determined by drive times. Orange County and the San Fernando Valley are severing themselves from Los Angeles, creating independent economies that are less integrated because it is too difficult to get from place to place. These developments undermine the ability to access talent that is the key business advantage of large urban areas. As each person's drive-time radius shrinks, Los Angeles loses the advantages of bigness and the disadvantages begin to loom larger. You can say the same about both Atlanta and Silicon Valley, though these are among the most heavily freewayed landscapes in America. For similar reasons, the economy of Long Island is becoming steadily more isolated from that of metropolitan New York, because sclerotic freeways and a lack of train service make Westchester County, southern Connecticut, and New Jersey suburbs all but inaccessible.

The changed way businesses interact with one another has become noticeable in the way companies build facilities in the megaburban hinterlands. Up until the 1990s, prestigious corporations erected self-contained campuses on vast acreages in tony suburbs, wrapping these emblems of success with private lakes, running trails, and impeccably groomed landscaping. The insightful urban observer William H. Whyte noticed that no one wanted to visit these intimidating redoubts, and the self-satisfied grandeur tended to focus business culture inward, while businesses that co-located with customers in downtowns or multiple locations thrived at the old-line companies' expense.[14] In the past couple of decades, those blue chip names vanished or shrank (AT&T, General Foods, Union Carbide), and many of the corporate showplaces have been torn down and sold off.

According to Fuerst, who did the research on firms that stayed in Manhattan after 9/11, there is ample, though anecdotal, evidence that too few businesses consider the potential for interaction and collaboration when they choose business locations distant from the center—and then pay the price. "The company moves back to the city after a while when it turns out that its business operations have become less efficient in the suburban location. The problem becomes apparent when employees report that they actually spend more time traveling to and from the new location, not less. For example, many clients are unwilling to travel to a remote suburban office park for a meeting and prefer to meet in a downtown location instead. Consequently, employees of the suburban company spend precious time traveling to and from inner cities for these meetings."[15]

Many megaburban realms are becoming denser—though rarely in a planned way, struggling to make interaction and collaboration easier, leading to what sounds like the oxymoronic notion of "dense sprawl," evident in Los Angeles, which has grown denser as people seek shorter daily travel times. Metrowide, Los Angeles is now the densest urban area in America. But the interactivity essential to urban health needs both density and mobility, and there's a limit to how dense such places can become without better access to auto alternatives.

With a sclerotic growth machine and an opportunistic, short-term, fragmented view of the future, we should not be surprised that the urban places we make are not adaptable—not really agile—in business terms, in quality-of-life terms, and in climate-adapting terms. The ecological notion of high-efficiency/low-impact aligns with the business case for urban density because urban places designed to allow lots of interaction are inherently agile and adaptive, just as reducing the land footprint and the ecological impact of cities is. You can reject climate-change science and still make a case for places that are compact and that enable the use of auto alternatives. Auto-alternative cityscapes permit many scales of interaction but exact no penalties if you hole up in your office and never see anyone. Megaburban settlement patterns are responsible for the fact that transportation costs for doing business (even with generally far cheaper energy costs) are much higher in America than in similar developed-world countries, and that energy use of all kinds is much higher than in peer nations—but without the payoff in greater wealth that cheap energy and unlimited auto mobility are supposed to confer.

Edge cities are beginning to recognize that they must transform themselves to continue to capture the advantages of proximity once conferred by the networks of open freeways, according to Virginia Tech's Robert Lang. He described a big computer-company enclave in Atlanta's beltway-hugging Perimeter Center. Staff resisted an expansion proposal because it already took twenty minutes to get down the freeway off-ramp.[16]

The transcendent megaburban issue is mobility. Experts and the traffic-weary commuter alike know that localities cannot build traffic lanes fast enough. Fewer understand that it is especially difficult to improve mobility if there is no means to address it systematically—at the metropolitan scale at which highways supposedly knit communities together. What we do, however wasteful and senseless we know it to be, is upgrade an intersection here or add a highway lane there. It should come as no surprise that an accumulation of such $100 million projects adds up quickly to billions yet only rearranges the traffic jams temporarily rather than actually alleviating them.

If mobility seems an obsession in these pages, it is because mobility is the centerpiece of urban success. Cities exist to collect people for a wide variety of exchanges. If you can't get to those cities, and if you can't get around within them, those exchanges simply move somewhere else. Older cities paid the price when auto mobility released people from dependence on train routes and schedules. Now the auto dependence of megaburbia has become a liability. Wealth building, mobility, and climate change are becoming increasingly inextricable. The urban places we make will largely determine our economic *and* ecologic future.

SUBURBAN VALUES VERSUS MEGABURBAN REALITY

Can small-town governance structures and suburban cultural ideals ("bathed in sunlight and fresh air," as suburban historian Kenneth T. Jackson put it) hope to deal with the form of suburbanism that has emerged? It has not been easy. The growth machine that makes megaburbia happen is on a collision course with the quality of life that has for so long animated the suburban dream. As people have moved from inner suburb to outer suburb, with the beltway loops, like tree rings, marking growth eras twenty, thirty, even fifty miles from the center, they settled down at what seemed to them a safe distance from stagnation and congestion, only to find the tsunami of traffic, growth, and urban anxiety rearing up right behind.

The land-use controversies that fill the pages of suburban local newspapers can be parodied as the selfless tree-huggers versus the evil developers or the heroic businesses bearing jobs versus selfish anti-everything activists. Instead, these are fundamental struggles over suburban values and identity. They are efforts to maintain stability and a sense of place—one might also say, a sense of civility—in the face of economic forces that only incidentally recognize these values. Business groups gripe that not-in-my-backyard (NIMBY) activists protest the roads, the office parks, the malls, and the airport expansions necessary for modern commerce to function economically—everything that makes their good life possible.

Suburbanites become activists to "preserve our quality of life"—by which some mean housing values, by which some mean a place where people like them will continue to feel comfortable, by which some mean a place where houses still open to views of farm fields or forests, and by which some mean a place that's as affordable to the next generation as it was to the last.

The ad hoc nature of NIMBY-style activism—moving relentlessly from the proposed subdivision to the proposed road widening—infuriates businesses that have already "jumped through all the hoops." It provokes heartburn at government agencies that find themselves endlessly mediating squabbles that have morphed into epic, to-the-death battles. These kinds of protests are classically suburban in character, however. The individualistic values embodied by such activism are ingrained in its DNA. They are no match for the vast economic forces roiling megaburbia, however.

Broadly speaking, the environmental activists and property-tax protesters are fighting the growth machine forces that have created megaburbia, but the culture of small-town home rule provides "weapons" capable only of winning battles here and there, not of winning the war for suburban quality of life. Climate change, along with taxes, traffic, and school funding, are all megaburban concerns that can't successfully be dealt with until suburbs come together to create a high-performance, low-impact future at metropolitan scale.

Suburbia's enclave culture plays out in various ways. It is difficult not only to efficiently consolidate government functions but also to unite so many entities to accomplish anything. Mamaroneck, a suburb of New York City, wanted to stop the construction of an Ikea superstore because the enormous traffic generated would clog its narrow, quiet streets. Unfortunately, the store was located a stone's throw away in neighboring New Rochelle, which wanted the tax receipts the store would generate. New Rochelle, not Mamaroneck, had the power to approve or nix the store. Mamaroneck tried to pass an ordinance to restrict the actions of New Rochelle, which New Rochelle rejected as a power grab.[17] This kind of land-use roundelay happens all over America all the time.

LOOKING FOR ORLANDO

Leaders in even relatively young metropolitan areas have recognized how hard it is to prepare for the future when you can act only as an assemblage of enclaves. Orlando is such a place. There's not much of a center, though I-4 takes you by a smattering of downtown towers. Most of "Orlando" lies beyond the city limits and is made up of small communities huddled along the I-4 backbone far to the north and south, or tucked around the dozens of sparkling lakes to the west and northwest, well beyond the freeways' reach. In the tightly packed subdivisions scattered across the square miles, middle-class retirees seek low-cost solace amid orange groves abandoned after freezes in the 1980s. To the east, the St. John's River, rimmed by wildlife-rich marshes, forms a watery, green barrier.

On paper, many places recognize that economically related cities and suburbs must work together on issues of common importance, but regional government is a concept beloved by planning wonks and few others. Federal transportation rules require metropolitan planning organizations to hammer out transportation priorities, but few operate transparently nor get beyond conventional political horse-trading. Many places form councils of local governments. Because each of their members answers only to their own voters, these aptly named COGs often accomplish little. Orlando has taken a different path, attempting to forge a metropolitan *identity*, which could lead in turn to the formation (or rearrangement) of government institutions to make that identity a reality.

According to Shelly Lauten, "Orlando" is actually eighty-six municipalities and seven counties. "We were a bunch of small cities," she explained when I visited some years ago. She is president of a group called MyRegion that tries to build a more cooperative attitude in such satellite Orlandos as Ocoee, Kissimmee, and Apopka.[18] She and her colleagues don't think the region can successfully compete, or maintain the quality of life that attracts people, or deal with global warming challenges, if all these little places won't work together. She recognizes that her vision is a minority one. Lauten and her colleagues at MyRegion know that most of the communities that make up this "city" don't see much value in working together or defining themselves as the united urban entity they are—economically anyway. "People don't want to think of themselves in terms of 'Orlando,' " Lauten says, "but there's nothing else."

The go-it-alone ethos is evident in the way metro Orlando flings itself outward with ever-greater centrifugal force. The freeway net stretches in an elongated thirty-mile-diameter loop, while the hottest growth zones are fifteen to thirty miles farther out. It's an ultra-low-density scatter, dissolving the edge of Orlando's megaburbia into what Virginia Tech urban analyst Robert Lang has called the "Edgeless City" (figure 6.2).[19]

Figure 6.2 Land development patterns in agricultural zones far beyond the urban edge often take suburban form, like this subdivided farmland in Southampton, New York. Credit: James S. Russell

Orlando has struggled to maintain a balance of growth, friendliness, and quality of life. "We don't want to become L.A.," is the mantra that has united the MyRegion project with its skeptical constituents. However, a conservative politics; a pro-growth ethos; cheap, plentiful land, and minimal government—little different from the ethos which prevails in Orlando today—did not keep the "L.A." people love to hate from happening.

When I checked back in 2010, MyRegion had succeeded on the transportation front because it helped build a consensus to link metropolitan Orlando and Tampa with high-speed rail (which will turn a one-and-a-half hour trip into a thirty-seven-minute one), and that corridor was the first one selected for funding in the Obama administration's intercity-rail push. "Orlando mayor Buddy Dyer told me that if not for MyRegion's efforts to help us collectively change our mindsets, we would have never gotten high-speed rail," Lauten said.[20] A local commuter-rail project has also been approved. "We were able to point out that our population may double by 2050 and serving that with new roads would require about $260 billion."

MyRegion had not yet been able to resolve squabbles about water supplies when I spoke to Lauten. And global warming skepticism has prevented greater

Orlando from developing a strategy on climate change, even though low-lying Florida could suffer gravely from rising seas. "Some people say all of south Florida is at risk, and we know it's hugely important, but a lot of people just want to ignore it," Lauten explained.

MyRegion is incrementally readying those eighty-six cities for the day when climate change and other metrowide challenges must be faced. The federal government has begun to offer what could become game-changing grants that unite pots of money from the Departments of Housing and Urban Development and Transportation, along with the Environmental Protection Agency. Instead of throwing money at fixing a traffic problem here or underwriting an urban-revitalization scheme there, these grants support regional planning that integrates economic development, housing, transportation, and environmental protection. They actually can address systemic issues. Unlike most metropolitan areas in the United States: "We have learned collaborative behavior," explains Lauten. "So what better region in country to test this planning approach than central Florida?"

THE CITY AS A MUTT

Rather than obliterate suburbia, reshape it in the form of a traditional central city, or throw a lot of ideas around and see which stick, we can more comprehensively envision higher-efficiency and lower-impact urban forms. Then we figure out ways to enable them to happen—which means rebuilding the growth machine from scratch. Subsequent chapters spell out a number of possible futures, none of them utopian. America has tended to discard places when they get older, moving on to something newer, greener, and shinier and trying not to see the mess that's left behind.

The cities we worship, though, the places we'll pay good money to go visit, are often old. They seem to have been built for the ages. Keep looking at those handsome streetscapes and you see that they are anything but pure. They are a mélange of eras, styles, and adaptations. Along the streets of Rome, you can see a medieval window arch that survived a Baroque-era makeover. A grand ancient Roman arch may form the ceiling of a basement restaurant. Places that build for the ages don't obliterate the past or leave it behind; they repurpose it. America needs to wreak a transformation of its communities over the next decades, but it is unlikely to make cities and suburbs as we know them vanish.

Instead, places will become more muttlike—less pure and more interesting—and we know that mutts are often healthier and less high-strung.

The single-family home may lose its dominance in the housing mix, and you'll live in it differently, performing daily errands with far fewer car trips because you'll park once and walk to destinations clustered in neighborhood centers. More people will choose to live in multifamily buildings of various kinds, where heating and cooling are far more economical and where maintenance chores are fewer, and in neighborhoods where most tasks can be accomplished without driving. Fast light-rail or bus rapid transit lines will link neighborhood centers to one another and to major destinations. Commuter rail and inter-city rail will link destinations of metrowide importance.

Asphalt acres should shrink in a more agile megaburbia, as reliance on autos declines. We can jackhammer parking lots in favor of suburban forests, We can widen waterside buffers so that streams and lakes run cleaner, linking them together in "green lung" corridors that serve natural and human needs together. Rather than fill wetlands for warehouse shopping, we can let them handle flood control and water filtering for us. The apparent paradox of "denser," more diverse megaburbia is the potential to reclaim the closeness to nature that was always at the root of the suburban dream.

Part 3

Agile Urban Futures

It is tempting to avoid engaging with an unknowable future that seems to ask so much of us as citizens. Challenges on the scale of climate change are not new to the United States, however. A century and a half ago, the nation's wrenching transformation from small villages and farms to a multiethnic industrial powerhouse overturned established identities and caused us to choose to be citizens in new ways. Rethinking our outlook and encouraging visionary ideas is actually time honored in America, even though today's political hard edges can make that seem hard to believe.

Devising an appropriate kind of citizenship obsessed America in the nineteenth century when industrial cities first developed to enormous size and immigrants flooded in. The city would cause the loss of the uniquely independent self-reliant American, social critics feared, and there was ample evidence to support their views in the dehumanizing grind of the filthy factories.

At that time, many observers, whether they loved or hated the city, decried its anonymity. Convulsive economic expansion tended to sever traditional ties to families and communities. Much of the effort of planners and visionaries in the late nineteenth and early twentieth centuries was devoted to carving out places that were safe—a civil antidote to the excesses of the industrial city. The historical suburban ideal, of course, posited closeness to "pure" nature as the antidote to the disordered industrial city, operating by a set of agreed-to rules and promising to nurture a moral person. This was, to put it kindly, naive, but the idea continues to work subconsciously even as suburbs have morphed into megaburbs defined by social, economic, ethnic, and moral difference rather than homogeneity.

In the cities themselves, Americans evolved a range of metropolitan identities. Clubs and civic associations nurtured urban civic ideals. Their leaders promoted the urban park systems that brought fresh air and greenery to the endless streets of brick and stone. Civic leaders created the settlement houses in the slums to raise up the poor. They created the monumental temples of secular art and culture during the turn-of-the-twentieth-century City Beautiful movement—inspired by the columned and pedimented White City of the 1893 Chicago World's Fair.

Farm people reinvented themselves in the city as ambitious entrepreneurs and journalistic provocateurs. Immigrants cast off their pasts to become American, both an ideal and a mystifying reality. Personal transformation, in fact, is the central American story told by our best writers and by playwrights and movie makers.

HOW TO BE A CITIZEN IN A TUMULTUOUS AGE

We Americans fiercely cling to our quintessential individuality—an individuality, to be sure, that has been a wellspring of vitality throughout our history in every sphere of life. But we have also become urban people who must cooperate and collaborate in myriad ways. Individualism, in urban terms, continues to lead to a fragmented view that is inadequate to a tumultuous and hard-to-predict future.

According to Peter Drey, an Atlanta urban designer, the privatized, individualist approach is so deeply ingrained in his city that an attempt to create consensus on growth, planning, or identity can barely be contemplated. The lack of respect for government is so instinctual that, as he explained, "people basically steer around governmental mechanisms to accomplish what they need to accomplish." There's little attempt to influence planning or development at any scale larger than individual parcels of land. As a result, said Drey, "people can achieve only incremental steps all over the metro area. I call it uncontrolled adaptation."[1]

Out of such an anti-collaborative ethos comes a proposal to widen a freeway corridor to a colossal twenty-three lanes. Most of the world sees such an idea as delusional, but it's hard to imagine a nonfreeway approach to mobility in Atlanta, so the idea is taken seriously. After all, as in most of the United States, more lanes are the default solution, the path of least resistance. By contrast, the city's BeltLine project founders, perhaps because it is a once-in-a-lifetime opportunity. That project would make a twenty-two-mile necklace of parks, transit lines, and commercial redevelopment out of obsolete rail corridors. It requires different kinds of collaboration, planning, and finance, but it could create significant development opportunities all over Atlanta while uniting dozens of neighborhoods (more about this project in chapter 8). We've got to ask ourselves why that's such a heavy lift. This is not to pick on Atlanta; the same story applies in much of America.

The deeper American problem is the lack of a collective ethos to insist that large-scale problems be addressed. In the political discussions around numerous issues that affect cities, someone is always arguing that Americans won't look at questions larger than their neighborhoods and their lives. Certainly, we can't "sacrifice" (in the political parlance, whatever that means) to build a better future. Government always fails, goes the claim, so we have to limp along with whatever mashup of brain-dead development, fragmented dysfunctional government, and ritualized unchanging interest-group battles we've lived with for decades. It's a strangely defeatist attitude for a nation that has long believed it can do what "they" said couldn't be done.

Though Americans lionize the iconoclast and the entrepreneur, the United States has invented some of the world's great collective places and democratic institutions. Pierre L'Enfant's 1791 plan for Washington, DC, was an imaginative invention dedicated to asserting the young nation's identity in brick and stone. Its diagonal streets, town squares, and great public spaces may have been derived from the baroque urban structures put in place by autocratic European courts and clerics, but L'Enfant repurposed those structures to create a rich urban network that expressed America's division of government power and its evolving public self. The monumental palaces and temples of Washington were self-consciously styled to evoke the great democratic moments of ancient Greece and Rome. These emblems of civic order, in contrast to the young nation's wilderness—which then seemed unknowably vast and dangerous—gave the architectural grandeur a deeper resonance.

The urban setpieces of Washington, as well as the National Park system, state forests, library systems, and public schools, along with the parks and parkway networks in Buffalo, St. Louis, Kansas City, Chicago, and elsewhere, helped us to see the world as larger than ourselves. Implicit in these acts was a belief that we—collectively, not just individually—create our destiny by what we do with the land and how we make cities. These landscapes and places were seen as vessels of our culture, defining our national identity, and passing on our values. They required a great deal of cooperation to come to fruition.

As we seek a sustainable path to the future, we're challenged to examine our values, our worldviews, and our role as citizens. Part 3 sketches agile urban futures to show what's possible and what living in communities adapted to climate change will be like. Many of the tactics described are pioneering or provisional: they are forays into the future rather than the future itself, since we'll have to try on many ways of doing things, then evaluate, tweak, throw out, and invent anew. What will guide us is an American citizenship that engages at the scale of the challenges we face, while we pursue our individual hopes and dreams.

Chapter 7 shows how each of us, in the individual buildings and places we inhabit, can take a holistic approach that harvests the unique qualities of climate and setting. We dramatically cut our impact on the planet's environment while shaping buildings that palpably belong where they are built and express the uniqueness of their place. The state of the green design art is moving quickly, so diverse technologies and techniques available today lay the groundwork for improved versions tomorrow.

These days, we often must look to cities outside the United States that have learned to transform themselves. Berlin has had to find an ideal for the future so that it could reconcile itself with a tragic past. Bilbao needed to build a viable new economy. The port city of Hamburg, a city that has adapted to changing trade patterns and technologies for centuries, now designs for more severe flooding as it builds a low-carbon future. The tasks in these cities were not all related to climate change, but the *means* by which such cities collaboratively willed a new future is the subject of chapter 8, because American cities can learn from their experiences and adapt them to our unique conditions.

"Loose-fit" urbanism, discussed in chapter 9, punctures the myth that the green city can only constrain individual enterprise in the service of a defensive environmentalism. The very notion of urban agility recognizes that places adapt to circumstances of all kinds. We hail cities that have recognized and quickly capitalized on new economic opportunities. Less often do we look at cities that squandered the riches their location provided and ignored catastrophic environmental change (deforestation and desertification most prominently), which would ultimately undermine economic success. It is already clear that the future will reward places that are entrepreneurial in both economic and environmental ways, since they will become both more resilient and more productive.

The global recession that began at the end of the previous decade should cause developed economies to reconsider long-held presumption that ever-growing consumption builds economic health. Chapter 10 shows the remarkable degree to which America's chimerical growth over the last three decades relied on a bubble ethos. America needs a new way to ensure its economic future, and more economists are coming around to the idea that uniting human well-being with environmental resilience is not merely a moral imperative (which we can condescendingly leave to do-gooders) but an economic one. The chapter considers economic models that depend less on heedless consumption of finite resources, since the world economy now consumes them so voraciously that small upticks in global GDP translate into commodity shortages and rapidly rising prices, dampening wealth creation.

An era of perpetual change requires a rich, ongoing dialogue, based on trust, among citizens, community leaders, and officials, and the epilogue proposes several means to hammer out the future in a constructive and collegial way.

7

BUILDING ADAPTIVE PLACES

A small house in Orient, a village on eastern Long Island, beckoned charmingly as a summer rental. It looked across the lawn of the village green to a sailboat-dotted harbor. A group of us moved in, and it grew on us throughout the summer in the way some deeply special buildings and places do. It wasn't a classic beauty. It had started out as a tiny, square 1840s saltbox built by a carpenter out of pattern books widely available at the time, and it had more than doubled in size through three idiosyncratic additions over a hundred years.

The unobvious wisdom built into its strangely colliding parts began to reveal itself. It had been carefully oriented on the lot to capture cooling breezes that predictably spring up on the Peconic Bay on summer afternoons. (The whole house was cross ventilated, which meant that only on the half dozen hottest days did you even need fans.) A charmingly odd door opened outside from partway up the stairway, aligned to the floor below; you had to clamber a couple of feet to use it. As the days warmed, its usefulness became clear: it routed that prevailing breeze up the stairs and into the bedrooms, pushing accumulated hot air out.

When the back porch grew too hot, we found ourselves moving to the street-side front porch, out of the sun. The watery quality of the afternoon light slanting in, filtered by street trees, invited a nap, a read, and quiet cocktail conversation. As the sun sank toward the horizon, it slipped between the trees, putting on a magical spectacle, it seemed, just for us (figure 7.1).

The point of this is not to wax poetic about a summer idyll but to recognize that one of the most environmentally responsible things we can do is live pleas-

Figure 7.1 Along the northeastern seaboard, climate-sensitive houses orient porches to capture summer breezes and funnel them through the cross-ventilated houses. Credit: James S. Russell

urably in closer cognizance to climate, weather, daylight, and breezes. In contrast to the ordinariness and sameness of most of our cities and suburbs, many communities and many natural environments seem to have an innate, soulful sense of place. Of course, a great deal of a city or town's uniqueness is formed out of culture, history, and habit, but its built form—like that of the Long Island village—can enhance its specialness or erase it. You would not mistake stretches of the northern Atlantic coast for anywhere else, because of the light, the color of the water, the shape of the dunes, the plants growing on them, the shingled houses hunkered down to survive storms. By contrast, you could never divine what is unique about much of Florida's developed coastline, since its unique flora and even the configuration of the beach itself have been so altered—if not obliterated—that the ingredients of "beach" have been degraded merely to water, sand, asphalt, concrete, and condos.

This chapter shows the enormous untapped and underestimated potential of buildings and sites to reduce carbon emissions and adapt to climate-change effects. Buildings and their settings can harness nature to do much of what in the past few decades we have handed off to costly energy-hogging machinery.

So I do not propose fifty ways to green your home through better lightbulbs and caulking your windows properly. These are valuable things to do, but plenty of guidance exists already.

You will see in this chapter many references to heating, cooling, and lighting. These are the biggest energy users in buildings by far, and they offer the largest opportunities for reduction. In most nonresidential buildings, cooling is very important because the lighting and equipment—and even human exertion—add so much heat to conventional sealed buildings that air-conditioning commonly switches on when the outside building temperatures are as low as the fifties. (As global warming adds a degree or two to warm days, we'll be pushing that air-conditioning harder, drawing more power, ejecting more heat and carbon into the atmosphere—an ever more costly spiral.) In homes, the energy used for heating hot water, cooking, and drying clothes may be much greater than that used for lighting.

The real opportunity to make deep cuts in carbon, and to live with much lower impact on the environment, begins not with technology but with place, with a holistic approach to understanding and making the most of every setting's unique qualities.

LOVING THE LOWLY SHUTTER

Designers of agile buildings and ensembles can "read" what the natural environment is telling them—whether in the windblown plains, under the South's dense tree canopy, in the sharp light of high deserts, in the misty Pacific Northwest, or in the chill of the upper Midwest and New England.

Let's start small, with a window protection that has existed for centuries: the shutter. Shutters are among the humble architectural devices that we discarded when we decided we could engineer our way out of anything (figure 7.2). Louvered ones keep the hot summer sun out while letting in cooling breezes. They can repel intruders. In Rome, shutter design for the enormous windows of the city's endless palaces has been honed to a fine art. You can open the top half to catch a breeze or rooftop view, and close the lower half for privacy. You can close the top and tilt out the bottom during the hottest part of the day to keep track of the doings on the street (an essential Roman pastime) while you remain shrouded in shadow.

Such historic architectural devices harness nature rather than defy it. By and large, they work because they were honed by time, experience—and

Figure 7.2 Louvered shutters cut the heat of the sun while admitting breezes and maintaining privacy. Sturdy ones can protect windows from hurricanes and intruders. Credit: James S. Russell

tragedy. In the hurricane-prone South, shutters were a home's first line of defense. When hurricanes threaten the Atlantic or Gulf Coasts nowadays, homeowners desperately nail plywood over vulnerable windows—including over modern useless shutters.

Those great colonnades of Deep South plantation houses were made tall and deep to shade grand windows from the sun. The high-ceilinged rooms stay cooler longer. Many southern homes featured upper-floor terraces. Giving relief from the heat, they facilitated nighttime trysts, fodder for endless southern novels. The great facades of the grand old homes were sometimes only one room deep so that the Gulf breezes would run refreshingly through. Other houses were stretched into a long T, so that every room could harvest the same precious cool.

I am not one for returning to the past or embalming it. But as we think about an adaptive way to build for the future, there's no reason we can't learn from these great traditions. I wrote about a distinctly modern house built not far from Charleston, South Carolina, to replace one swept away by Hurricane Hugo in 1989. It has tall ceilings and high windows, but a contemporary informality. A handsome wood latticework protects those windows from storm-driven debris while providing dappled shade to a wraparound porch. Unlike its neighboring McMansions on stilts, it's carefully proportioned to look good even though it is raised nine feet above the ground so that the kind of surging waves that regularly level Atlantic coast communities could pass beneath. The house drew a great deal of attention at the time, and its architect, Ray Huff, of Charleston, was instantly deemed a hurricane expert by the press. He was not, and did not pretend to be; he just followed the traditional rules and applied them in an especially inventive way.[1]

As mechanical air-conditioning has become universal, the South has replicated the look of history endlessly but stopped installing working shutters and rarely builds deep porches or breeze-harvesting floor plans. That damaged the great social traditions honed by hot climates: the art of deep-into-the-night conversation and music making. But it's understandable. The most sensitive architecture can't duplicate the comfort provided by a humming compressor.

Air-conditioning is great, but it's cheaper to run if we protect windows with shutters. It's even cheaper if we turn it off in the evening and hunt for the breeze on a capacious front porch.

For all the variety in the New Orleans designs for Global Green, the Make It Right prototypes, and the model home projects in Biloxi, they shared climate-sensitive design themes. Many attempted in various ways to update the long "shotgun" types, a modest form of housing historically built in the Gulf south. Shotgun builders simply strung one room in back of the other in a long, skinny line from porched, street-facing parlor to back garden. They're called shotgun because you can shoot a bullet from one end to the other unimpeded as each room opens into the next in a straight line. They have long served as a cheap means to funnel fresh air. Among many permutations, some alternated rooms and tiny gardened courtyards.

The modern prototypes adapted the advantages of older shotguns to fit modern lifestyles, creating houses that have more privacy yet are airier, energy efficient, and more wind resistant, and that place neighborly porches close to passersby on the street even as they hike themselves above potential flood levels (or, in the case of one Make It Right house, float).

However many tactics and technologies they use, all the post-Katrina prototypes also used what is always provided free: sun, daylight, and fresh air. Writ just a bit larger, that means making the most of the location: orientation, topography, soils, vegetation, cultural traditions, and so on. Shaping a house and correctly orienting it to minimize both winter heat loss and summer heat gain can deliver double-digit energy savings no matter where it is. The savings are all free, but too often we just don't bother. If you take the same house and make it a town house, so that it shares two of its four main exposures with neighboring dwellings, you can save from 40 to more than 50 percent of the heating and cooling energy needed by a single-family house designed heedless of its place. If you add high-performance mechanical systems and upgraded windows to the well-oriented house, they perform better with quicker paybacks.[2]

The result does more than put dollars in your pocket. You inhabit a building, a site, and a community that isn't *in* a place—it *makes* a place. Why would we build the same home-builder's box everywhere when we could be building homes that, like our little Orient house, clock the seasons and reveal the uniqueness of their location by how they catch breezes, harvest winter sun, and husband shade in summer? As a bonus, we will have made lower-carbon communities with a far richer range of experiences and social amenities.

TRADE WIND TECHNIQUES COOL CALIFORNIA

Let's have a look beyond the South at the diversity of adaptations you can find among America's vast range of climates. It should be simple to all but eliminate heating and cooling in most of coastal California. The boxy, stucco-sided houses roofed in red tiles that dot the endless hills have learned nothing from the traditional Mediterranean architecture from which their look is cribbed, and so demand expanses of tinted glass and hefty air-conditioning machinery only because they are not oriented to use sun, shade, and breezes.

The San Francisco federal office building, designed by the Los Angeles firm Morphosis, shows what's possible. It uses south-facing metal screens to repel unwanted heat, and glass fins to the north to bring in daylight. Inside, the undulating concrete ceilings encourage cross ventilation through windows that open. The concrete itself absorbs heat from people and machines and radiates it during the cool nights. (In warm, dry places with cool nights, there are many tactics that can be used to "store" the evening coolness in massive masonry or rammed-earth walls for use in the daytime.) The narrowest sides of the building face east and west so that the least possible wall area faces the heat of the morning and afternoon sun. The thin form of the building means that people work in daylight rather than electric lights (figure 7.3). Almost everyone has a view. The main elevators stop every third floor, which not only saves energy but encourages people to get a bit of exercise as they encounter coworkers on wide, handsome stairways that open to bay panoramas.

Almost every technique I just described is ancient, though this eye-catching building's form and use are utterly contemporary. (While walking around it, I overhead a passerby comment "very military-industrial complex.") The building could effectively harvest breezes and daylight because it applied rapidly advancing computer-aided analytical software to make the old techniques work with today's expectations of comfort.[3]

Much of inland California, where the coastal cooling of the ocean is less pronounced, can still forgo mechanical air-conditioning if well designed or sensitively remodeled. Minimizing broad expanses that directly face the sun is a much more powerful tactic than rule-of-thumb cooling-machinery calculations credit. If the view or the prime frontage can't avoid facing into the sun, protecting walls with external awnings and shutters (the old-fashioned solution) or suspended louvers (the 1950s solution) or adjustable external blinds (today's solution) not only saves energy but means you can get rid of the dreary internal environment created by tinted glass. With shaded clear glass, you can use daylight and switch off lights near the windows, ramping up savings. (Lights use power and add heat that must be removed). You can dare to open the window because the sun on an 80-degree day has not heated the glass to 120 degrees.

Figure 7.3 In the San Francisco Federal Building, north-facing windows permit work by daylight with only minimal use of electric lights (Morphosis, architect). Windows at top and bottom open to naturally ventilate the building. Credit: James S. Russell

Ensembles of buildings can be arranged to shade one another during the hottest periods of the day yet grab light during the short days of winter. They can connect to one another through appealing, shadowy courtyards or trellis-covered passages. (Plopping buildings willy-nilly and wrapping them in surface parking takes no thought at all but is wasteful by every measure: isolating people, throwing away useful land, and building in wasteful energy use.)

SEEKING SHADE IN THE DESERT

The windshield-exploding heat of the desert in places like Phoenix and Las Vegas would seem to defeat any energy-conserving regime. But people have lived for centuries in the world's hottest places and have honed numerous architectural means to beat the heat. High buildings shade narrow streets. Thick walls absorb daytime heat, then release it in cool evenings. Shutters, veils of curtains, and decorative perforated screens orchestrate layered thresholds from hot, bright streets to cool, shadowy private realms in Spain, Africa, and the

Middle East. Overlapping expanses of fabric dapple traditional souks with light and waft in fresh air. Tall chimneys capture rooftop breezes to draw out heat rising from lower floors.

People who have lived for centuries without cheap fossil-fuel energy have not plopped the same boxy buildings you'd find in damp, dim climates in the middle of sun-seared, heat-capturing parking lots. That's what we do in the United States. Of course, massive air-conditioning units must roar atop such climate-ignorant buildings.

Cruising by the headquarters of the Endesa power company on Madrid's M-40 beltway, you would not naturally think of the traditional Spanish patio. Horizontal blades of translucent glass project from its long, six-story bulk to cut the western sun. Behind the facade, the building wraps a city-block-long courtyard, covered by a high-tech roof framed in massive steel trusses. The courtyard was built as a gathering space that would remain comfortable even in Madrid's dry, searing summers. Instead of the traditional patio's trellis of wood or roof of canvas, the Endesa courtyard has a system of louvers and translucent glass that shade the courtyard and diffuse daylight, which offices around the courtyard borrow to largely replace electric lights (figure 7.4). Air cooled by the earth seeps into the courtyard through the paving. Solar chimneys draw hot air out of the top of the atrium.

The design does not avoid the use of mechanical air-conditioning but minimizes the amount of space that must be cooled. The extensive use of shading devices all around reduces external heat buildup. I've long admired this building because of the inventive way architects Kohn Pedersen Fox (the London office of the New York firm), the local architect Rafael de La-Hoz, and the London natural-ventilation consultants Battle McCarthy combine so many tactics of traditional hot-climate architecture in a building of utterly contemporary use.[4]

It's extraordinary that in hot-weather America such techniques have been adopted only rarely to make buildings and streetscapes more comfortable, even in the absence of an urgency to reduce energy use. Yes, residents of Tucson or El Paso can live their lives almost entirely within air-conditioned cars and air-conditioned buildings, but traipsing across the acres of arid parking lots to do everyday errands eradicates much of the comfort advantage. For many months of the year, a stroll down the street, through a public square, or into a park is not a pleasure but an ordeal. It is not surprising that people flock to pedestrianized shopping malls shaded by porches and cooled by fountains or trellises networked with misters.

Figure 7.4 The glass roof of the Endesa headquarters outside Madrid both shades an internal courtyard and supplies daylight to offices that wrap its perimeter. Solar chimneys temper the space by exhausting warm air (KPF and Rafael de La-Hoz, architects). Credit: © H. G. Esch courtesy KPF

THE EAST: HEAT FROM THE EARTH AND PASSIVE POWER

It's not easy to harvest climate forces for energy conservation in much of the eastern United States—St. Louis, Philadelphia, New York, Boston—where you have low winter temperatures and humid, high summer heat. As you move north, traditional houses become tighter and boxier to minimize building exposure to the cold. That's why additions to farmhouses in Vermont or New Hampshire seem to huddle together for warmth. Windows grow larger on the south and north sides to draw in elusive sun on short winter days. It's easy to cut heat energy simply by insulating well, using an efficient furnace, and switching it off where and when you don't need it. In old houses of the East, only a few cozy, well-insulated rooms might be heated.

Summer breezes are nice but can only minimize the discomfort of high-humidity days. That's why many engineers in the humidity belt regard natural ventilation as suitable only for the all-too-brief "shoulder seasons," when summer humidity diminishes but the winter heating season has yet to begin.

As elsewhere, traditional architecture offers cues to "broaden" the shoulders: porches offer summer respite though they are shallower than their southern counterparts. If you are willing to open and close windows and shutters, as the seasons dictate, and use ceiling fans and whole-house fans, you can counteract the discomfort of all but the hottest humid days in much of the East, minimizing the need for air-conditioning in buildings carefully oriented and shaded from summer heat.

The East has climate advantages, too. Much of it is lush, so carefully placed trees can shade the hottest building exposures. The push to "forest" Philadelphia, Chicago, New York, and other cities can knock a few degrees off of sultry days while making people feel psychologically cooler. Conveniently, eastern tree leaves fall off in winter, replacing shade with useful daylight and welcome solar heat.

While solar and wind energy offer great localized potential, geothermal heating and cooling is fast becoming the renewable-energy source of choice in the humidity belt. A system entails many tiny wells drilled into the earth under a garden or parking lot. In winter, pumps withdraw warmth from the earth, usually an unvarying fifty-five degrees, adding it to the heating system, which then must do much less to bring the rooms up to a comfortable temperature. In summer, the system essentially pumps heat back into the earth, replacing the high energy demand of conventional cooling machinery. It's more powerful and consistent than either solar energy or wind.

These days, geothermal systems are complex, and costly up front. However, they cost next to nothing to run. If there is space for the wells and the geologic conditions are right, they can be installed to serve a single home or a complex of large buildings. They deserve a major research effort aimed at bringing costs down because they have the potential to replace a great deal of the dirtiest energy the nation now uses: heating from high-sulfur fuel oil and electricity generated from coal. Geothermal energy at large scale applied to cut cooling energy loads could allow cities all over the East to shut down the dirtiest power plants—ancient, high-polluting relics fired up only to supply electricity for the summer peak, which in many places lasts only a few days or weeks, though the plants must run much longer to accommodate sudden temperature spikes and extended heat waves. That's a lot of wasted load.

Passive House techniques, which dramatically lower heat-energy requirements, promise the next significant steps to lower energy use in cold climates. The idea, pioneered decades ago in Scandinavia, is to build super-insulated, nearly airtight buildings that therefore demand very little heat energy. (Hence the term *passive*; it doesn't rely on solar panels or other renewables.) Though the techniques are usually used for homes, I visited the Riedburg primary school, outside Frankfurt, Germany. Grey and low slung but brightened by orange panels, it was built around a broad, landscaped courtyard. Daylight lit the hallways. Broad, tall windows lit a typical classroom.

Alex Bretzke, a Passive House design expert at the Biberach University of Applied Sciences (though not the designer of this particular school), demonstrated some of its features. The wood-window construction is massive, with two layers of glass widely spaced (a level of insulation essentially unknown in even the coldest corners of the United States, let alone mild Frankfurt). I could not see the heavy layers of insulation applied to the walls and roof, but it is almost double the thickness typically found in Germany. Bretzke drew our attention to small air returns that draw used air out of a classroom and run it across heat exchangers that extract the heat generated by children, teachers, lights, and equipment. That heat warms an incoming stream of 100 percent fresh air that enters the classroom through a long slot. (That means that this super-tight building actually ventilates more fresh air than conventional ones.) Most of the time, that's all the heat the building needs. There is a small radiator that can augment the heat on the coldest days, fed by a boiler that cleanly burns renewable wood pellets.[5]

The Passive House measures reduce heat-energy needs to negligible levels. (It is as yet unclear how well they will work in warm climates.) With its relatively simple techniques, it can come close to more elaborate low-energy office buildings, such as Unilever, described in chapter 3—around 120 kilowatt hours per square meter per year. The Frankfurt school's energy use is low enough that the addition of some solar panels would make it a net-zero-energy-use building. Passive House buildings cost slightly more than conventional buildings, with the additional money put into insulation, airtight construction, the high-performance windows, and the heat exchangers. They also eliminate the cost of large, conventional boilers, as well as a great deal of ductwork and heating infrastructure.

Passive House design bursts certain myths about how energy savings work. In conventional construction, those hefty windows would probably take so long to pay back that you wouldn't buy them. But when several techniques are combined so that the value of each builds on the others, you can achieve much higher performance at the same or lower overall cost. That's why common presumptions that only at best 20 or 30 percent of energy can be saved by conservation alone, or conservation combined with the use of renewables, will likely prove seriously low.

CIVILIZING A SEVERE CLIMATE

Building designers increasingly use biological metaphors, such as skin or lungs, to describe the techniques they develop to harness natural systems to heat, cool, ventilate, and light buildings. Winnipeg, in the eastern prairies of Manitoba, offers an almost literal interpretation, designed for one of North America's most extreme climates, where temperatures dip to around minus thirty-one degrees Fahrenheit, accompanied by icy winds. Spring and fall are volatile. Summers can be both searing (ninety-five degrees) and humid.

On frigid days, no one hunkers behind windowless super-insulated walls. Instead, sun pours into the office space from all sides through floor-to-ceiling untinted glass. (Winnipeg is quite a sunny place for all its weather gyrations.) Dependable winds from the south push fresh air into sunny, multifloor winter gardens that act as a combination of sunny porch and giant air-mixing box. Heat from the low winter sun angle augmented by warmth captured from the ventilating system's exhaust tempers the air (figure 7.5). It moves horizontally northward through the office spaces, which are protected on their east and west

Figure 7.5 The tall winter gardens in the Manitoba Hydro building act as a thermal blanket in winter, "preheating" the building with a combination of strong winter sun, heat recycled from air exchangers, and heat generated from a geothermal well system. Credit: © Eduard Hueber, courtesy KPMB Architects

sides by three layers of glass separated by a three-foot-wide insulating blanket of space. The used air is drawn up and out through a solar chimney on the northern edge of the building.

When the warmth of spring comes, flaps open in the long glass walls of the building's east and west elevations—just as the pores of our own skin open up—and staffers can operate windows in the inner wall to bring in as much natural ventilation as they like. Shades inside the insulating space drop to reduce solar glare and heat.

In summer, the atriums become the cooling lungs of the building. Chilled water drops down suspended Mylar ribbons, precooling and dehumidifying the intake air. Water from the geothermal wells runs through the concrete ceilings of the office space, absorbing heat. The air flaps in the window walls close to keep heat out.

Geothermal wells add heat in the winter and take it away in summer. Heat exchangers grab excess heat before it's exhausted. Manitoba Hydro Place can afford to supply continuous 100 percent fresh air (in most buildings, 80 percent of the air you breathe is recycled), because most of the energy used to heat and cool it is free.

Manitoba Hydro, as the name implies, is a power company that sources almost all of its electricity from hydroelectricity, a renewable resource that could already be deemed essentially carbon neutral. But there are only so many streams that can be dammed, so the company ensures its "supply" by reducing power demand.

Clearly, a building so versatile in its approach to climate doesn't come cheap, especially because the calibration of its many conservation measures is anything but simple. The building design came out of a closely integrated team effort. Design architect KPMB, of Toronto, worked with climate criteria and concepts developed by the New York City office of Transsolar, a "climate engineering" firm based in Germany. Additional architects and engineers worked together with the building contractor to construct the eighteen-story building at a reasonable cost to Manitoba Hydro.

Much of what was done in the project is not new but is a pioneering adaptation to a severe climate of techniques more commonly used where milder weather prevails. The building, completed in 2008, achieves that now-familiar goal of requiring no more than one hundred kilowatt hours per square meter of energy per year. A few years ago, not many experts would have predicted that the forces of Mother Nature could be harnessed so successfully to the creation of the consistent lighting and comfort conditions we've come to expect in our mechanically serviced age. It should be an easier task to hone these techniques to deliver them widely at lower up-front cost.[6]

SEEKING THE ELUSIVE SUN IN SEATTLE

The climate of the Pacific Northwest (as well as some parts of New England) is much like that of Northern Europe. Measures that are now widely used in the United Kingdom, Germany, and the Netherlands will be widely adopted in the United States once we recognize that buildings can pay back investments over more than two investment cycles. Multilayered, naturally ventilating insulating window walls, the use of daylight instead of electric lights, and strategically placed external shading (like those found in Unilever; see chapter 3) will quickly become common.

Some buildings have pioneered environmental tactics even under today's low-upfront-cost, cheap-energy expectations. The broad, planted roof of the Ballard neighborhood library in Seattle curves gently up on its northern edge, opening clerestories underneath to sweep northern daylight inside (figure 7.6). This building, completed in 2005, does not depend on innovative technologies or complex building assemblies. The roof profile, developed by architecture firm Bohlin Cywinski Jackson, expresses the environmental agenda, but most people will simply see it as a welcoming gesture.

Seeded with drought-resistant local plants, the roof absorbs 86 percent of the site's storm runoff and insulates the interior. The high, sheltered glass walls underneath grab whatever daylight the generally thick cloud cover delivers, augmented by carefully placed clerestory windows and skylights. Sensor-driven dimmers turn off electric lights when they're not needed, creating a pleasingly balanced light inside.

The architects pushed the building to the western edge of the site and extended the roof to form a sheltered entrance porch that cuts both the local drizzle and the setting sun. People naturally gather underneath. The porch unites entrances for the library, a neighborhood service center (shared by several city agencies), and a metal-shingled meeting room that can be used even when the library itself is closed.

Showing off the building's green tactics became an educational aspect of the library that increased patronage. "If you interest kids, they bring their parents,"

Figure 7.6 The planted roof of the Ballard Library in Seattle absorbs rain runoff and curves up to admit daylight to the reading room. Its wide roofs shelter patrons from the city's perpetual drizzle. Credit: Nic Lehoux Courtesy Bohlin Cywinski Jackson architects

explained Robert Miller, Bohlin Cywinski Jackson's project manager. These educational possibilities encouraged Seattle City Light to help amortize the additional cost of some conservation elements, such as the photovoltaic panels mounted on the roof.[7]

The building cuts energy use substantially using high-efficiency but conventional systems, since the city did not waive strict construction-cost criteria for the building's green features.

DESIGNING DENSITY

Place-sensitive design especially applies to that essential element of agile design: density. You cannot fault people for abhorring higher-intensity development when it comes in the form of blank-walled, ill-proportioned buildings pushed to the edge of the property lines that offer neighbors views of garbage dumpsters and parked cars. And yet, far too many communities offered as green award winners deliver precisely such urban insult. To the street, they present the now-stock elements of the neotraditional catalog: a cute massing of gable ends, and a porch. Houses may surround a tidy little public lawn with the inevitable Disneyland gazebo. In side yards or backyards, though, you find expanses of asphalt, the noisy air-conditioning units, and rows of repellent garage doors.

Density can be done gracefully without sacrificing the amenity that people reasonably expect, but only if developers are sensitive (even if that sensitivity is mandated by government) and local residents are open-minded enough to value community-spirited, larger-scale development when they see it.

From time immemorial, building designers have struggled to make dense places amenable, so there is much wisdom to draw upon. Until the advent of modern plumbing and sanitary sewers, density was a killer, because packing people tightly together made them ready victims of waterborne and airborne disease. With modern sanitation a given, the job these days is much easier. There are just two keys to building density with dignity: light and air. These, not coincidentally, were among the earliest concerns of civil jurisprudence as urban crowding spawned disputes between property owners. Countless disgruntled owners have petitioned countless courts with the question, how high can my neighbor build? The answer: never so high as to block your access to essential daylight and fresh air.

Yet that left plenty of room for controversy as well as ingenuity. The need for daylight and fresh air led designers of Roman palaces to wrap rooms around quiet, beautifully proportioned courtyards. It's why everywhere the bay window is among the most richly varied architectural element: it captures both light and breezes, and broadens the view. Depending on where you are, shutters or glass doors can move aside to create a summer terrace. With those doors closed, the opening becomes a winter greenhouse. A window stretched to the floor and provided with a railing becomes a Juliet balcony, a romantic aperture to the world that usefully snatches passing breezes. Factories and artist garrets were long designed with sawtooth roofs angled north, to capture the best light for sculpting, painting, and assembling Fords. (Albert Kahn, America's greatest industrial architect, created long, light-filled sheds shaped not just to light the auto assembly process but to vent the heat and fumes of manufacturing.) It's why domes, appropriately called "lanterns," crown churches. They are daylight distribution devices, not merely symbols. It is only a slight exaggeration to say that the history of architecture is the history of lighting and ventilating buildings in cities.

Density needs to take form that is responsive to climate and latitude. You need more light in cloudy northern cities where winter days are short. Shadow is more welcome in hot, southern locations. Architect Lorcan O'Herlihy has built a contemporary, low-rise take on the courtyard apartment houses of 1920s Los Angeles in a project called Gardner 1050. It wraps apartments around a lush courtyard crisscrossed by external corridors and bridges. Vines have crept up to the third floor on stainless steel wires. Each unit is bright yet protected from too much direct sun. Each apartment has a private terrace and two or more exposures, so they cross ventilate. The courtyard is shaped as a welcoming enclosure, a leafy, calming threshold between the public street and the private home.[8]

Dense developments too often fail to gracefully accommodate vehicles. Californians have become adept at tucking them away. Some sink cars a half level below the first floor, disguising the presence of vehicles with attractive landscaping and architectural grilles and louvers. On steep slopes, architects can wedge them into hillsides. Even when surface parking is unavoidable, the space they occupy can be elegantly landscaped so that they become part of the view, rather than a dispiriting outlook of metal and asphalt. Better, agile city techniques, in the long haul, will make parking fewer vehicles a necessity.

PRESERVING THE POWER OF THE OLD

Perhaps the best argument for sensitive, future-focused, low-impact design lies, ironically, in our deep and increasing regard for the past. Both historic preservationists and environmental activists correctly make the point that preserving old buildings, by reusing the valuable materials and tremendous energy embodied in their construction, is an act of environmental stewardship. Much of the building stock we'll be living with for the next generation or two is not only environmentally (if not otherwise) obsolete but also not readily adapted. Ranch houses don't cross ventilate, and many admit little daylight. Offices have deep floors, with sealed exteriors so windows don't open, and tinted glass so daylight is more an idea than a reality. As we shift our growth machine incentives, we'll find the agile buildings lurking under the ranch's hip roof and behind the flimsy office curtainwalls.

Though real estate wisdom deems old buildings poor candidates for energy-conservation retrofits, Anthony Malkin, president of Malkin Holdings, set out to find whether such a project could save real money in his trophy property, the 1931 Empire State Building. I met him one day, and he took me not to the famous observatory (which Malkin had recently refurbished) but to a window factory on the fifth floor.

A "green-collar" workforce of forty stripped old windows out of their frames, hung a new heat-reflecting film between two panes of glass, puttied sealant along the edges, and installed them back in the cleaned old frames. They were wringing affordable energy savings out of the eighty rentable floors of New York's most beloved 102-story-high landmark.

The little—and temporary—window factory was one of the unexpected outcomes of a months-long analysis. Malkin partnered with the Clinton Climate Initiative, founded by former president Bill Clinton, which puts together teams to tackle global warming challenges. The Initiative brought in the Rocky Mountain Institute (an environmental think tank based in Aspen, Colorado) and real estate advisors Jones Lang LaSalle.

Over several months, the team considered dozens of ideas, and Malkin has gone ahead with those that best balanced cash flow, energy savings, and greenhouse gas reduction. Another partner, Johnson Controls, which makes thermostats and building-management systems, guarantees the energy performance.[9]

The windows, though they had been replaced in 1992, glowed brightly in infrared scans of the outer walls, which meant they leaked heat. After looking at a variety of possibilities, the Rocky Mountain Institute proposed retrofitting the frames, which remained in good condition, while replacing the glass units with highly insulating ones. In the end, Malkin found it less expensive to hire a company called Serious Materials to redo all 6,500 windows in-house.

He was abetted by the building's original design. The tower famously rises in elegant slablike setbacks that seem carved from some primordial geological formation, but original architects Shreve Lamb and Harmon had calibrated the setbacks and recesses to capture daylight and breezes before air-conditioning had become common.

I saw tenant spaces that gloriously restore the light-filled interiors—and take advantage of their energy-conserving potential. Daylight alone was ample enough to light workspace most of the time. (Regrettably, too many commercial buildings built after air-conditioning became standard can't take advantage of this retrofit advantage.) In the prebuilt space, desktop "task" lights use less energy than the few ceiling lights, since a sensor can turn them off (along with computers and other equipment) when the occupant is out. The ceiling lights dim when not needed. People can open windows when weather permits. Johnson Controls monitors heating and cooling consumption and shares the information with tenants, who compare consumption with one another, helping to develop an ethos of conservation, according to Paul Rode, a Johnson Controls business development director in energy efficiency.

Combining this and several other energy-saving measures, Malkin's $20 million retrofit delivers an impressive 38 percent energy savings, putting building usage at about 174 kilowatt hours per square meter per year. Malkin found he could entirely forgo a planned expansion of the building's cooling capacity, saving $7 million. He'll lop $4.4 million annually off his utility bill, he said, and avoid generating a minimum of 105,000 metric tons of carbon dioxide over the next fifteen years. He'll amortize his investment in just a few years, demonstrating that hefty savings can pay even when energy is relatively cheap and incentives to conserve are few.

Malkin says he could have done even more, especially in carbon-emission reduction, if investment incentives and disincentives had shifted to encourage investments that are more productive environmentally *and* economically. The team considered LED lighting, even more advanced controls and windows, and innovative ways to retrofit the exterior walls, among others. The Rocky Mountain Institute calculated that "technically we could have reduced energy use 65 percent," according to Carol Fluhrer, the institute's consultant on the project, if costs and paybacks had not been such a concern.

Malkin's energy investment was small, however, compared to the $500 million he spent refurbishing the Empire State in total. While conventional analysts deem the floors of the Empire State too small for modern business needs, Malkin felt he could sell the building's iconic status as probably the world's most beloved skyscraper. Malkin simply validates what's long been proven but easily forgotten: the power of historic preservation. The historic-preservation movement has done more to extend the longevity of cities, to enrich their existence, and to attract reinvestment and growth than the billions allocated to urban renewal, not to mention the endless tax goodies and zoning gimmicks officials regularly offer to spur investment.[10] In New York, for example, a pair of activists launched a campaign to save a rusting, long-abandoned 1.5-mile stretch of elevated railway. That has been turned into the wildly popular High Line Park. The City of New York estimated that it will ultimately spur as much as $4 billion in new development.[11]

Preservation became an ethos about the public value of architecture that united people. So not only have we saved great churches and civic ornaments, we've preserved beefy, red-stone warehouses squatting on great brooding arches and decorated with whimsical floral terra cotta. We've designated entire neighborhoods of houses both humble and grand as worthy of preservation, backing up our national commitment with tax breaks and grant programs to help people restore and maintain their community's patrimony. Once-abandoned small-town downtowns all over America have found new life thanks to the National Trust for Historic Preservation's Main Street program.

Our passion for old buildings, even ones many would deem ordinary, unfortunately draws from a widespread belief that what we build today is simply not as good as what came before, so we better save whatever we can. If we created buildings today that deserve a future, they may actually have one.

LEARNING FROM LOFTS

A building seems fixed, immutable, or at least not readily changed. New techniques and technologies will come along, but over history, certain kinds of buildings have adapted again and again to changing needs and technologies. An environmental and economic era that may demand constant adaptation will prize buildings that gracefully accommodate to changing circumstances.

In America, that means considering the humble, multistory industrial loft. The earliest lofts came of age in the nineteenth century as industrialization demanded big spaces with high ceilings unencumbered by interior walls and columns. As the industrial city grew, massive masonry structures with timber columns and beams gave way to thin, cast-iron columns supporting fire-resistant, brick-vaulted floors. In such spaces, almost anything could be—and was—made and sold. The street facade was the chief means of advertising the quality of the owner's goods or the importance of the location to tenants. A walk through SoHo, Manhattan's district of cast-iron lofts, gives an idea of the endless possibilities.

Lofts needed skylights and high windows to provide good room light and ventilation in the decades before electric lighting and mechanical fans. As manufacturing environments, lofts gradually became obsolete after Henry Ford's pioneering horizontal assembly lines became widespread. But the multistory urban loft has proved resilient: as a warehouse, as a retail store, as a clothing factory. Today, the high ceilings, good ventilation, flexible open spaces, and ample daylight have attracted artists and designers, who started the live-work loft trend that has sent the value of old lofts steadily skyward. What once was a sweatshop is today a multimillion-dollar residence big and open enough for children to skateboard in.

Lofts can be continually adapted to new needs because they provide daylight, good natural ventilation, long-lasting construction, and flexible, adaptable space. These are the very few essentials for agile buildings.

8

CREATING TWENTY-FIRST-CENTURY COMMUNITY

The world was riveted to the horror and heroism that followed the destruction of the World Trade Center towers in New York on September 11, 2001. It applauded as officials at every government level determined to rebuild the site. But the world averted its eyes as the rebuilding effort foundered. Too many entities were in charge. Officials did not know how to convene people with a stake in the site, especially when some deemed it a sacred graveyard and others regarded it an essential element of the downtown economy. For all the expertise assembled, plans kept stalling, costs ran ever upward, and management of the enormously complex building site bogged down in political and money disputes.

When completed, perhaps by 2015, the rebuilding of the World Trade Center site won't be a shining example of what New York could be, nor will it galvanize the world's aspiration to end an era of global terror. It will be an appallingly expensive, overscaled real estate development little different from mediocre real estate developments found anywhere, with a memorial museum secreted beneath a large, useless plaza.[1] In that span of time, the massive job of reuniting West and East Berlin—the equivalent of dozens of Ground Zeros—was largely completed.

Once floodwaters at last drained from New Orleans weeks after the passage of Hurricane Katrina in August 2005, the city, state, and federal governments that had negligently permitted underdesigned levees to breach found themselves lacking the planning acumen and the political and civic infrastructure to rebuild the city. The state's Road Home, a program of bridge loans intended to help homeowners rapidly rebuild, was instead extraordinarily slow to get moving and delivered too little too late to thousands of homeowners.[2] As weeds grew around abandoned homes, seven separate and competing official planning processes grappled with the city's future, along with dozens of "visioning" processes undertaken by foundations, universities, and some three dozen architecture schools around the country. Five years after the disaster, the city still struggled to regain its footing and almost one hundred thousand of its prestorm residents had decided not to return.

Then came the Deepwater Horizon oil-spill disaster that began in April 2010. Lax rig procedures at the well being drilled on behalf of British Petroleum (BP) were the proximate cause of the disaster, abetted by a lack of oversight by the federal Minerals and Management Service. But the nation found yet again that it was ill prepared to cope with a disaster much larger in scope than the sanguine emergency plans of BP, its competitors, and regulators. The nation, and especially Gulf residents, breathed a sigh of relief that the worst fears about the spill were not realized, but the rapid vaporization of the spill was largely a product of nature, not human foresight.

The lack of preparedness and poorly coordinated response to these iconic urban disasters of the first decade of the twenty-first century should teach Americans that they lack the capacity to take on challenges—those made both by nature and by man—at the scale and complexity that the world now demands.

Most communities will never face the dire events that befell New York and the Gulf Coast. Or will they? Global warming and other kinds of environmental change may well damage agriculture, deprive communities of clean water, or subject them to alternating floods and drought. Preparing for such catastrophic events means more than boosting emergency response. Communities must figure out how to systematically prevent them or minimize damage. Long term, that means incubating new ideas that build urban and environmental resilience at the scale of transportation systems, metropolitan regions, coasts and rivers, and the quilt of ecosystems that thread through our developed landscapes.

DALLAS: TWENTY MILES OF GREEN

Hunting for a project big enough to meaningfully influence a metropolitan landscape took me to a place that thinks big: Dallas. The Trinity River project is a highway project. Or it's a flood-protection project. Or it's the transformation of a twenty-mile stretch of largely sterilized river bottom into a ten-thousand-acre necklace of wetlands, parks, recreation spaces, forests, and wildlife preserves—a green lung that arcs through the center of one of America's largest cities. Its global warming benefits are not advertised in a state where noisy climate-change deniers are prominent, but they could be substantial. However, it is unclear at this writing which of its identities the project will ultimately assume.

The three branches of the Trinity River that meet in Dallas meander in a flat, treeless, grassy plain along the southwestern edge of downtown. The river is all but invisible, though, walled off by high, wide levees. Dallas wants to add highway lanes and needs to upgrade its system of flood-control structures, and the city hopes to piggyback neighborhood connections to the river and develop its recreational and ecosystem-resilience potential. Near downtown, the project plans to add a meandering, braided watercourse between an "urban" lake and a more naturalistic one for canoeists and kayakers. The renderings by the landscape architecture and planning firm WRT show rowers skulling along a new course, with spectators ranged along a grassy amphitheater that offers skyline views. Reunion Plaza, at the edge of downtown, will extend across the highway and the levee to a terraced, sheltered esplanade opening to an expanse of river backdropped by the four interlocking arches of a span designed by the celebrated architect and bridge designer Santiago Calatrava (figure 8.1). Chains of constructed wetlands will "polish" the treated effluent from the city's gigantic central sewage-treatment facility. South of the city, six thousand acres of bottomland hardwood forest already have been preserved in what's called the Great Trinity Forest.[3]

I fear this vision may fall victim to business as usual. An impetus of the project is a proposed six-lane, high-speed freeway that would run between the river and heavily populated neighborhoods. It would make accessing the river bottom intimidating. (It is supposed to relieve traffic on overburdened I-35E, which parallels the river a short distance away, pursuing the senseless notion that building more urban freeway lanes will "relieve" anything long term.)

Though the river's thirty-foot-high levees already divide Dallas as effectively as the Berlin Wall, the US Army Corps of Engineers wants enlarged and lengthened levees, cutting off even more of the city from the river. The levee could be gracefully sculpted to weave in the graceful curves of a sensitively scaled parkway, using the earthen mass to screen the road from view and reduce noise. The

Figure 8.1 A bridge designed by Santiago Calatrava is one feature of the Trinity River project, in Dallas, which mixes environmental restoration and new parklands with extravagant highways and upgraded levees. Credit: Courtesy Trinity River Project

design could attractively integrate appealing ways for citizens to cross both road and levee on foot and bike to get to the park.

The Army Corps of Engineers apparently does not see things that way and has insisted that the levee and road be built separately. So the usual overbearing, clumsily engineered road structure will run inside the ridge of the levee, itself a looming intrusion. If access points turn out to be just a bunch of chain-link-fenced concrete bridges accessed by long concrete ramps running high over the highway, the city will still feel walled off, and the great potential of this multibillion-dollar project to pull the riches of the river environment into the very fabric of urban life will have been squandered.

Other metro areas are taking on projects that have a similarly large-scale potential to transform their urban identities in the way Boston's necklace of Olmsted parks and parkways did. The Atlanta BeltLine intends to take a twenty-two-mile ring of obsolete railroad rights-of-way and use it as a way of tying the city together with new transit lines, biking and walking paths, parks, and development sites. Even its tentative early phases have spurred growth in a dozen neighborhoods. In California, the Orange County Great Park will repurpose 1,300 acres of the El Toro military base with such park amenities as a botanical garden, sports fields, and a great lawn for gatherings. But it will also restore native landscapes and set off parts of the park as a migration-corridor preserve, reweaving long-severed links between inland mountains and sea by connecting the Cleveland National Forest to Crystal Cove State Park. A variety of natural-treatment landscapes will leave water flowing out of the park cleaner than it came in.

Like the Trinity River project, both efforts have proven difficult to finance.[4] Great Park, which may cost as much as $1.5 billion, was set up to rely on the spinoff from the added value of commercial development elsewhere on the base, which collapsed along with the real estate market. Lacking a dependable flow of dollars and the coordinated participation and commitment of transportation and economic development agencies of the kind one finds in international large-scale development, the once-in-a-generation undertakings in Dallas, Orange County, and Atlanta have proceeded slowly and uncertainly.[5]

None of these projects was hatched with the primary notion of addressing climate change, but all developed with a potentially transformative environmental component. They are the kinds of metro-scale opportunities that challenge cities and suburbs to work together to recognize the value projects like this can create and to address the barriers they face.

BUILDING THE FUTURE WITH PAINT AND LAWN CHAIRS

In the United States, a wide variety of small local efforts are trying to make citizens more comfortable with large-scale transformation. A guerrilla action by, of all things, New York City's Department of Transportation struck a blow for people over cars. Over just a few days, crews pedestrianized much of Times Square with green paint, orange traffic cones, some shrubs in planters, and dozens of inexpensive lawn chairs (figure 8.2). Shopkeepers and cab drivers reacted with horror to this violation of the auto's sacred ground. Pedestrians, who had long overflowed into the streets from mobbed sidewalks, were thrilled. The department's director, Janette Sadik-Khan, was not shoving a carbon-reduction strategy down citizens' throats, but was cutting through a bureaucratically encrusted process that had made a task as minor as relocating a curb as complex as negotiating a major international treaty. The Times Square strategy, inspired

Figure 8.2 Though sidewalks had been overcrowded for years in New York's Times Square, little was done until paint and lawn chairs pedestrianized Times Square virtually overnight. After a trial period was deemed successful, design began to create a permanent streetscape. Credit: James S. Russell

by a street-design innovator from Copenhagen, Jan Gehl, was driven by the need to smooth traffic flow, which was done by reducing the number of intersections that were too close together and making pedestrian movement smoother and safer—both, incidentally, carbon-reduction tactics.

Skeptics were determined to find Sadik-Khan's tactics a failure. "There are 8.4 million New Yorkers, and some days I think there are 8.4 million traffic engineers," Sadik-Khan told me in an interview. "But that's not surprising. Streets are our front yards." After looking at street-flow data, the city made the Times Square changes permanent, with adjustments. In similar fashion, Sadik-Khan's department painted two hundred miles of bike lanes in three years, paved fifteen miles of protected bike lanes, and expanded dedicated bus lanes. Some of these moves have been controversial: for example, orthodox Jews in Brooklyn's Williamsburg neighborhood depicted the lanes as privileging underclad hipsters. (One of the lanes was subsequently removed.) By and large, the effort has been welcomed, however, and has wrought a subtle but important change in attitude: upending at long last the long-embedded notion that streets are only for cars.[6]

Diversifying street layouts is one of the signature accomplishments of PlaNYC, the city's ambitious blueprint to cut carbon emissions by 30 percent by 2030. While many of the plan's tactics directly address energy and climate change by targeting building-energy use and polluting vehicles, it is moving ahead because most of the measures it envisions address issues that many New Yorkers find more pressing. Efforts to increase affordable housing, for example, will pay off in climate terms by putting more people closer to jobs. More than a fifth of the city has been rezoned in the past few years not just to achieve lower carbon emissions but because the code had been outdated for years. Some neighborhoods have been zoned for greater density (even though communities tend to strenuously resist bigger, bulkier buildings), but the highest densities have been located adjacent to primary, transit-served streets—reducing people and traffic impacts on quieter secondary streets—with thought given to how large buildings can be accommodated while minimizing the shadows they cast and the views they block.[7]

PlaNYC also seems to be working because like-minded department managers cross disciplinary boundaries to magnify the benefits of a given idea. City Planning has devised guidelines for storm water–retaining parking lots, in the process uniting agendas that serve a variety of environmental and livability goals that concern at least three city departments. None of this should be news, but the cooperative attitude of city departments remains a rarity in America.

Shaun Donovan, among New York's pioneers of cross-disciplinary coordination, moved from the city's housing agency to become secretary of the Department of Housing and Urban Development (HUD). There he worked with other cabinet secretaries to create the Interagency Partnership for Sustainable Communities, which coordinates the work of the Environmental Protection Agency with the diversification of transportation options promoted by the Department of Transportation, and transit-sensitive HUD housing policies. The initiatives were small in scale as this book went to press (like the grant MyRegion's Lauten sought; see chapter 6) but are promising.[8]

WHAT LOW-CARBON LIFE IS LIKE

It's tempting for many of us to want a magic clean-energy bullet because curbing climate emissions may require such major lifestyle changes. How major, really? Consider Dockside Green, the carbon-neutral Victoria community that was introduced in this book's prologue. You may give up a house set in a big plot of land to live in Dockside Green, but you get easy proximity to both the city's attractions and the rugged scenery of Vancouver Island. Your heating bill will be a fraction of what a typical single-family homeowner pays. Climate as well as climate-sensitive design means you'll never switch on air-conditioning. (It's not needed and not provided.) Dockside Green achieves carbon neutrality—a standard thought unattainable within a spec community only a few years ago—not with a lot of high-tech bells and whistles but through its community design. Only a large-scale development could support the biomass heating plant and the on-site sewage treatment that sends the stream of almost-drinkable water burbling amid reeds in front of terraces. Once you move in, you may sell one of your cars because you've set up your business in the small office building across the street. (It has special shading devices and windows that open so you'll run few lights and avoid most air-conditioning costs.) Or you'll take a passenger ferry a few minutes to downtown. You'll run errands by using the waterfront bike path. Dockside Green involves changes in lifestyle without the "sacrifices" that energy conservation doomsayers say North Americans will never make.

Dockside Green is not a futuristic project; it is being built with today's technologies under today's development rules but has begun to pioneer tomorrow's kind of environmental sustainability. Dockside Green is one of a few dozen pioneering projects tentatively certified under a new community-design rating system called LEED ND. (ND is for "neighborhood development.") A program of the US Green Building Council, it takes the best-known environmental rating system for single-building designs and scales it up. (LEED's virtue as an engine for innovation is discussed in chapter 9.)

LEED ND, since it is a voluntary rating system built by consensus, identifies dozens of ways that many experts think communities will change in a low-carbon future. Some are obvious, such as connecting communities to transit and building neighborhoods that are compact and walkable so that people take priority over cars. Developments also score points when they preserve valued landscapes, such as wetlands, water edges, and migration routes. Many LEED measures subtly undermine wasteful standard-development practice. You can't get certified under the rating program with wandering, dead-end cul-de-sacs; developments must knit themselves into the surrounding neighborhoods with a great number of street connections, so that you can get to local destinations by bike, by bus, or on foot.

It strongly encourages developments that fill in abandoned sites in already built-up areas, both discouraging the leapfrog pattern of "drive to qualify" development at the urban edge and making efficient use of infrastructure (like water and roads) and services (like schools and libraries) that have already been paid for in existing communities. Instead of strip highway stores separated from one another by seas of surface parking, commercial development hugs the street to invite the pedestrian and encourage neighborly hanging out.

The program demands a mix of uses within developments so that there is at least the opportunity to run errands, get children to school, and work within walking distance of home. The minimum residential density is seven dwellings per acre, almost double the density of the once-standard suburban lot. That density wastes less land and can turn an empty-feeling subdivision into a lively neighborhood. It accommodates a diversity of dwellings (single houses, town houses, apartments, and hybrid types like homes with "mother-in-law" units in the rear yard) serving a range of incomes. (Standard developments usually target one market.) LEED ND won't certify developments of houses on one, five, or ten acres, even ones designed to work off the grid, because the extensive roads and acres of mown lawn fragment exurban landscapes and require long auto trips even to run simple errands.

LEED ND, when you take its requirements together, rejects the kind of podlike subdivisions of single-family houses that are plowed out of forests or farms heedless of nearby, essentially identical subdivisions. It rejects the standard builder product of more than four decades, which has been premised on a kind of exclusivity that comes with the subdivision that consciously separates itself from everything else.[9]

Will the United States ultimately be coerced to abandon its love affair with the suburban house and yard? The couple with children that suburbia has built itself around is already a minority of homeowners, and demographic trends already favor a much higher percentage of multifamily dwellers. Further, the romance of the house on a landscaped lot is already over in most places. Where land is costly, road dollars are short, and water scarce, builders shove boxy, beige-stucco houses close enough together that the eves almost touch. Bulging garages dominate the street and the SUV-depth front yards. In dry places like Las Vegas, gravel replaces lush plantings. The lots have shrunk to the degree that outdoor space consists of a walled yard big enough for a not-too-smoky barbeque. This knee-jerk version of suburbia is so degraded that its advantages have all but disappeared.

Some LEED ND communities handle density awkwardly. Few of the program's early participating communities preserve important landscape features and intact natural systems, such as wetlands. But the beauty of LEED is that it is not fixed. It is an agile model of growth because it is capable of course corrections. In general, that cannot be said of government regulatory processes or the rigid underwriting rules of the real estate development industry. The LEED model has proven so compelling that it has gone global, with programs founded even in countries like Germany that have well-developed low-energy and climate-change regimes.[10]

Though LEED is a powerful agent of change for the reluctant real estate industry and for often-antiquated local systems of land planning, it is far from a panacea. It is comforting to think, as many of the New Urbanist planners and developers behind LEED do, that a neighborhood is the building block of urban development. After all, a neighborhood feels bounded, understandable. The disasters along the Gulf and in New Orleans and New York remind us that climate change—and other urban challenges, for that matter—requires us to think about urban and natural systems on the scale of a watershed, say, or a metropolitan region, comprising city, suburbs, and exurbs.

A community designed around transit derives no benefit if no bus line is put in place. A green city can feel smug about its accomplishments, but that will mean little if the much-larger suburban ring doesn't buy in. You can't fix the Gulf Coast without effort on a wide range of levels.

That takes Americans well out of their comfort zone. You can say that action at the community and the regional and the state and federal level is too complicated, too inefficient. There's not enough political will or money. There are too many special interests lined up against the little guy. The inevitable conflicts between needed action and private property rights are too difficult to untangle. And all these things are true, if we remain passive about them. All can become excuses for inaction.

Increasingly, cities worldwide are undertaking transformation at a scale that makes Americans' heads spin. Not all of the examples below target climate-change transformation per se, but it's worth considering both what they are doing at such large scale and how they go about doing it.

BERLIN: A TRAGIC CITY'S NEW GREEN IDENTITY

When the Berlin Wall came down in 1989, history forced a reconsideration of the city's identity. Facing a different future was not a choice but a necessity as a vast program was undertaken to reunite a city that had been divided for almost half a century. The job could not stop at linking up streets, utilities, the subway, and the railways—vast as those undertakings were. Berlin had been the nerve center for the deadly world-conquering aspirations of not one but two twentieth-century autocracies, and the city had to find a way to transcend those tragic aspirations, even though they were coded into the city's layout and architecture. The streets weren't merely wide, for example; they were suited to military parades and the rapid deployment of troops.[11]

The world would not let Berlin forget its history, but Berliners, too, felt that the effort of reuniting what had been the communist East with the democratic West was an opportunity to define a future-oriented city, one that could reconcile the wounds of the past. As neighborhoods were redesigned and megaprojects were proposed for public review (for an inter-city rail station, a new government quarter, and so forth), people turned out in droves to consider what each one would mean.

As the effort to reunite got under way, questions of how to rebuild got framed in cultural terms: Should it define a twenty-first-century glamour tuned to a globe where culture and entertainment were powering urban economies? Was Berlin to be the gateway to an Eastern Europe transformed by capitalism and democracy? Debating the means by which the city's physical form should reflect a brighter future consumed Berliners in the late 1990s.

The confidence to engage in such debates, and to trust government to get it right, came about because public and civic involvement in reinvigorating Berlin was pretty much a constant theme, even during the divided-city era. Virtually the entire Western side of the city had been reconstructed in the decade after World War II ended. Some of it was significantly reimagined with slim towers and row houses shot through with trees and gardens—a rejection of the old city, notorious for its densely packed tenement buildings facing warrens of dim, fetid courtyards. Not all this worked; the progressive enthusiasms of architects and planners often created impersonal, amorphous neighborhoods. But neither Berliners nor Germans ever gave up on Berlin, even when its position as an island of Western values surrounded by the Communist East demanded ongoing subsidies.

Reweaving East and West in the 1990s was not nearly so large a physical enterprise as the 1950s rebuilding—even though it involved every form of infrastructure, the resolution of hundreds of thousands of decades-old property claims, and thousands of individual building projects—but it was a difficult emotional one. Virtually every point of view about the future was realized at least in part. Daniel Libeskind's Jewish Museum confronted Germany's geno-cidal history directly: it is both spectacular and menacing, powerfully evoking both the glories and the tragic fate of Berlin's Jews. A railway hub bombed in the war was at last reestablished and connected to a lost north-south trunk line by a tunnel under the Spree River and the Tiergarten. Architect Norman Foster reinvented the burnt hulk of the Reichstag, giving the city an idealistic new icon—using glass literally to symbolize political transparency in the united gov-ernment. The dour pile's modern dome transformed its old bombast, making it a symbol of environmental sustainability by simultaneously ventilating the leg-islative chamber below by natural means and using a giant sunscreen and mir-ror system to light the chamber with daylight rather than electric lights.

Indeed, a greener, less energy-intense city became the essence of a new self—an ideal that would carry the city forward, so that it would not wallow in the past. Not everything went perfectly. In the short term, official assumptions about the city's economic growth proved far too optimistic. (It has not become the gateway to the former Soviet East, as it had hoped.) Critics took issue with a redevelopment process that was very top-down.

Out of this gigantic endeavor came a city that is fundamentally new and different yet respects the layers and complexities of history, one that offers big-city bustle and quiet neighborhoods of tree-lined streets (figure 8.3). It has no dominant downtown district, but several centers, each with a distinctive per-sonality, and all of which are well connected by bike paths, streetcars, elevated trains, subway trains, and regional commuter trains. You can get to most of Germany's largest cities in less than four hours by fast inter-city trains.

There was plenty of debate about style and how much money was being spent, but creating the basic ingredients that would permit Berlin to thrive were never in question, even if Germans could never be certain that ideas about the city's economic future would work. Design competitions for whole blocks and individual buildings perpetually injected new ideas into the debate. Extensive public involvement checked architects' and developers' worst excesses, and a constant rebalancing of taste and scale and approach to history also enriched what was built.

How did Berlin do so much? It wasn't just money, though plenty was spent. Libeskind described to me an attitude to the city that made such a brilliant and pluralistic rebuilding possible. "Berlin, like many European cities, has a civic dimension that American cities don't have. When I use words like 'public space' in America, clients are appalled. They are afraid pubic places will attract

Figure 8.3 Berlin's Potsdamer Platz was for decades a no-man's-land tangled with barbed wire and gun emplacements. Since reunification, the city has built a lively mixed-use community that links what had been West and East Berlin. Credit: James S. Russell

homeless people and others who will do things they are not supposed to do. Every building in Berlin, even an office building, has some visibility, and people ask if it is the right building. Does it belong? They see these buildings as expressing the force of history."

"In Europe, in Berlin, public space and civic space are of concern to everyone," Libeskind added. "You, the architect, have to address that—whether you do it badly or well. In America, the private world of power and money is seen as the inevitable force that dictates the form of the city. So architecture becomes no more than advertising."

In contrast to Berlin, Americans could not find a means to truly rebuild New Orleans—a city one-fourth Berlin's size—after Hurricane Katrina. The city has not found its economic footing in spite of having one of America's largest ports, among its most appealing neighborhoods, and a rich culture of food, music, and architecture. The civic infrastructure of police, courts, libraries, and schools still functions poorly years after the flood. Its defenses against future floods may be insufficient.

Historian of modern art Karl Scheffler in 1910 famously wrote that Berlin is "forever to become and never to be." In terms of that particular city, especially in the twentieth century, this turned out to be a serious understatement. But it could be seen as a good description of any vital urban region now. The cities that attract the best and brightest, and that produce the ideas and products we want, will continue to dance as fast as they can with growth and change. The agile city will unleash this dynamism in facing global-warming challenges.

VANCOUVER GOES SKYWARD

Vancouver, British Columbia, has created a widely admired model of government partnership, colluding benignly with private interests to nurture a civil form of high-density center-city growth. Wedged between downtown and the gorgeous near-wilderness of Stanley Park, a high-rise residential core has risen as dense as anywhere outside Manhattan, but it is density driven by amenity. Developers must follow urban-design guidelines that allow them to build tall buildings as long as they respect "view corridors" established by the city. Those tubes of space within which no one can build ensure that both new and existing buildings continue to have largely unobstructed vistas to the stunning surroundings of mountains and bays. It's not a simple approach; a given development can entail some serious negotiation with the city to determine whether the complex criteria are met. Projects often involve some architectural acrobatics: squeezing the building's bulk this way and that to stay clear of the view corridors. But developers and buyers sign on quickly because this is one of the few high-rise districts where everyone's interest in the view (a key to each unit's value) is protected. It's a win for city and residents alike. The lesson is not profound, though understood surprisingly rarely. Everyone cooperates and everyone harvests the value of a well-understood amenity (figure 8.4).[12]

Vancouver's appealing form of high-rise living did not happen primarily in pursuit of environmental goals, though the city was well aware that such high density adjacent to the commercial core put thousands at walking distance to jobs, shopping, restaurants, the city's transit nexus, one of the world's great city parks, and an extensive public waterfront: in other words, a rich and appealing lifestyle that was "green" primarily by the lower energy use innate to apartments over houses, and to walking and biking over driving.

For Americans who fear that their quiet suburban streets will be turned into roaring hordes of vehicles, and that lumpy twelve-story condos will loom over their once-private backyards, Vancouver should offer solace. From a dis-

Figure 8.4 High-density towers in downtown Vancouver were designed to respect the amenity everyone seeks to share: the extraordinary views to bays and mountains. Credit: James S. Russell

tance, Vancouver's downtown towers look crammed together. Close up, you find that most are fairly slim and have a lot of space around them, so that neighbors are not cast in perpetual shadow. Trevor Boddy, a local architecture critic, says that the view-corridor regime led to the creation of a unique high-rise type he calls "Vancouverist," which has now migrated around the world. It is a slim tower mounted at one end of a row of town houses and stores. The townhouses form a low wall that shapes the street and enlivens it with small-scale activity, which has the effect of humanizing the big scale of the towers.

Since 2008, Vancouver has extended the design capacity and acumen developed downtown to encourage density with amenity in its predominant neighborhood pattern of modest single-family houses. The city has tied the agendas of its EcoDensity initiative explicitly to carbon-reduction goals and increasing the supply of affordable housing. So the plan encourages building modest rental units along alleys (called "laneways" in Vancouver) and townhouse construction on infill sites. Owners can add rental units to existing homes as long as they don't overwhelm neighboring properties. Higher-density developments can be built along main arterials and near transit stations. And the city promises to supply the public facilities required as neighborhoods grow denser.[13] Greater urban density is essential to a greener, more adaptive future, and Vancouver's lesson is that higher density need not come at the price of local qualities that are desirable, such as views.

BILBAO: FROM GRITTY TO GLEAMING

Dream for a bit. Imagine half a dozen blocks in an industrial waterfront of abandoned shipyards and crumbling blast furnaces transformed into a thriving district of museums, theaters, hotels, and shopping. Such transformation, especially over just a few years, is almost unknown in the United States. When you look at the sheer scale, quality, and ambition of what was undertaken in the steel city of Bilbao, Spain, you have to ask yourself why America is unable to take on endeavors of comparable scope and complexity.

The narrow valleys and tumbled hills of Bilbao, in the Basque country of northeastern Spain, strikingly resemble those of the Monongahela Valley around Pittsburgh—as does the town's historic reliance on steel. Unglamorous Bilbao became a household name in late 1997 when Frank Gehry's sculpturally spectacular branch of the Guggenheim Museum put the city on the international culture map. American cities have tried to jump on the Bilbao bandwagon since by frantically fundraising for glitzy culture projects to jump-start moribund local economies. But Americans smitten by the so-called Bilbao effect too often fail to recognize that the transformation of this once down-at-the-heels center of steel and shipbuilding counted (and still counts) on much more than the presence of an eye-popping museum (figure 8.5). The city was already building a new subway system, an airport terminal, and many other infrastructure improvements by the time the Guggenheim opened. The heavily used Metro, for example, has helped pull together a string of communities stretching along the Nervion River. Isolated by steep ridges, these enclaves had declined rapidly with the departure of their traditional industries.

The city completed a massive river cleanup while the local port authority undertook the gigantic job of moving the shipping facilities out of the space-squeezed center and into a vast new container port on the Bay of Biscay.

"We've been lucky," Carlos Gorostiza said on a tour of Bilbao. "The Guggenheim was a much bigger success than we anticipated." He's a spokesperson for Bilbao Ría 2000, a private redevelopment agency responsible for coordinating public redevelopment efforts. In its first two years, Guggenheim visitors

Figure 8.5 The Guggenheim Bilbao museum has galvanized interest and investment in a once-declining steel city. But it is only one element of a comprehensive redevelopment that includes building a transit system and a new airport. Credit: James S. Russell

added 433 million euros (about $570 million) to the local economy, paying back the project's 132 million euro investment ($172 million) more than three-fold, according to an analysis by KPMG Peat Marwick. As important, it changed the city's picture of itself, from high-employment hopelessness to a "faith in the future," according to Ibon Areso Mendiguren, an architect and director of urbanism for the city of Bilbao.[14]

The stiff resistance that had first greeted the idea of a splashy branch of the Guggenheim melted once visitors began flooding in. With broad public support, the pace of urban revitalization has increased since the museum opened. The Guggenheim, large as it is, occupies only a fraction of what had been the derelict Euskalduna shipyard. Since the museum's opening, a new tramline extends a handsome riverside esplanade from the Guggenheim past a new shopping mall and a new hotel to a new theater and congress-hall complex. Twin commercial towers by one of Japan's most respected architects, Arata Isozaki, have gone up, taking advantage of a view created by the arresting presence of a pedestrian bridge designed by Santiago Calatrava.

On the other side of downtown, a railway trench has been reconfigured to accommodate commuter-rail lines that once blocked the waterfront where the

Guggenheim now stands. A new street lined with new housing and dotted with new train stops lids the old trench. It's hard to imagine any city of three hundred thousand in the United States attempting rebirth on this scale.

The process in Bilbao is as significant as the product. The scale of urban regeneration has been made possible because Ría 2000 has been able to sell redevelopment sites, most of them controlled by the city's port commission, at a profit, according to Angel Nieva, the general director of the agency. But it is also uniquely well coordinated. Key agencies participate, according to Nieva: the port, the railroads, the housing ministry, and local government. The Basque regional government and the Spanish national government cooperate, even as the Basques continue to insist on greater political independence from Madrid. "Participation is at the highest level—the heads or seconds-in-command of each stakeholder," Nieva added emphatically. The European Union sweetened the pot with a grant.

By comparison, it is almost inconceivable in the United States for a transit agency to be party to a major urban redevelopment or that an American port commission would cede power over its properties to a separate redevelopment authority. (The political turf battles at New York's Ground Zero are perhaps the most publicly depressing face of this dysfunctional state.) The cooperative nature of redevelopment in Bilbao is even a bit unique in Spain, observers say, driven in part by the Basques' desire to show a "can-do" attitude in the face of widespread resistance to their separatist ambitions.

Bilbao has not yet transformed itself into Silicon Valley or a biotech haven, as it hoped, but it has succeeded in retaining sophisticated industrial technology and increasing some white-collar jobs. Although the metro area is not growing, which is common in Europe, Bilbao is not losing population, as many obsolete industrial centers in Eastern Europe are—and as most heavy-industry cities in the United States continue to do. Its residential center has been shored up, and residents are rediscovering overlooked neighborhoods in the old city and outlying districts. None of America's industrial cities has found a comparable engine of rebirth; there are lessons to be learned along the Nervion.

HAMBURG: THE GREENEST DOWNTOWN

At the edge of the Elbe River, I stood on a handsome, terraced esplanade that swirled with pipe sculptures that played off the endless expanse of harbor cranes you could see in all directions. Hamburg, Europe's second-largest port, has built a thrilling infrastructure of transaction. The view was new. The city is recapturing obsolete inlets and narrow strips of land once devoted to shipping for public and commercial gain. I stood at the edge of HafenCity, a $10 billion, twenty-year, 390-acre redevelopment of old docklands a short walk from the city center. This is redevelopment with an ambition inconceivable in America, and its green aspirations are impressive. It will make downtown Hamburg 40 percent larger, adding up to two million square meters of buildings (twenty million square feet in round numbers), forty thousand jobs, and 5,500 residents when it is built out.

HafenCity is a pleasant walk from downtown through the Speicherstadt, the mile-long complex of high, turreted brick warehouses ranged along Elbe canals that were the nineteenth-century answer to moving goods from ships to warehouses to city. (They are still used by importers.) It reminds you that this city has perpetually adapted to new circumstances since its strategic role in the Hanseatic League, a trading confederation founded in the thirteenth century that lasted until the nineteenth. You may notice as you cross through the Speicherstadt that the handsome trusses of the pedestrian bridges hold up pathways at two levels. The upper layer of circulation has been built to create an escape route in case of flooding that occurs when storm surges magnify the North Sea's dramatically high tides and collide with rain-swollen volumes of water headed downriver. Both the swollen river and the higher tides are deemed climate-change effects, and HafenCity is designed with the assumption that these effects will magnify over time.

The first floors of a well-ordered mix of midrise residential and commercial buildings face streets and walkways that run above flood levels, at about twenty-five feet above sea level. Hamburg did not want to extend its levee system—at huge cost—to wrap the new development, so its lower elevations have been made handsomely flood tolerant instead. Set among courtyarded apartment buildings, small squares open to river views and cascade down about twelve feet toward the waterside, via broad stairways that invite people-watching. (The impish squares and esplanades were designed by the Barcelona architect EMBT.) The esplanades get people close to the water and the views and so are immensely popular (figure 8.6). Rippling benches, warped into potato-chip form, and tubular steel light fixtures that recall shipping cranes can survive floods. You'll find cafés with heavily armored doors that move into place when waters rise.

Figure 8.6 While buildings at HafenCity, in Hamburg, are raised above flood levels, a lower-level esplanade is resilient to floods. Heavy doors slide into place in the event of high water to protect cafés that line the walkway. Credit: James S. Russell

Turning flood-safety tactics into a delightful waterside sequence of public paths, plazas, and parks is but one of HafenCity's impressive accomplishments. Hydrogen-powered buses will soon loop through the development. A subway-line extension is being scooped out of the perpetually wet soil to augment stops on existing lines nearby. In other words, a car will be largely superfluous.[15]

HafenCity is turning to cogeneration to dramatically reduce energy and carbon emissions. Such plants, which produce power, heating, and cooling centrally and distribute them to a complex of buildings (for example, a college campus, office-building development, or medical center), can be much more efficient than the best technology available to individual buildings. (Powered by advanced biomass combustion technology, they have helped well-known eco villages like Växjö, in Sweden, get off the grid.) To serve a large community with a wide mix of uses, HafenCity's plant creates heat, which generates electricity through a turbine, augmented by local geothermal-well systems and solar and fuel-cell technology. HafenCity's management says its plant is 27 percent more efficient than conventional models. A second system will burn biomass fuel and use biomethane fuel-cell technology and a heat pump to derive almost all of its heat and power from renewables.

Guidelines encourage developers to exceed Germany's already strict energy codes. A variety of shading devices, from external venetian blinds to sliding panels of metal and reflective glass, cut the summer sun's heat enough to make air-conditioning almost superfluous.

It is in HafenCity that you'll find the regional headquarters for Unilever, the low-energy building wrapped in rippling sheets of the transparent "foil" described in chapter 3. Over time, HafenCity will tighten its energy standards by embedding stricter criteria into its developer-selection process. Already, the city uses a two-track procedure, one of which establishes a land price. Then developers compete on the basis of quality, amenity, the way they have mixed uses, and the environmental sustainability of the design.

HafenCity is one way metropolitan planners are shifting city growth inward, reusing obsolete land rather than plowing under more farmland. To be sure, it doesn't look much like an American city or suburb. The density is quite high, yet this is no skyscraper downtown. Only a couple of buildings exceed seven or eight stories. Americans would find the level of amenity appealing. With ample courtyards and public green space, a high percentage of both apartments and commercial spaces looks out to harbor views.

European and Asian nations have developed the engineering and management capability as well as government structures, financing models, and community-consultation techniques to make large environmental and public works possible, and they have continued to redevelop cities at large scale as economic change has created huge obsolete industrial landscapes. Nowadays, declining air and water quality spurs remedial action even in a country as historically heedless of pollution as China. Dallas, Atlanta, Orange County, Vancouver, and New York have chosen to participate in the invention of their future. Now America needs to adapt the best tools out there to broaden these efforts and pave the way for their success.

9
LOOSE-FIT URBANISM

The 1950s bestowed the American dream of homeownership on millions of families living in crowded city tenement apartments across the United States. That seems very distant now. Only in television shows and movies does the new wood grain–sided station wagon, stacked with kids and boxes, pull out through the crowded streets to the new highway or parkway and then to the Cape Cod–style subdivision outside Chicago, the shingled ranch on Long Island, or the low-slung picture-windowed modern house in California.

Those postwar suburbs were more spacious and greener, with ample roads and affordable houses. That vision still constitutes the American dream for many, but these days it's mostly just a dream. America will have to devise an alternative to "drive to qualify" growth—a pattern that long seemed as inevitable as the ossified real estate growth machine on which it was based. Disguised by all the financial shenanigans that created the mortgage meltdown was the fact that throwing up new subdivisions at the distant urban edge wasn't working anymore. Builders kept building bigger big boxes, often on bigger lots, even as demand had begun to taper off.

Massive efforts to bail out the 2000s-imploded housing economy couldn't restore the dream. Urban growth analyst Arthur C. Nelson, who had documented McMansion overbuilding before the mortgage meltdown, predicted in 2009 that the rate of homeownership would continue to drift downward over time, which means little new supply may need to be created until 2020.[1] Aside from the dampening effect on an economy so dependent on housing-related spending, planners and economists are going to have to start considering what will replace the exhausted growth machine real estate model yet achieve the economic advantages it was supposed to confer: affordability, mobility, simplicity.

For decades, we've made the urban edge inexpensive to develop by providing ample, easily accessible land and low barriers to business entry as the communities on all that land compete for growth by limiting regulations and taxes. I call these "loose-fit" engines of urban growth. Must we open ample land for development only with beltways? Can we make housing affordable only by building it on former farms and forests? Must growth always go only to the undeveloped edge? No. In most of the world, you'll find the most dynamic, fast-growing communities not in far-flung exurbs or boomburgs but in cities. Cities throughout history have succeeded by perpetually adapting themselves to new economic realities, which is one of the reasons some cities in the United States are resurgent in spite of the hostility of growth machine forces. There's no pre-ordained place, scale of development, or kind of density necessary for the loose-fit city to thrive. Rather, it is a set of conditions.

PORTLAND: INVENTIVE INFILL

Should you have to go to the hospital, there are worse ways to get there than the aerial tram that accesses the Oregon Health and Science University. It departs from the Willamette River waterfront in Portland and rises five hundred feet above the city, opening panoramas of downtown, the river, and the Cascade Mountains. About three minutes and two-thirds of a mile later, the tram arrives at a silver and red station perched on high angular legs (figure 9.1). From it, you stroll to your destination on the Marquam Hill campus.

The tram is a novel way to enable growth of the Health University, which had become landlocked atop its hill. The tram links the hospital to a redeveloped riverfront brownfield parcel called the South Waterfront, where expanded medical and teaching facilities mix with high-rise residences and parks. A new streetcar connects the development with downtown, which conveniently links the hospital to all the city's light-rail lines.[2]

The tram, streetcar, and South Waterfront development, taken together, are a creative way to bring denser development gracefully into already-built parts of the city, and they are a riposte to those that claim the United States can only build at the urban edge because there's no space left in existing communities.

Figure 9.1   A stylish aerial tram links the hilltop Oregon Health and Science University and expanded facilities in the South Waterfront mixed-use development, in Portland. Credit: James S. Russell

Few communities are truly built out; in most, vast tracts go wanting but look valueless so they tend to be forgotten. They are worth so little because the growth machine focuses investment on the urban edge. When a healthy city puts the vast forested and farmed tracts beyond the urban edge off limits, as Portland does (chapter 1), wasted land becomes valuable land.

On paper, confining the geographical extent of metropolitan growth by any means looks like a tight fit. There's always been concern, and much debate, about the potential of Portland's urban growth boundary to drive land prices up.[3] For years, Portland grew at densities and with the same kind of development as other cities because the urban growth boundary took in a lot of territory. In recent years, the city has grown faster and the boundary has expanded more slowly, which at first spurred infill development on sites that would be overlooked in most places. One-story commercial strips along transit lines sprouted four-story apartment buildings atop stores. But the need to accommodate still more growth has spurred amenable innovation, like the South Waterfront and tram. Portland was the first place I ever heard a development-savvy architect, Gary Reddick, promoting the idea of building housing over a supermarket parking lot. Local developers didn't get it. They were used to building either housing or supermarkets, not combining the two. Once he convinced one of his clients to do it, the idea took off.[4] Lately, the Pearl District, a neighborhood of derelict warehouses that attracted artists, has fledged into a popular mixed residential and commercial neighborhood.

The growth boundary has the effect of shifting growth machine priorities, making it safe to invest in mature communities and to innovate. Portland could not succeed if it was promoting infill growth that people didn't want. Instead, it unleashed the market conventional developers have ignored. It was hard for pioneering developers trying to build differently, but lenders have been chasing Portland projects not just because they can't plow up exurban forests but because people like the new Portland, and the fact that land supply is limited gives developers, lenders, buyers, and tenants faith that values will grow over time. By shifting growth machine incentives (by growth boundaries or other means), many other cities can develop Portland-style success.

For contrast, cruise central neighborhoods within Houston's I-610 inner beltway and you will find vast empty tracts with "for sale" signs so old the paint has peeled and the wood is split. Since metropolitan Houston perpetually opens lightly regulated new land to development with an ever-growing freeway network, land is indistinguishable and utterly commoditized. There's far too much generic land, so little of it can be made to pay, and innovative approaches are too risky.

The growth boundary has generally worked for Portland, but because it is a political construction, there have always been tensions about just how big the boundary must be. Draw it too tight, and it will only enable high-end growth. Draw too loosely, and the standard inefficient patterns of American growth reassert themselves. It's a balance that must be struck, then struck again.

Just as an ample supply of open land spurs outer-suburban development, an ample supply of land can be created through creative redevelopment and in-fill opportunities in mature communities. Vancouver has created enormous growth downtown through its inventive urban-design guidelines, and the new EcoDensity initiative aims to increase affordability in town by increasing the supply of developable area through selective increases in density. New York has rezoned about a fifth of the city to create opportunities for desirable development to proceed, "as of right," which means that projects that follow the zoning rules can move swiftly to approval, while developments that want to be taller and bulkier than rules permit must go through a long planning and community-consultation process called ULURP (Uniform Land Use Review Procedure).

GROWING MATURE COMMUNITIES:
RETROFIT, REPURPOSE, REINVENT

As we shift the growth machine's incentives and disincentives (in the tax code, in how we value investment, in how we provide transportation and infrastructure), we'll hasten a realignment of development opportunity that is already under way. The space for denser, less car-centric development in the "built-up" cites and suburbs is everywhere. In places like Bellevue (chapter 3), belatedly acknowledged market forces have already caused suburban downtowns to trade in their vast parking lots and oversized arterials as they consolidate into denser downtowns. Made more systematic, with trunk transit lines linking them to other centers of activity, remodeled suburban business districts can flourish while reducing auto emissions and congestion.

If you knew the old Villa Italia, in Lakewood, a close-in western suburb of Denver, you might not guess at the redevelopment potential of a once chic but long obsolete shopping center from the tailfin era. Villa Italia is now history,

Figure 9.2 The Belmar development, outside Denver, replaced an obsolete shopping center surrounded by parking with a mixed-use community that includes lofts, artists studios, and an art museum ranged along a network of streets and squares. Credit: James S. Russell

though familiar upscale big-box stores such as Whole Foods have risen out of the blacktopped acres. But you'll also find narrow streets with wide sidewalks lined with shops and artists' studios, surmounted by apartments and lofts (ultimately 1,500 units in a variety of styles; figure 9.2). Residents can hang out on a public square and walk to shopping, dining, movie theaters, and a bowling alley. The developer, Continuum Partners, underwrites a small branch of the Museum of Contemporary Art Denver. Belmar's hipness is soft-edged and carefully cultivated, but the $850 million development has made a big impact on an older suburb that was on a slow trajectory of decline. Most important of all, Belmar has created a residential and commercial node with the critical mass to deserve high-frequency transit. The opportunity to make more Belmars is endless.[5] Drive along any mature commercial arterial, and you will see just how much space is wasted, and how much aging highway-strip development is ripe for redevelopment.

The housing market has so obsessively supplied single-family houses that many sites will merit conversion to environmentally efficient apartments.[6] The market has been slow to realize that single-family houses make less sense for active young people who nowadays marry less often, have fewer children, and have them later in life. Nor are houses necessarily the right choice for couples after children are raised, who may not want to spend decades painting siding and clearing gutters. As in Portland, cities will discover that wasteful acres of parking are actually land banks that can generate cash when redeveloped.

Increase Development Opportunity by Mixing Uses

For decades, zoning ordinances tried to eliminate the kinds of industrial neighborhoods found in nineteenth-century cities, where factories, half a block in size and four stories or more in height, interrupt rows of houses. That factory might once have belched lung-searing smoke, and so segregating it into a separate industrial area made sense. Today, we need not worry about stirring workplaces into the residential mix because most commercial and many industrial uses today are clean enough to share streets with homes, and such mixed neighborhoods can cut traffic and commute times and permit walking to jobs. You can find cast-iron loft buildings in New York, Boston, Philadelphia, and elsewhere that layer a garment-sewing operation, studios for artists and designers, and wide-open residential lofts above street-level stores. Mixing living and working within neighborhoods suits the way small businesses incubate today, but officials may have to adjust fire codes, parking requirements, even bus schedules as eight-hour neighborhoods become twenty-four-hour ones.

Make Brownfields Desirable

Many cities possess square miles of once-industrial waterfront—sites that should offer the highly desirable combination of environmental restoration, high-value development potential, and public access to the water. Some leftover industrial space can get redeveloped in what have become high-value locations under today's accounting methods—such as Stapleton, in Denver, which was an obsolete airport close to downtown and now is a huge new neighborhood. Most brownfield plans founder, though, because the sites are too expensive to clean up.

Cities should be able to reinvent the water's edge—as they did in the early twentieth century—by threading parks, promenades, bikeways, and boat access through rebuilt natural wetlands and waterside plantings. The result would be a natural-system restoration project that creates a major public amenity but also happens to create high value for developers inland, helping to defray site-cleanup costs. New York is gradually sculpting a vast mountain of garbage on Staten Island into Freshkills Park, restoring wetlands and inlets along a saltwater channel that is recovering from a past as a fetid industrial sewer. But progress is slow because the city has only the most limited means to capture the value it is creating for the surroundings. Philadelphia has even greater potential, with miles of fallow Delaware riverfront that could host stunning redevelopment.

Every community should be looking at how to junk outmoded growth machine incentives in favor of tax and subsidy techniques that reward redevelopments—like brownfields—that can offer extraordinary value for the subsidy buck because they are not just an eco-fix but nurture stronger neighborhoods and can host very large-scale development where urban services and infrastructure already exist.

EASING ACCESS

High growth could never happen at the urban edge without a steady supply of new freeway lanes and beltways. Older cities struggle as the nation continues to underinvest in auto alternatives. The private sector can build (and, to some extent, has built) higher-density housing and closer-in businesses, but if the public sector fails to supply more buses, tracks, and trains, communities reap problems, not benefits. San Francisco, New York, and Seattle have seen rapid growth, but traffic has simply worsened and parking has become impossible because needed transportation investments have not been made.

Offering more transportation options to more people may prove to be the most important loose-fit strategy of all. An auto-only transportation system forces a singular, very low-density kind of development. Think of denser cities and suburbs served by several transportation modes as "bus to qualify," "rail to qualify," or even "bike to qualify." Making more of our metropolitan areas accessible in more ways in effect increases housing supply (and therefore restrains prices) because more people can get to more destinations from more neighborhoods. These days, neighborhoods well served by transit tend to be expensive because the supply of good transit is so limited.[7] The answer is to supply transit to more areas.

GOING WITH THE GRID

In the interests of making suburbs more walkable, bikable, and transit friendly, urbanists have declared war on the cul-de-sac, those streets that dead-end like so many loose threads after looping around a subdivision enclave that's disconnected from everything around it. These layouts are suited to one thing: minimizing traffic within subdivisions. Many cheer quiet streets, but they come at a cost. The streets that wind aimlessly through the woods eventually collect and dump into a big noisy arterial—the opposite of quiet.

Streets in a grid or web form a loose-fit pattern because they replace the dysfunctional duality of single-use residential streets and single-use commercial arterials with neighborhoods that can host a wide variety of uses and a wide scale of residential and commercial development. Coffee shops, dry cleaners, and book shops survive in strip malls, but they tend to thrive in intimate, side-walked neighborhoods with lots of houses and apartments nearby (figure 9.3). If the blocks aren't too big, and the streets not too wide, a pleasantly walkable scale can develop. You can zigzag through the blocks on foot to a nearby school or transit stop, rather than be nowhere after traversing a mile of looping subdivision street. Walkable cities develop economic ecosystems based on proximity: for example, districts that sell designer furniture and high-end clothing. Bars and clubs tend to cluster, too. You park once and find what you want at the price you want by visiting many competing businesses. These zones rarely develop in far-flung, auto-oriented metros.[8] Street grids use land far more efficiently, even when overall densities are not higher. Curvy subdivision streets tend to leave unusable chunks of land behind.

Spreading traffic across a grid of streets means main arterials need not be wide and intimidating culverts of traffic that moat communities, but can be developed as green streets (as described in chapter 4): inviting, tree-lined boulevards shared by cars, buses, bikes, and people. Traffic-calming design details, such as landscaped medians and sidewalk bump-outs, can keep largely residential streets from becoming drag strips.

Does the layout of communities really make that much difference? Consider two places built about the same time: Santa Monica, in Los Angeles, and Seattle. Both were laid out after the turn of the twentieth century on a grid with mainly single-family houses on small lots. The streets in Seattle are fairly narrow, many with only one traffic lane with parked cars on either side. Arterials wider than four lanes are a rarity. In Seattle, people walk, bike, and take buses,

Figure 9.3 By narrowing streets and building over parking lots, Mercer Island, a suburb of Seattle with good transit access, has become pleasingly walkable and less auto dependent. Credit: James S. Russell

especially to run local errands, because streets are pleasant and mainly quiet (the narrowness and a variety of traffic-slowing devices keep speeds down). Most neighborhoods are served by village-scaled, one-story commercial centers, where it is a pleasure to walk. In spite of their narrowness, Seattle's arterials rarely clog, though parking can be frustrating. (Seattle's ghastly traffic is confined mainly to freeways, which is where mobility breaks down.)

Such streets were not good enough for California street engineers. Decades ago, they cut Santa Monica streets much wider, so traffic moves much faster, even on residential streets. These streets are intimidating, not intimate. In Santa Monica, people mostly speed through residential neighborhoods by car to commercial destinations located behind parking lots on huge, traffic-clogged avenues that repel walkers, bicyclists, and transit users. Though there's much more "throughput" in terms of lane miles, the overall driving experience is far more frustrating than in Seattle. Both the arterials and the freeways gridlock.

We need not make the grid rigid (you can even have a cul-de-sac or two!). They can warp into webs of streets to follow slopes and orient to views. The blocks can be proportioned to catch prevailing breezes or to shade buildings from summer sun. We need not wipe the slate clean, but, like the most dynamic cities in history, we need to learn to overlay what works atop what doesn't.

AGILE REGULATION

In times of high growth, local leaders pat themselves on the back for creating a "business-friendly" atmosphere and a pro-growth community consensus for the shiny new malls next to the still-black asphalt of the just-completed off-ramps leading to the bright rooftops stretching toward the horizon. But as communities mature, especially communities that have created a great deal of wealth, people tire of the eternal disruptions of growth. They watch in dismay as the forests, rolling fields, or majestic desert recedes. Citizens' natural reaction is to demand tighter regulations to preserve the peace they feel they've paid for, and to demand that developers preserve more and build less.

Some businesses, especially well-heeled ones, will jump through more hoops, especially in the communities that have historically attracted the affluent. Others will throw up their hands and head to more-distant, less-restrictive pastures. The number of hoops, the uncertainty of the outcome, and the time it takes can be what's costly—and what makes a city that once welcomed entrepreneurship seem a tough, tight-fit place. The degree and arbitrariness of restrictions demanded by localities becomes a deal breaker for all but those who can coin cash in high-cost, highly regulated, high-wealth communities.

In a global warming age, many see tighter regulations—on megahouses, gas-guzzling autos, all-glass buildings, and power lawnmowers, to name a few—as the key to lower energy use and a carbon-neutral future. Regulations must play a role, but they must operate strategically in a dynamic, adaptive economy and support a sustainable community-investment strategy.

Regulation is a dirty word in a traditional loose-fit context. But an agile era (in truth, any era) demands carrots (incentives) and sticks (regulations) to shift behaviors toward results that nurture all communities rather than the urban edge at the expense of everything else. *How* regulating is done is important.

Keep Rules Simple

Regulations that are straightforward, understandable, and focused on the truly relevant are loose-fit tactics that lubricate development while preserving key values. Cities often have to learn this lesson the hard way. In the 1970s, New York City developed a very sophisticated and well-meaning program to reward developers for including desirable public amenities, such as atriums and small pocket parks, in crowded Midtown Manhattan. Developers could even reap rewards for building new Broadway theaters into the bottom of an office tower. Planners devised elaborate formulas to allow builders to exceed the allowable building size by X square feet if they included Y square feet of plaza or a Z-sized glass-covered walkway through the middle of a long block. The requirements were so detailed—spelling out how many trees, planters, and linear feet of café frontage was needed—that a great deal of negotiation had to go on to determine whether the city was getting the value it expected for the incentives.

It turned out to be a tight-fit strategy that developers resisted because it was so complex. They skillfully managed the negotiation process, offering little at the start and settling for not much. The stillborn parklets and grim public spaces mostly turned out to be more meager in fact than they had seemed on paper. After a few years, the city largely abandoned the idea and stopped negotiating. Instead, it wrote into the zoning some much simpler requirements, asking developers to provide some straightforward amenities to compensate for the very large size of some projects. If developers followed the rules, they'd receive permits quickly, "as of right," with no haggling and little official fuss.[9]

The revised approach wasn't as subtle, but it worked better. Developers liked it because it laid down understandable ground rules to which they and their competitors would have to adhere, and it was quicker and cheaper.

Keeping it simple, however, calls for the community to decide what is really important to regulate rather than what it would like to regulate. You don't want development by Lake Wilderness? You don't want high-rises blocking a beach view? Then zone the lake and the beachfront off-limits. Then write into codes where builders can build (in a less-sensitive place that gives views and easy access to either lake or beach, for example).

To places long armed with complex regulatory regimes, a place like Las Vegas seems anathema. Certainly, many in the environmental community would be pleased to see its neon-sign extravaganzas and synthetic stucco pretensions bleach abandoned in the unforgiving desert. Too often, urban experts fail to learn from such freewheeling, high-growth places. I visited local officials in Las Vegas in 2005, when the city was convulsed by the latest in a regular series of transformations—from dusty crossroads in the 1950s to a global casino capital. Planners were not only trying to deal with tremendous, never-ending (it

Figure 9.4 Planners recognized that protecting views to the Red Rock Mountains out-side Las Vegas was one of their most important duties, since locals value them as an an-tidote to slot-machine bustle. Credit: James S. Russell

seemed) growth, but they were watching the nature of that growth change al-most before their eyes. Along the Strip, developers had started adding high-rise condos catering to retirees and frequent visitors. The proximity to shopping, restaurants, and casinos made the punishing traffic not such an endurance test. In a city where loose slots and loose regulations go hand in hand, regulators permitted the transformation to happen virtually overnight with little hand-wringing. Here was a city that didn't care how developers handled the kinds of issues that in California could induce swarms of homeowners to take to the streets. It didn't matter how small lots were or how tall a building you might erect on it.

What citizens—and therefore regulators—cared about was the view to the Red Rock Mountains (figure 9.4). They regulated buildings that might block views because that's what locals held sacred. And they began to understand that the urge to go high-rise could help create neighborhoods with real urban life—a quality the youthful city of gated subdivisions had never had.[10]

As they looked ahead, they asked developers to break open the priva-tized high-rise enclaves, fortified by walls and parking garages, and provide an appealing pedestrian connection to the street, so that all this new development could someday have the potential to be walkable and served by expanded transit.

To say this style of development was enlightened is going too far. The city had not diversified its economy beyond the casino-shopping nexus and had never learned to create the amenity and city services that encouraged people to stay after they'd made their packet, so it has always been among America's most transient cities.

Over decades, though, Las Vegas has proved adept at turning on a dime, as the casino economy convulsively evolved, and locals credit the hands-off regulatory ethos for making that possible. "You can get things done here at a speed that you can't do in other places," explained James Murren, the head of MGM Mirage, when I visited again in 2009, with the city in a deep slump. He and his wife, Heather, were instrumental in the financing and building of a local cancer center, for example. It took three years from start to finish—shorter than the permitting process alone might have taken in many other places.

Murren is ready to help move the city to a lower-impact future, and people listen because his company is the largest landowner in Las Vegas and the state's biggest taxpayer. Profligate water use was no longer center stage in his CityCenter megadevelopment, as it was at the Bellagio casino complex next door, an MGM Mirage property built just a few years earlier. He described an expansive civic vision for relentlessly privatized Las Vegas. A metro region of 1.8 million people could not pretend to be a small town anymore, he said. "We've got so many needs here, we've got to catch up on basic services." He advocates rail transit to link the city with the Strip, an idea vehemently opposed by his competitors. Murren's approach is radical only within the hothouse culture of Las Vegas, where a natural gas–powered limo is considered green. With its willingness to make big-scale change, though, you can't count Las Vegas out.

Keeping it simple also means rewarding performance rather than mandating specific actions. Setting household energy-efficiency goals, for example, rewards performance while permitting any number of ways of achieving those goals. It is better than mandating the use of compact-fluorescent lightbulbs, because regulatory mandates never update as quickly as technology advances. (As I write this, LED light sources are quickly closing the cost and performance gap with the fluorescents and will probably supersede them.) Rewarding performance also spurs innovation, and that innovation could come from sources that even the most enlightened regulator could not anticipate.

Regulating at the Right Scale

Too many well-meaning tools operate on the wrong scale, such as environmental impact statements, which assess environmental effects of development on a project-by-project basis. The incomprehensible technocratic language of these massive documents can be massaged to make just about any development a candidate for sainthood, and the process too often gives a pass to developments that are harmful in the aggregate rather than individually. (One strip mall matters little; miles of them matter a lot.) On the other hand, projects like the long-stalled redevelopment of Penn Station in New York develop environmental benefits that are best captured by a regional-scale lens. The Moynihan Station project, as the rebuilding is now known, could move hundreds of thousands of daily passengers faster at less cost and with lower carbon emissions over a good portion of three states. Environmental-impact tunnel vision frustrates Vishaan Chakrabarti, who tried to move the project along before he became director of the Real Estate Development program at Columbia University. "Moynihan has by my count gone through three and a half environmental impact statements, probably $12 million worth of reports. It makes no sense that both the public sector and the private sector have had to put so much money into that kind of reporting for what is ultimately a green, transit-oriented project."[11]

We would know so much more about what kinds of development communities should encourage if we looked at the big picture with good baseline information. What areas are most precious? What ones most need redevelopment? What kinds of projects will reach our goals? What kinds should some carefully tailored regulation discourage? In this way, communities signal what kinds of development will be approved as of right, eligible for incentives, or publicly financed. That's a loose-fit approach. Then we can subject lazy, business-as-usual projects that build in high reliance on energy and chip away at valuable resources to a process that makes transparent the damage they do. Localities can then either reject them or subject them to very substantial requirements to mitigate that damage (think highways that fail to improve mobility or cul-de-sac subdivisions located where they require extraordinary public investments).

Regulating Affordably

One reason farms beyond the urban edge are so appealing to developers is that a field of asparagus will never show up to protest development at a public hearing. Human neighbors—especially neighbors who can afford top-drawer lawyers—are a pain in the neck most developers would prefer didn't exist. Where you have affluent neighbors sensitive to the environment, to recreational advantages, and to burnished historic neighborhoods, you tend to have restrictions, regulations, and prohibitions, along with high costs and a tangled development process: the opposite of the lightly regulated, development-friendly ethos that prevails at the exurban edge. Yet, such tight-fit cities—most of them on the coasts—are often wealthy, successful (at least by some measures), and appealing to live in. To create cities that are loose fit, that are entrepreneurial in the environmental and economic sense, requires unpacking these sets of apparent contradictions.

Over the years, both the state of California and many of its cities passed a panoply of strict environmental and growth-control regulations, accompanied by elaborate citizen-review processes. Localities became adept at slowing residential growth (which was perceived as adding traffic and costing tax revenues whatever their environmental impact), unpredictably rationing building permits, and making developers jump through more plan-review hoops. It got to the point in San Francisco that neighbors were given veto power over the style and even the color of an addition you might want to build. The rallying cry for such invasive regulation was always "preserving quality of life," but slowing growth also had the unspoken purpose of propping up property values—a foundational value of suburbia, especially in California, which got used to putting rising property values in the bank, even as costs to first-time buyers moved inexorably out of reach.

Many experts think lots of regulations, especially environmental-preservation ones, drive up costs.[12] In California that would appear to be the case, but the equation is more complicated. People aren't unhappy watching their homes appreciate. They willingly pay more to live in the Victorian hills of San Francisco or near the stunning bays of Marin County, and nature is not making any more of those places. Cities have also created a lot of wealth, which makes it possible for more people to pay more for amenity, and to pay more to defend it from the next wave of growth.

That combination powerfully reinforces the regulating urge. Rising values, though, come with rising taxes, stirring anger. In 1978, voters passed Proposition 13, which cut property taxes by a stunning 60 percent, curtailed their future growth, and rearranged who paid them. It protected longtime residents from dramatic property-tax spikes. It has long been regarded as the opening salvo in a nationwide tax revolt that has since intermittently swept the nation. William Fulton, a longtime observer of the urban-planning and development scene in California, described Proposition 13's most profound consequence as depriving the suburban growth machine of the cash it needed to keep on running.[13] Fulton shows how Proposition 13 inspired all-out fiscal war in the suburbs, as municipalities encouraged developers to plow under valuable farmland for sales tax–generating auto malls and shopping centers to pay for the American suburban dream without appearing to resort to the evils of greater taxation.

Such development obliterated fragrant orange groves and blighted the misty slopes above the ocean beaches, and Californians wanted to stop it. Each development's come-on promised closeness to nature, but inevitably the bulldozers came and carved the view of chaparral-covered hillside into dirt platforms for the next rows of houses.

The result is a tight-fit development environment: roller-coaster (but generally high-priced) housing costs *and* an oversupply of tax receipt–generating auto malls that jockey to steal business from one another. This contradictory, capricious development economy constrains growth, experimentation, and entrepreneurialism as it pushes moderate-income people to drive dozens of miles from job centers to find an affordable home (if they don't simply move to a state where life is simpler and cheaper). The farthest-out communities, where cash-strapped home buyers stretched themselves farthest, foreclosed fastest in the mortgage meltdown.

For all the rampant NIMBYism, California's environmental and quality-of-life victories tend to be pyrrhic, coming one isolated tract at a time. Then communities rise to fight the next battle. The blatantly unfair property tax structure has induced regularly scheduled fiscal crises and ruined once-great schools and universities. Phoenix, Las Vegas, and Denver have all grown on California outmigration.

California's contradictions are made more lurid by its tradition of government by citizen ballot initiative, but clashes among fiscal, land-use, environmental, and regulatory cultures plague many metropolitan areas—and the price is often paid in affordability, especially in the high-achieving cities on both coasts. In New Jersey—the most suburbanized state and, by some measures, the nation's wealthiest—the state's thousand-plus localities wield antidevelopment regulations to preserve disappearing farms and woodlands, and to keep out families with children of modest means as a way to reduce public-schools costs. The state's property taxes remain punishing. "Driving-to-qualify" in New Jersey can mean going as far as eastern Pennsylvania, more than sixty miles from jobs in New York City and its suburbs. To reduce congestion and encourage conservation, the state wants more people to use its statewide rail- and bus-transit system, but it regularly starves NJ Transit of operating cash while encouraging driving on its jammed, underengineered roads with among the nation's lowest road taxes.

The innovations in Vancouver, Portland, and New York suggest ways to preserve and enhance what communities value and to do it better than relying almost entirely on regulations. Letting developers know how they can build quickly and easily is a looser-fit strategy than rules that are complex, micro-managing, and ambiguously worded. Communities that prescribe a long list of required building attributes and mandates, followed by a long series of reviews by community groups and an assortment of boards with wide discretion and no time limits, may preserve only what they know, in a very limited way, usu-ally at high cost.

LEED: HOW TO WIKI INNOVATION

If you are a man, you may have recently encountered your first waterless urinal. No flushing necessary. Or, as a woman, you may have been offered, via coy graphics on the toilet-flush apparatus, the choice of a little flush (when liquids alone are concerned) or a normal flush (for "solids"). I briefly invade your per-sonal privacy to illustrate the power of LEED, the Leadership in Energy and En-vironmental Design program of the US Green Building Council (USGBC). The waterless urinal and the dual-flush toilet save water, and they have made their appearance not due to plumbing-fixture obsession or top-down regulation but voluntarily, one building at a time. By the time you read this, such fixtures may have become mandatory in water-challenged jurisdictions because they have proved their worth when introduced through LEED's standard-setting process. Or that process may have found something better.[14]

In a loose-fit context, the beauty of LEED is that it amalgamates the wisdom of many experts to quickly mainstream useful innovation. For cities, it offers an analogy that can address a wide variety of questions and test good ideas.

LEED is a checklist created by volunteer architects, engineers, and building experts to represent their collective assessment of best practices in environmen-tal sustainability. It is intended to widely address environmental issues, not simply focus on climate change. Volunteers on USGBC's numerous LEED committees propose, debate, and adopt measures by consensus. When a building or remodeling project's designers and owners seek LEED certification, they choose the measures that best fit the building—functionally, economically, and environmentally. The more measures they undertake, the higher the rating: from certification, the lowest standard, to silver, gold, and platinum.

Water-efficient toilets made their appearance as an approved LEED measure and rapidly moved into the mainstream because they proved cost-effective, easy to install, and reliable. Other measures have fallen by the wayside because they have not proved out or are too onerous. LEED standards have moved such products as advanced air filtration and solvent-free paints from outré to mainstream and have made construction-site recycling common, even on noncertified projects. Local requirements or tax incentives for green design can move this process faster, demanding (as many municipalities now do) that a higher LEED standard like gold or even platinum be met.

The USGBC's vision of environmental sustainability is exceedingly broad, encompassing site development, water efficiency, building materials, and fresh air, among other issues, so it was slow to reflect the importance of climate change. Until 2007, buildings could get certified without receiving any of the energy points aimed at reducing carbon emissions.

I was initially a LEED skeptic. Its checklist approach seemed mechanistic, and it seemed to reward what critics derisively call "point mongering": cherry picking low-effort strategies—a bit of bamboo flooring, some never-used bike racks—that figure heavily in project marketing campaigns but raise the score without having much environmental impact. However, LEED has proven to be flexible and dynamic—in other words, loose fit—as it has responded to criticism, with, for example, a mandatory focus on energy efficiency.

Douglas Farr, an architect and community designer in Chicago, sums up how LEED moves innovation forward: "You need to make it legal, make it easy, then require it." As a useful sustainability measure is identified, such as the waterless urinal, the first step (to many advocates' surprise) is to make it legal. Newish products often fall outside hidebound local building or local zoning codes. Negotiating approval can take time, but then what was once new and mysterious becomes mainstream and less expensive. Farr and architect Joe Valerio (of Chicago's Valerio Dewalt Train) had to convince city officials in Troy, Michigan, that reducing paved parking in favor of native grasses and wildlife-attracting ponds in the 2006 LEED Platinum headquarters for the

Kresge Foundation (chapter 5) was a good thing. They were just ahead of their time. It's largely because of LEED that many cities and communities have rewritten regulations and incentives to encourage designs that retain or divert storm water from overburdened sewer systems (figure 9.5). LEED has an invisible multiplier effect. Innovation gets built, and is therefore testable. If successful in one project, it migrates to others (whether subsequent users bother to certify or not) as owners and communities look for solutions, whether in flood control, energy conservation, or air quality.

This leads to Farr's second step, making adoption of new products easy. LEED has encouraged the geothermal well system industry, which didn't even exist in the United States a few years ago. Now, local suppliers and contractors all over the country have developed the capacity to produce and install them. More research and development—which LEED cannot fund—could make them less expensive and more efficient. LEED, however, helped identify their transformational potential.

Many jurisdictions have taken Farr's third step by making mandatory measures that have high value and are inexpensive. Construction recycling is now required in many places, since an infrastructure has developed for it (thanks to LEED) and contractors and local officials alike have recognized the high value and low cost of separating valuable metals, woods and so on. (In some cases, recycling makes money for the contractor.) You can earn LEED points for engineering in better indoor-air quality than today's building codes now require. If these measures prove to truly advance health (reducing asthma, say, or increasing alertness), officials might well make them mandatory.

LEED has had its growing pains. At this writing, only a few thousand buildings have been certified (though the number is growing exponentially) because it is neither an easy nor an inexpensive process. Architects not only have to design a better building but have to copiously document it and then await the USGBC's judgment on whether they've actually achieved the rating they sought. Its impact, however, has proven to be much larger than the number of certified buildings suggests. It has spurred broader acceptance of many green techniques even by owners who have no intention of doing the paperwork, because the scoring system creates benchmarks that corporate decision makers can understand and compare. It reduces greenwashing—the marketing of faux green tactics—because a disinterested third party is certifying performance. For companies who want to show their commitment to broad well-being rather than just profits, LEED is a brand with credibility.

Figure 9.5 Although storm water–absorbing rain gardens, like this one in the High Point redevelopment in Seattle (Mithun, architects), are rapidly becoming popular, they must still be made legal in many localities. Credit: James S. Russell

Though it can identify the potential in emerging technologies, LEED cannot replace government research investments or a useful regulatory role. Should Congress pass a program that allows polluters to buy carbon credits (called "cap and trade"), and some of that cash is used to underwrite green innovation, LEED could become a means to funnel that cash to products and concepts with high potential but that require R&D.

LEED's success suggests that there are numerous other ways to similarly wiki environmental innovation. As described in chapter 8, the USGBC has scaled up LEED in its Neighborhood Development program to capture large environmental efficiencies—such as cogeneration plants, mobility enhancements, and on-site green sewage treatment—that can happen only at the scale of a neighborhood, college campus, or office park. The organization ICLEI–Local Governments for Sustainability is using LEED as a model for its new STAR Community Index, intended to rate the environmental performance of entire communities in such areas as natural systems, planning and design, economic development, health, and social equity.[15] That's a tall order, but if the rating system catches on, there is no limit to the agile creativity that could be unleashed.

10

GREEN GROWS THE FUTURE

In 1990s Berlin, tower cranes silhouetted the sky in every direction as the city remade itself, presaging square miles of instant tower skylines in Dubai, Singapore, Seoul, and dozens of cities in China as the globe bound its economies tightly together.

It was a strange time for a Berlin real estate developer to tell me, "Europe's closets are full." By this he meant that most western Europeans owned what they needed, and that those mature economies would not grow on a diet of new and bigger cars, televisions, houses, and so on. Being a developer, though, he was optimistic about the prospects for growth—at least in the short term. He thought united Germany would supply the consumer economy's bounty to former East Germans, lifting them and the nation's economy together.

Though Berlin grew, it still struggles to find a firm economic footing. But he was right about the closets.

He expressed a quiet consensus that has developed in much of Europe that mature developed economies cannot thrive just by getting their citizens to buy more stuff. It's not just Europe's closets that are full. So are Japan's, Canada's, Australia's, and America's. The idea that growth in domestic consumer spending will power economic growth forever is about as widely rejected in Europe as it is received wisdom in America.[1] It's one reason many European governments resisted the buying binge urged upon them by American economists after the finance bubble burst. Europeans have long had their stimulus plan in place: an extensive social safety net and hefty spending on public works. They don't need more highways, because they've built them everywhere. They also have built

221

the future-focused infrastructures that America has chosen not to invest in: buses, trams, bike lanes, high-speed rail, up-to-the-minute rail and air hubs. While many American communities don't even have sidewalks, nations with a third of America's personal income cobble them.

Though some countries used ample global capital to finance a housing bubble as America did, Europeans generally save more and are becoming more anti-consumption, which is why governments did not urge greater purchases of cars and televisions to end the recession. This kind of stimulus would add to debt without generating sustainable growth, they felt. In general, the deal Europeans have made with their governments is to accept low basic wages in return for government-paid health care, subsidized housing, child daycare, schools, job-security measures, extensive unemployment insurance, long vacations, and a secure old age. These aspects of life have become much more important than more and bigger gadgets.[2]

There's also a cultural dimension. Consumption of goods and services does not drive most developed-world economies to the degree it does in the United States both because of the graying of populations and because of a deeper concern about global warming. The advanced European economies are at least a decade ahead of America in energy-conservation technology and carbon-emission policy. There's an ethos—in wealthier, better-educated Northern Europe especially—of living lighter on the earth. (There's also an economic dimension in the commitment to carbon reduction: ramping up green technology reduces energy imports and boosts exports, especially in Germany, which became a solar-panel leader in spite of having a cloudy, solar-unfriendly climate.)

The United States has not seriously questioned its prevailing consumption ethos: that people buying bigger houses and furnishing them with more gadgetry will somehow power economic growth, and thereby lift general well-being. It was precisely that ethos that fed the real estate bubble. The bust shattered Americans' faith in ever-spiraling real estate values as a magic growth serum, but we still avoid the key question: where will growth come from?[3]

One does not need to be an economist to recognize that the developed world will have to find a postconsumption growth model. That model must entail reweaving natural systems and human endeavor at a very large scale, because resuming business-as-usual consumption-based growth, assuming it can be induced over more than a brief period, will hit a wall of global warming effects and diminishing resources.

This chapter shows how the many tactics and policies described earlier in the book can put off that day of reckoning. Transforming our buildings, communities, and infrastructures to nurture natural systems and use precious resources efficiently can become an economic-development strategy as well as a sustainability strategy. More important, it can be a strategy that grows by improving well-being.

It's a tall order, but not an insurmountable one. First, we—especially in the United States—must wean ourselves from reliance on bubble economics.

THE REIGN OF BUBBLENOMICS

The case for a postconsumption economy will strike many as faddish or apocalyptic. But the lurid excess of the most recent American bubble, and the heavy price Americans are paying for it, undercuts the idea that America can build economic strength by a return to "normalcy." At this writing, more than two years after the United States entered the worst slump since the Great Depression, economists and politicians largely argue over what kinds of growth nostrums will get businesses and consumers to spend. America has been able to sustain the fiction of a successful consumption-driven economy only by inducing three bubbles to form over three decades, all of which popped with varying levels of damage. There's no "normalcy" to return to. Overconsumption, besides ignoring the environmental damage it caused, got America into its current mess.

The 1980s Reagan Bubble

I have vivid memories of being toured around the edges of Phoenix about 1991. Nothing looked amiss until my guide, a long-term resident, pointed out the brand-new strip malls with no cars sullying the parking lots' clean white stripes, and empty new office buildings you could see through. The savings and loan scandals that rocked the late 1980s left a residue of vacant stores and offices all over the country.

Tax shelters and regulatory relief unleashed in the early years of Ronald Reagan's administration lushly benefited commercial real estate, and developers threw up office buildings, subdivisions, and shopping centers with abandon. They did not sign up tenants in advance, because they could afford to build and wait a year or two for them to come along. Savings and loan associations, the chief sources of local finance at that time, and historically among the most conservative of lenders, joined the party with a vengeance.

The denouement bears a remarkable resemblance to the much larger housing bubble that would burst twenty years later. An overheated market and gagged regulators made life easy for S&L crooks. Congress reined in the costly tax breaks in the late 1980s, but the damage had been done. Construction volume, which hit records in 1986, crashed, shrinking by two-thirds in five years. The collapse took the savings and loan industry and its shoddy lending practices with it, costing the taxpayers some $160 billion. Commercial construction did not recover until the mid-1990s.[4]

The 1990s Dot-com Bubble

It's San Francisco, year 2000. I had visited a stylish loft building renovated in a matter of months to accommodate Internet startups that were growing so fast they were snatching up every square foot of space they could find to house people they hadn't hired yet to do tasks not yet defined. The rise of the personal computer and the Internet seemed to change the rules of investing, not only having created enormous wealth for Microsoft's Bill Gates, Apple's Steve Jobs, and AOL's Steve Case but also enriching software engineers and secretaries lucky enough to be in on the hatching of Windows or Netscape. It was a much-touted New Economy, an entirely unprecedented era of wealth creation, according to industry shills. The growth and innovation were real, but by the late 1990s, investors bid up companies like AOL to values rivaling longtime blue chips like Exxon or General Electric, which were deemed part of an antiquated "legacy" economy. Stock prices need not reflect dull "old economy" profits, the New Economy advocates said, as the stock market bounded to record after record.[5]

When I visited that loft building, only about a third of the building's space was occupied, because tenants would sign leases then realize they needed even more space and would sublet to another startup. In one space, several transactions had taken place with not a soul actually having moved in.[6] Out on the bustling street, early mobile-phone adopters were frantically deal making. The air was so infused with instant-millionaire dreams that I looked up, half expecting the sky to rain money. A boom has never felt so palpable to me before or since—nor so fragile. The bubble burst later that year, with the tech-heavy NASDAQ exchange plunging from a peak of over five thousand points, wiping out billions in paper value.[7]

The 2000s Housing Bubble

Given the lives and fortunes ruined in the previous two bubbles, we should have known better in the 2000s. The twenty-first century's first bubble was a product of the twentieth century's last one. House prices in many markets had risen with the dot-com ebullience and began a precipitous fall as the tech bubble burst, especially in overheated markets in California and New York. With the 9/11 attacks further shaking faith in the American economy, the Federal Reserve goosed the housing economy with big interest-rate cuts. The rest is still fresh history: The subprime lending sector, in spite of critics who said terms were abusive, grew rapidly, with mortgage makers reaping huge profit on buyers shut out of the housing market by the 1990s price runups. The Federal Reserve interest cuts propped up those prices, and regulators looked the other way as buyers, hoping to scramble into the middle class, signed onto mortgages with rates that pretty much guaranteed they'd never cash in.

Wall Street packaged loans in new exotic investment products that brought in huge amounts of new cash to lend. House prices, especially in desirable markets, rose rapidly. People could keep up only by taking out high-risk loans. Again, pundits claimed the rules had changed, that America had this time for sure found a new road to wealth. Regulators sat back, accepting the specious notion that markets were transparent (which they were not) and self-regulating (which, as in previous bubbles, they weren't).[8]

To keep the new mortgages rolling in, lenders pushed new loan "products" that could remain viable only if home prices rose forever. People tapped the growing paper equity in their homes to pay college and medical bills, to buy yet larger homes, or to take Vegas flings.

It was all, of course, a colossal house of cards, built on greed and dishonesty. The cracks in the edifice started to appear in 2006, and the damage spread wider in 2007, leading to the precipitous economic crash that began in fall 2008.

During these three growth spurts, the US economy seemed to outperform those of most of the developed world, leading to the belief (still widely held) that growing consumption would lead to economic expansion, which would feed yet more consumption, and so on. Evening out the bubbles and declines, US economic performance would not look impressive. The bubbles simply disguised the fact that consumption would otherwise have risen little, not enough to raise standards of living or keep the economy vibrant. This was especially the case in the 2000s, when the bubble expanded and the economy seemed to grow even as wages stagnated.[9]

The United States has had to keep bribing citizens to spend by cutting taxes and pushing new deregulatory gimmicks.

LIMITS TO GROWTH

In the early months of the housing-bubble bust, a paradoxical debate played out. Reacting to job losses and the crashing value of their homes and investments, Americans rapidly cut spending and started saving to cushion the bad times. Economists cried, wait! wait! People needed to keep on with their bad old habits just a bit longer to keep the economy from spinning into the abyss. The experts were admitting that the consumption basis of the economy had failed (propped up only by a bubble), but they needed people to keep it going while they thought of something new. Americans, it turned out, could not afford to keep spending, and the government's ability to spend for them was severely limited by accumulated deficits. The recovery got off to a slow and rocky start.

The barriers to long-term sustained growth through consumption have become formidable, however, and we'll see below how that takes us back to the environmental challenges I spelled out in the introduction.

Developing Giants

In today's tightly integrated global economy, Brazil, China, India, and perhaps Indonesia and Mexico are among several populous nations that will grow at least partly at the expense of mature developed economies. On a per-person level, incomes are not large, but cumulatively, these economies are already huge and have—or are gaining—a productive capacity that is able to undercut Europe, Japan, and America on price.[10] In a few years, they may well compete in the high-tech sectors and service sectors that the developed countries have traditionally dominated. (Solar-panel manufacturing dominance, to name just one example, shifted from Europe to China in just a few years.)[11]

Resource Shortages

As these large economies shoulder their way into the world economy, the globe demands correspondingly enormous amounts of mineral and natural commodities. As growth rates increase, expect rapid rises in the price of oil, copper, steel, and numerous other commodities essential to our economy as it is now structured. Even in the absence of literal shortages, a combination of speculation and higher extraction and processing costs will create periodic commodity price spikes, much like those the world witnessed at the peak of the 2000s economic boom.[12]

Nature Bites Us Back

Until economic activity accurately prices the value of natural resources, the forests, fisheries, and agricultural land will continue a spiraling decline, exploited beyond the point of no return by unprecedented levels of world demand. We're watching entire water systems, fisheries, agricultural regions, and forests die before our eyes, which means they can no longer support productive human endeavor, which impoverishes us and leads to even heavier exploitation of the natural systems that remain, hastening the appalling specter of large-scale environmental collapse.

Taken together, these factors will make it much harder for developed economies, especially America's, to grow their way out of recession, particularly through the purchase of consumer goods. Climate change may remain a hazy abstraction to many people, but building an economy that is resource efficient as well as energy efficient may be the only way to address economic well-being. The issues of resource shortage, pollution, and pricing will become more evident as large swaths of the world's population achieve a lifestyle beyond privation. There is a real risk that business-as-usual, GDP-focused, high-impact/ low-efficiency growth cannot long sustain itself.[13]

A NATURAL RECKONING?

The scale of the 2010 Deepwater Horizon oil-spill disaster may at last force an accounting of these risks. BP's catastrophic mistakes in the incident cannot be ignored, but neither should America's larger failure to appropriately balance the subsidizing of cheap oil with the risks of drilling for it a mile beneath the sea. At this writing, the ultimate cost of the Deepwater failure is not yet known. But the cost goes beyond sullying some of the world's most beautiful beaches and undercutting the economies of three states. It could include the disruption of one of the world's most essential ecosystems.

We could have been up front with ourselves about the risks of drilling versus the costs of making that drilling unnecessary through energy conservation and alternative energy sources. The United States still chooses not to make that calculation. Had we done so, the course of action would have become much clearer. We may have come to terms with the real risks and the real costs of resource extraction in an era that demands ever more risky procedures. (Drilling in Arctic seas? Blowing up West Virginia mountaintops for coal? Shattering underground northeastern geological formations to extract natural gas at the risk of essential water supplies?) In its ignorance of the scope of such risks, America *enables* Deepwater disasters to happen.

GREEN ECON: COSTS AVOIDED; MULTIPLE, SYNERGISTIC BENEFITS

To an extent rare just a few years ago, economists have begun to embrace green investments as essential to advance conventional growth as the benefits of including the cost to the environment in pricing has become more obvious.[14] They are also recognizing that conventional analysis often fails to capture the unique benefit of green investments.

Costs Avoided

Many environmental-repair efforts produce positive economic outcomes because we stop having to pay for the secondary effects of consuming resources destructively. In other words, if we don't have to drill, we don't risk the Gulf's ecosystem and economy. If we save water, we don't have to pay the punishing costs of finding more fresh water. We could price coal to reflect not just the cost of the GHGs it emits but the cost of cleaning up the pollution caused by its extraction, processing, and burning. After all, if a company blows up a mountaintop to extract coal, and clogs streams with the debris, just what kind of economic future can that place have once the miners leave? I thought of this when I visited the listless copper-mining town of Anaconda, Montana, where my mother grew up. It would be a thriving place, since its setting is one of the most eye-popping natural landscapes in the world, but for the mile-long pile of mine tailings that defaces it.

The green economy avoids costs by preserving resources or not using them up, primarily in energy and in reducing the percentage of GDP devoted to transportation (which, in the United States, is larger than most other nations). The dollars we don't spend are available to us for other essential or more desirable purposes. Consider the comparison made in chapter 4: the gas-guzzling SUV costs the owner a lot of money to fill up, pollutes the air, worsens global warming, contributes to traffic congestion, and puts more pressure on a finite resource (oil), helping to push the price up. In America, much of the cost of every oil gallon doesn't circulate in the economy but heads offshore to oligarchic nations whose interests are often opposed to America's and who use American cash to achieve them.

By contrast, Americans in large numbers could halve the negatives by buying cars with double the mileage. If one member of an American family switches to the bus and sells the car, he not only reduces the negative effects to a fraction of what the SUV owner creates but gains the ability to save $10,000 or more annually or spend it on things that may have more beneficial economic and environmental effects. If a significant percentage of Americans made such a choice (readily doable within a decade), you get the idea that transformative results, especially in global warming terms, are not far from reach.

Benefits Multiplied

When the United States and other developed nations committed to cleaning their water and air in the early 1970s, few people were optimistic enough to imagine benefits beyond better health, modestly prettier lakes, and fewer brown skies. But the results went beyond almost everyone's wildest dreams, a lesson worth revisiting as we confront environmental challenges that feel less personally urgent than choking on smog. We're used to accounting for actions in simplistic monetary terms: if I invest X, will I get back a 20 percent profit on it? By that measure, many green tactics at best pay back. Instead, green investments tend to offer broad benefits that we rarely measure (like selling the SUV does). To set effective priorities for ourselves, we need to account for these real, if sometimes indirect, benefits because they can be so substantial.

As small children, my brothers, sisters, and I splashed the summers away in the murky waters of Lake Washington, next to which we lived, not far from Seattle. Each year, the beaches were closed for more days, since raw sewage from the growing city and its suburbs poured into the lake untreated. That began to change in the early 1960s as a local effort to build sewers led to the treatment of almost all industrial and domestic sewage in just a few years.

Our family welcomed the cleanup, obviously, but we expected little beyond safe swimming. Over the years, though, we witnessed an extraordinary transformation. The murky green water turned to blue, and that blue kept deepening. Where before, at best, we could see a few inches into the water, visible depths grew to more than ten feet—the kind of clarity you expect to see in a remote mountain lake.[15]

Wildlife multiplied. We were stunned to find salmon spawning in a shallow, sandy cove in front of our house. Bald eagles, which had all but vanished, now roost in the high firs above the house and even scour densely built-up neighborhoods in Seattle for unsuspecting prey. The lake is a playground, hosting all manner of boats. Bass have returned to the lake in such numbers that the high-tech skiffs of sport fisherman clog the shoreline.

Real estate values near the lake zoomed, as what had been an unofficial open sewer became a desirable and finite amenity. At this writing, my childhood home is worth almost ten times its 1953 value (inflation adjusted!), a rate of appreciation that dwarfs properties lacking waterfront. Would the likes of Bill Gates and his Microsoft cofounder Paul Allen have built multimillion-dollar residences along the lake if it had been allowed to putrefy? Multiply the seventy-five miles of shoreline by these kinds of numbers and you have an amount of value creation no one expected that alone dwarfs the cost of building the treatment infrastructure.[16]

Then multiply this story all across the country, where rivers no longer reek, industrial cities have emerged from soot and grime, and yellowish smog no longer shrouds suburbs. To my knowledge, the real estate value preserved and created by clean air and water has never been estimated.[17] Imagine how enormous it is.

What if those sewers had never been installed and the tailpipe exhaust from hundreds of millions of autos had never been scoured? Lake Washington would be dead, and that waterfront we grew up on would be worthless. Countless cities would have been abandoned because the air was unbreathable. We'd have very little clean water for drinking.

When clean water and clean air legislation was being debated, it seemed hard to believe that the Cuyahoga River in Cleveland—where a mélange of toxic chemicals actually caught fire—could be saved.[18] Now, with the river significantly restored, Cleveland has built stadiums, the Rock & Roll Hall of Fame, the Great Lakes Science Center, and other attractions along the river. Who then could have imagined that the Towpath Trail would make the Cuyahoga Valley

National Park one of the most visited in the nation? Who would have dreamed back then that the hills of Pittsburgh, for decades seared of vegetation by pollution, would now be lush with trees, and that many of the neighborhoods above the old factory sites would be more desirable than ever?

Experts have estimated the cancers that have been avoided, the many lives not cut short, the health care and hospitalizations we didn't need. Who has ever looked at these numbers? Most of us take for granted the notion that the good outweighs the bad; we can see it with our own eyes. The statistical tally does not capture the well-being created from millions of children swimming in heedless pleasure in clean lakes, streams, and coastal beaches on a hot summer day.

California's experience shows that similar benefits can develop from aggressive energy conservation. It has been a leader in curbing energy use, with per capita consumption rising not at all since 1974 while the nation's use has risen 50 percent. Think of the power plants not built, the pollution not generated, the cash Californians have been able to commit to other goods and services that in other states goes to building power plants and buying fuel. (Indeed, the state redoubled its conservation efforts after Enron and other energy-service companies conspired to fake a power-supply crisis, leading to huge, artificially induced utility-rate spikes that were later rolled back.) If the harm to the state's economy was as large as naysayers have claimed, the state would never have set aggressive targets for greenhouse gas emissions and set out ways to meet these goals through a planning framework called Vision California.[19]

Benefits That Build on One Another

Both the economic and environmental benefits of incremental conservation measures and technologies may be much greater than we can reliably estimate now because of the way one technique can add value to another. Improvements in overall building or vehicle efficiency are not linear or geometric but can be exponential.

Let me stitch together the synergistic (if not obvious) relationship of a smart electrical grid, better building controls, and electric cars. Owners have for some time used automatic controls for lights, heating, and cooling in houses and office buildings. From a touch screen or mobile phone, you can set your house to minimum-heating "vacation" mode, or preheat the place when you are about to return. In large structures, computerized building-management systems regulate lighting, heating, cooling, and many other functions.

Control systems in homes and businesses become far more useful when connected to a smart grid hooked to renewable sources. That's because a smart-grid electric utility doesn't just send power to customers from large generating stations; it also receives power from customers selling the excess from large wind farms and small home-solar arrays. Smart controls can make energy-consumption choices for you that take advantage of the smart grid's dynamic fluctuations in supply, demand, and pricing. Large companies already get big power-price breaks if they agree to reduce energy use during demand peaks. With a recent retrofit, the Empire State Building's (chapter 7) advanced controls permit both the building and its tenants to cut peak power use as much as 1.5 megawatts, a much larger savings than would have been possible just a few years ago, and to share a hefty check written by Con Ed, the electric utility.

The smart grid can extend the idea to small users and homeowners, instructing your appliances (unless you override them) to heat water, wash dishes, and dry laundry when wind farms are whirring and pricing is most advantageous. In this way, smart grids working with smart controls considerably reduce the disadvantages of wind and solar, which are not consistently available.

Solar and wind energy fed into the smart grid can enable a proliferation of such load-shifting techniques. Solon, a German solar-power maker, demonstrated a prototype of what they called the "solar shuttle," a portable power source you could charge when demand and prices are low, then roll out to your workplace to power desktop computers and lighting.[20] Using many such techniques, buildings can sip energy during heat waves (when electricity use—and prices—usually peak). Reducing peak-period usage across the board is especially valuable (and cost saving) because a considerable amount of generating capacity must be built and maintained (much of it burning the dirtiest fuels) just to serve that peak, which is usually 5 percent of the time or less.

Now to the electric-car connection. The smart grid and electric cars will need each other, because we'll have to add a great deal of generating capacity if an electric-car power-distribution system isn't priced to encourage charging at low-demand hours. Once electric vehicles become a significant percentage of the market, all those batteries connected to the grid also become a useful source of reserve power. That's because about 1 percent of capacity being generated at any given moment is power that's essentially thrown away because it is produced only to stabilize the grid as demand changes. That reserve could readily come from idled electric cars.[21] That means, in the worst-case scenario, the grid would borrow only a small percentage of the battery's capacity.[22] In sum, the consumer able to shift loads and the car able to contribute idle battery power both help the grid work more efficiently and make solar and wind energy more valuable. Indeed, it's a "sum" that considerably exceeds the value of its parts.

The economic implications, however, are as significant as the environmental ones: smart grids, electric cars, and building-control systems are each markets that will thrive with the right incentives, each innovating, each creating jobs and technologies. And this is but a tiny part of the carbon-reduction pie.

Motivated entrepreneurs can create and refine many green measures with relatively small up-front investments if we align growth machine incentives to help them find a market. The United States can create these markets and these technologies, or it can wait for circumstances to force them on us, when we will have to import them from nations that had the foresight to invent them. (Indeed, America is such an energy-innovation laggard that it already imports dozens of technologies for advanced rail and green building.)[23]

HOW GOOD IS GROWTH?

We assume that fast-growing urban regions in America are becoming wealthier, drawing people because of the opportunities they offer. In reality, the first does not automatically lead to the second. Some slow-growing metropolitan economies (in terms of population) have created a lot of wealth (like the big cities of the Northeast), while some fast-growing areas (in terms of population) create wealth at a much slower rate than population grows (the case for Phoenix and Las Vegas, even before their precipitous crash).[24] Europe may have grown GDP only modestly, but its performance looks better considered in the face of population decline. The lesson: countries can grow in wealth without growing in population and, by implication, without increasing consumption.

Regrettably, the fastest way to grow in both wealth and well-being has been to rise from subsistence agriculture by amalgamating in cities workers willing to perform labor-intensive tasks at low wages and to industrialize by taking on the world economy's dirty work. The Kuznets Curve, named after Nobel Prize–winning economist Simon Kuznets, posits that economic inequality increases as countries industrialize. People demand a bigger piece of the economic pie once education levels increase, the economy diversifies into services and knowledge work, and people achieve comfortable lives. The Environmental Kuznets Curve proposes that pollution increases with industrialization and then declines as people can afford to become more concerned about human welfare and the environment. Both propositions appear to reflect imperfectly what actually happens as a nation's GDP grows, but they both start from the assumption that moving a society from rags to riches via rapid growth in energy-intensive and polluting industry is a given—which has dire implications for the planet.[25]

It's unclear, however, whether sufficient environmental resilience exists for the wealth-via-industry route to remain viable. Just a few years ago, Chinese efforts toward reducing its stunning levels of pollution seemed largely window dressing. But the sheer scale and ubiquity of pollution and the economic potential of green technology seem to have pushed a rapid change of heart. Now China is rapidly closing its most polluting steel and power plants and trying to leave its basic-industry engine of growth behind. This effort could prove to be one of the most significant steps in reducing global greenhouse gas emissions.[26]

Further, a different wealth-building route suggests itself in the case of some countries as diverse as Norway, Botswana, and Malaysia. Botswana and Malaysia have used income from mineral riches to fund broad economic-development efforts, rather than funnel them to elites or corrupt government officials as has happened too often in Africa and the Middle East. As cash rolled in from oil discoveries in the North Sea, Norway chose to invest a considerable percentage of the proceeds on energy conservation and other greening tactics. The result will be to maximize export earnings from the natural gas while creating a low-energy infrastructure that will carry the country forward once those sources are exhausted.[27] Careful stewardship of resources may pay off big as global demand grows and viable mines, forests, and fields decline. Of course, preserving and enhancing key natural resources realizes multiplier effects, like reducing greenhouse gases, keeping water cleaner, and making possible a greater diversity of agricultural production.

Many people recognize these opportunities, but the global, liberal-economic growth machine can't value resource stewardship that prepares for a future of more people putting more strain on finite resources. Liberal economics, a predominant ethos among developed nations, presumes that free markets will distribute production to the most efficient producers. Maybe an iPhone could have been invented only in Cupertino, a Camry only in Toyota City, and movies only in Hollywood (and now Mumbai). The liberal economic model rewards places that can amalgamate intelligence to produce unique products, but for the most part, its "efficiency" operates purely in terms of production costs and has no means to account for environmental costs or human costs. The result has been to reward the lowest-cost producer no matter where they are or what methods they use.

SLOW CITIES AND LOCAL FOOD ECONOMIES

Some cities and regions are trying to step away from the GDP-at-any-cost, global-economy treadmill. The "slow food" and local food movements in America and elsewhere started the trend. The focus is on high-quality, organic, locally produced food that thrives in the uniqueness of a given locale's climate and soils: *terroir,* in the new parlance.[28]

To some extent, it works. The organic-food movement was the first to reverse the widespread "race to the bottom," in which food was produced at lowest cost, with high reliance on chemical fertilizers, pesticides, and growth hormones. Organic and local products found a market in those leery of the tastelessness and questionable healthfulness of globalized, industrialized agriculture. Huge food producers belatedly recognized that the USDA Organic label distinguishes a healthier, often better-tasting product and sells for up to double the price of the "commodity" item, whatever the actual difference in production costs. Big Food has rushed to embrace organic production.

Slow food goes beyond the product to include a more personal transaction. Customers can buy directly from producers in farmers' markets and learn how a pig was raised or why a given cultivar thrives in upstate New York and not in the irrigated expanses of California's central valley or some unknown place in Peru. With such close interaction, people cook in new ways and producers add more "heirloom" products that expand possibilities: for example, not just organically raised pork but sausages made from that pork. Local wine production begets local cheese production, and so entire micro-economies of locally produced products develop. Food becomes a way of life, not simply a package opened and popped into the microwave.

Slow food begat Slow Cities, a movement that got its start in Italy.[29] Italy had built a widely admired "economic miracle" in the postwar era largely on the basis of clusters of industries (fashion, designer furniture, lighting, household objects, autos, and stylish ceramics, to name a few) that were based on merging industrial techniques with passed-down craft cultures in certain cities or clusters of cities, mainly in the nation's heavily industrialized north. By the end of the twentieth century, the globalized economy, with its unrelenting focus on production cost, punished Italy's high-skill design industries as factories moved inexorably to developing countries with labor costs a fraction of those found in Italy.

At the same time, the world seemed to fall in love with the Tuscan lifestyle, with its slow pace and its artisanal approach to food and everyday life. This combination of events has caused many in Italy to conclude that competing directly with low-cost producers elsewhere is senseless. They have decided to try to create a high-amenity economy based on localness.[30]

The Slow Cities idea may never get beyond a lifestyle choice, but its ecological ethos taps into powerful economic forces (as the runup in Tuscan property values attests) because buying food, clothing, and furniture made locally feels like an authentic kind of life that yearly becomes more difficult to find. A "slower" life means depending less heavily on imported goods and energy. You walk, bike, and respect history. The Slow Cities idea links to the green-architecture thrust of sourcing materials and products locally as a way to reduce transportation energy and avoid products that are extracted or manufactured unsustainably.[31]

Like the environmental movement, the basis of local food and slow cities has been moral rather than economic, but the economic case only gets stronger. Portland, Oregon, with its mild climate and outdoor enthusiasts, has developed a high-end bicycle culture and nurtured a local bicycle-building industry. (It's "slow" because it is local, low-tech, and green.) The industry is as yet tiny and will not ever compete with low-cost mass producers in Asia. It is, importantly, a local industry that previously did not exist. It is not alone. Nike, the sports apparel giant, was founded and bases itself in Portland, and specialized outdoor-equipment makers thrive all over California and the Pacific Northwest. The synergistic local effects are clear: the ample national parks, wildernesses, and national forests attract outdoor-focused people, which in turn generates an economic cluster based on serving their desires.[32] Local economies could develop to serve the climate-specific building practices (shutters and other shading devices, windows, and so on) described in chapter 7. They would count as "slower" products than high-tech windmills made in China.[33]

Localized industries cannot be seen as an ecological or economic panacea, but the success of such a wide variety of endeavors shows that it may be time for the liberal-economic pendulum to swing back. After all, such economies may be a source of economic resilience given the fragility of a supply chain spanning oceans and continents. Globalized sourcing has relied on low transportation energy prices, which are unlikely to last. Climate effects, like rising seas, shifting ice flows, or intensified storms, may have a variety of unforeseen consequences for ports and shipping.[34]

Growing crops that are local, unique, and redolent of the region may be the economic salvation of rural places that have not been able to compete in a hemispheric, commodity-agriculture economy—especially if Congress aligns agricultural subsidies to help health-focused producers reach consumers of modest means. Localized agriculture, whether you call it slow food or not, has long been integral to agricultural policy in much of Europe, where regulations against towns sprawling into farm fields and an infrastructure of farmer's markets in town squares have aided artisanal production of cheeses, meats, fruits, and vegetables.[35]

From a global perspective, short-circuiting the Environmental Kuznets Curve by helping people achieve well-being through environmental conservation and restoration may prove the most economically viable course. Rejiggering global economic norms (through trade agreements, treaties, and other policies) to encourage sustainable practices in poor countries can help them earn nonexploitative export earnings.[36] That may not develop "consumers" of soft drinks, television shows, and SUVs but could create a much larger class of people who grow in wealth by "consuming" many more green "soft" goods and services of a global economy dedicated to creating a world we can all live in.

CONNECTING WEALTH TO WELL-BEING

Environmentalists lock horns with economists and advocates of business-as-usual by proposing that cities and nations look for ways to increase wealth and well-being by different economic measures that have lower impacts. We would focus not just on production and consumption of goods and services but on what it takes to raise people's well-being: adequate incomes, shelter, health care, personal safety, and so on. This is often portrayed as a "triple bottom line" that holds a company or organization to a measurable commitment to enhance economic, environmental, and social value.

As in localized economies, policies focused on improving well-being are looking better as an economic strategy, even if based on a social-justice idea. GDP is supposed to approximately measure well-being by accounting for wealth created in the economy, but too many expenditures that look like growth erode well-being rather than enhance it. The world spends more for fish, but that reflects a shortage economy created by destruction of the resource, not value or wealth created. The explosion of American health-care costs in the first decade of the twenty-first century goosed GDP while eroding the good life growing GDP is supposed to nurture.[37]

Certainly, rebuilding natural systems cannot be morally or politically justified if the developed world continues to shunt dirty duties to the world's poorest and most politically helpless. Nor can just some communities (especially the least well-off) be stuck with new burdens when fixing forests or diversifying transportation causes economic shifts. Improving human well-being and the environment at the same time is a lot to ask of any of us; juggling the good with the dollar isn't easy, as organizations who have signed on to triple-bottom-line efforts have found. But the effort to balance investments in people and nature may well prove economically essential, if for no other reason than that such efforts create new consumers for developed-world goods and services when people rise from the status of the desperately poor.

HOW MUCH DOES URBAN AGILITY COST?

The Agile City has constructed a big solution out of many incremental measures. The sheer quantity and diversity of strategies can be hard to price; it's complicated to neatly total benefits. That can tempt the hard-nosed accountant to default to the relative economic (though not technological) simplicity of sweeping alternative-energy concepts—whether clean coal, hydrogen power, or nukes.

None of these technology-intensive approaches is likely to create enough jobs to significantly power the economy, especially because high costs must be paid up front and may not result in much job creation. The benefits begin to accrue only after the technologies are fully tested, operational, and mainstreamed. Gathering the enormous up-front investments needed is a heavy lift for a United States that spends a pittance on energy research and can't come to consensus on more than the lowest-cost conservation efforts. There's no low-hanging fruit here.

By contrast, conservation tactics, many small and diverse in scale, can be developed in the same way as many of the wildly successful innovations of the personal computer and Internet age: by geeks tinkering in some garage (solar-powered, of course).

Consider the economic potential that could have been unleashed by the green and storm-resistant prototype houses created in Biloxi and New Orleans after Hurricane Katrina. Besides housing displaced people, just these few houses brought innovative products, building techniques, and expertise to a city that had not seen any influx of innovation in decades: geothermal well systems, dual-flush toilets, solar panels, rainwater harvesting systems, storm-resistant building techniques, traditional climate-appropriate building forms, new kinds of rot-resistant woods, and factory-built, low-cost, high-quality modular construction—among others.

In New Orleans, city officials realized that innovative housing tuned to the subtropical climate, the high winds, and the propensity to flood could become a catalytic group of industries, building on research expertise that already resided in local universities. The city put environmentally sustainable design and building into its economic-development plan.[38]

No growth machine infrastructure or significant government rebuilding dollars supported the green-economy aspirations, and so the city was unable to capitalize on the job-creating benefit of green technology, even though the house prototypes have inspiring stories to tell the visitor—among the few such stories the city has to offer.

IS CHANGE TOO TALL AN ORDER?

I've made an economic case for inventing and refining hundreds or thousands of small tactics and technologies rather than placing our bets largely on a few speculative big technologies. Since making large-scale investments in slowing climate change and dealing with its effects is essential, they should pay off in as many ways as they can.

Global warming skeptics who argue that greater investments in a cleaner environment today are misallocated make essentially the same arguments that were used against clean-air and clean-water investments. As this book demonstrates, leaving the mechanics of the growth machine untouched is certainly not an economic-growth strategy. One of the reasons we have needed three bubbles over the last three decades is because we've been unwilling to look at the wasteful investments promoted by today's regulations and incentives. If we managed to come up with some perfect clean-tech energy solution and plugged it into the grid, we would still leave many of these problems unaddressed.

Is creating a greener future simply too tall an order for an America facing challenges in every direction, where too many families barely cling to a middle-income lifestyle and so many others seem destined never to achieve it? Here's where we call on Americans' deep-seated inventiveness. It's not too much to ask ourselves how to manage decision making and how to invent and reinvent government. It has been at times a mantra of both conservatives and liberals, so there is a common ground to be found. (Politicians need outside stimulus since they tend to be acutely aware of the degree to which they can be reinvented out of a job.)

The same kinds of design acumen and analytical prowess that the nation regularly invests in biotechnical breakthroughs or in building a better portable music player can be applied to cities and the environment. We simply have not chosen to focus our talents in this way. If we can make athletic shoes for every sport, for every taste, and for every conceivable training environment, we can make cities and nurture diverse natural systems, too. We can develop citymaking models that take into account evolving business needs, residential diversity, and environmental appropriateness. We just have to decide that this is a task deserving of our attention and resources. I do not intend to trivialize the complexity and potential cost of thinking anew about growth, entrepreneurialism, and public investment. But business-as-usual is simply failing to deliver.

Can we really know the net employment or wealth-creating effect of refocusing our human endeavors to rebuild natural systems? No matter what anyone says, it's too soon to say. In fact, we'll likely have to make many important decisions on the basis of incomplete information. The data will never be good enough.

The big decisions will ultimately be ours as a society to make: What kind of people do we want to be? What kind of place do we want to have in the world? What resources are we conserving? What natural environments are we leaving less sullied for our children? After all, in an economically close-knit world, America's choices have powerful consequences.

EPILOGUE
Tools to Build Civic Engagement

In taking action, especially large-scale action, few communities know how to reconcile change with the understandable fear of neighborhoods and individuals that they will bear the brunt of the burdens. Since climate change and other environmental challenges will force large and complex actions upon us, it is essential to improve the way citizens and leaders work with each other.

Many cities inspire take-no-prisoners, stop-everything activism because they rely too much on public hearings, a classic top-down, "we know best" technique that asks citizens only to respond to proposals. Hearings are supposed to inform officials, but there is no real dialogue and almost no way that citizens can be involved from the beginning of the development process or in weighing alternatives. At best, hearings become a forum for citizens to put pressure on officials, usually to say no.

Other cities have built so many overlapping layers of citizen consultation that it seems process is the only product and citizens' entire power lies in gumming up the works. To no one's surprise, people involved in planning that is only consultative and "bottom-up" usually endorse the way things are because they fear the new. In citizen-driven processes, no one is empowered to lead, it's not easy to vet ideas, and different ways of thinking have a tough time penetrating the defensive carapace. "Yes" too often entails a Solomonic division of interest-group spoils, which can be disastrous in urban-design terms: a commercial project too compromised to succeed economically, a precious piece of land "saved" but with no financial resources for its upkeep or to let it serve its intended public function.

Neither top-down nor citizen-driven ways of operating are up to the challenge of the future by themselves. Here are a few ways to inject innovative and dispute-resolving ideas of entrepreneurs, experts, and leaders into debates that fully and honestly engage citizens in taking the future of their communities in hand.

CHARETTES

Contentious project? Get everyone who has a stake in a project in a room (whether disposed to be pro- or anti-), and get them to work intensively together. Though it sounds like a recipe for a riot, it's a charette, a workshop with the power to end fulminations and find common ground.

Citizens want to know how big? How dense? How much traffic? What happens to the view? When well led through the issues ("facilitated," in the wonky parlance), the workshop answers everyone's questions and engages concerns in concrete terms that everyone can understand. That's because sketches, models, and maps are the tools of the discussion. People are much more likely to understand their opponents' point of view when they work together and see the implications of actions (in those models and drawings) and when they can explore what-ifs by playing with blocks standing in for buildings and by sketching over maps.

Citizens find out that developers are not ogres, and politicians find out that constituents can utter words other than *no*. At the least, charettes discover areas of common agreement among many parties, which allows the workshop to hone in on the difficult issues. The group will often find an answer to a difficult question that no one would have come up with alone. The outcome inevitably entails compromise but typically identifies a more direct and compelling course of action than would have come out of the usual adversarial political process.

Charettes are especially useful as a visioning tool, or to address key questions when a development, say, or a rezoning is first considered: What do we want this place to be? How do we address this problem? A charette can come up with a set of recommendations or a broad vision; it can express a consensus.

Charettes do not replace conventional planning processes. They are a way to get stakeholders involved and to clarify the nature of the problem or the issue. Charettes run by self-organized planning teams after 9/11 dug up many meaningful ideas that would ultimately inform official plans for Ground Zero—but only after official plans, conceived without significant public consultation, foundered.

In late 2006, twelve planning teams fanned out all over New Orleans and successfully used charettes to create visions for rebuilding after Hurricane Katrina. The neighborhood plans helped bring to the fore all kinds of unique local qualities that, if nurtured, could attract residents and investment. These plans were amalgamated into what would become the Unified New Orleans Plan. The charettes could have engaged the really difficult political question of how to rebuild in low-lying, flood-vulnerable areas, where many people might never return. It would have been a very difficult and wrenching process, but one that could well define a viable, consensus-driven future for low-ground areas and dispel people's enormous distrust of officials' intentions by getting clear commitments. Officials feared engaging this question, and it was set aside. Avoiding that issue stunted the city's rebuilding.

CONVENING LEADERSHIP

Cities need not recruit a new Robert Moses (the New York City building czar who built parks, rammed through highways, and mowed down slums, displacing hundreds of thousands in often futile urban "renewal") to bulldoze our way to gleaming new eco-cities. We don't need messianic certainty about what must be done. Cities need to convene leaders, foster innovation, and seek consensus to cope with diverse problems at diverse scales. There are surprisingly few ways to do this systematically now. After seeing the Mayors' Institute on City Design in action, I became a convert. A partnership of the US Conference of Mayors, the American Architectural Foundation, and the National Endowment of the Arts, the Mayors' Institute does one simple thing: it puts a mayor with a carefully honed project or problem in a room for a couple of hours with a dozen experts in the fields of architecture, planning, landscape architecture, art, and urban development. There's no political entourage permitted, no audience, no press. The participants toss the issue around in a freewheeling, no-holds-barred session. The mayors discard stump-speech rhetoric because none of their voters are in the room.

Few political figures know the power of design to unite constituencies, to create energy, and to resolve sticky problems. So the mayors usually leave their sessions surprised and energized, not with a fully formed answer to the problem but with some smart ways to get to the answer.

I was particularly impressed by what happened to one mayor. He had arrived with considerable skepticism, fearing that the Institute was a hot-air, big-government waste of time. He emerged from his session with wonderment, having understood a completely new way to engage a problem that had vexed his city for some time. Another mayor asked: "Can I bring my whole city council?" That was not a bad idea, though no one's figured out how to replicate the experience with a group rather than a single political leader. The program has grown to include a governors' institute.[1]

A short session with experts can't solve a problem, but it opens many possible solutions. That's a starting point. The most brilliant idea cannot come to fruition until it gets funded and survives the political process. That is an ongoing effort, not a one shot. Urban expert Michael Gallis has devised a compelling means to amalgamate the wisdom of citizens, experts, and leaders in an ongoing way. In the process of creating vision or framework plans that place the issues of cities, regions, and even states in a global context, he solicits wide-ranging viewpoints, as many planners do, but in a unique manner.

For a project in New Jersey, I observed a workshop on education. He had gathered people concerned about all levels of education from public institutions, private firms, foundations, advocacy groups, and government agencies. Before he asked the participants to contribute, he took them through a presentation of what he had already learned from data gathering and previous workshops. He talked about education, but also about the state's economy, its cultural and recreational resources—some dozen categories of issues in all. I was mystified. What do educators care about convention centers or economic development? The participants were riveted, however, and the conversation became more animated, insightful, and candid because they had learned a great deal and they had realized that they could participate outside their areas of expertise. They were thrilled to put their aspirations and concerns into broader, more integrated contexts—ones that offered alternatives to tired, unending debates.

Gallis presents his information graphically, primarily in maps, which helps people instantly understand the scale of large, otherwise abstract issues. He could show that the state's costly and much-touted farmland preservation plan had failed to reach its potential because the program had purchased discrete plots rather than parcels that could be chained together into an economically viable agricultural zone. No one had ever mapped the farm program holdings before. In another state, Gallis mapped the road projects of three counties. It showed that the new roads would collide in an unholy mess. None of the counties had realized this because they had never looked at what their neighbors were doing. More to the point, people who participate in workshops on a single concern could see the larger patterns that Gallis was able to reveal. They could see the common roots in what had always looked like separate problems. Certain issues were amenable to resolution in ways no one had thought of.

There is no reason communities and regions cannot convene themselves in a similar but ongoing way. The metropolitan planning organizations that decide how billions of urban transportation dollars get spent operate in a vacuum, usually out of public view. That's how wasteful decisions get made. Cities and regions can build collaborative, systematic planning infrastructures that involve citizens, civic leaders, business, and government and that cross disciplines and political boundaries to consider issues at the scale at which they present themselves. Such a way of focusing on the future can lead us away from the tunnel-vision, problem-focused, reactive ways communities operate today.

DESIGN COMPETITIONS

A public design competition can be a useful yet economical way to bring new ideas into the development mix. Instead of hiring an architect through qualifications, referrals, and interviews alone, an owner of a building site, whether public or private, can invite landscape architects, planners, urban designers, architects, and any other design professionals to submit a design that responds to the owner's program. When competitions work well, the winning design will come up with an utterly new synthesis that responds to the owner's needs in some unanticipated way. It took a design competition, won by Daniel Libeskind, to move the rebuilding process at Ground Zero from a fast descent into stalemate to one that united people's diverse aspirations. (It didn't work out as well as planned, but that's another story.)

Arguably, the best park built in the last decade or so is Olympic Sculpture Park, in Seattle, which repurposed a long-derelict oil-storage site near downtown into a richly varied landscape where art resonates with the restless activity of downtown and bracing panoramas of Elliott Bay and the distant Olympic Mountains. It was the kind of design, by New York City architect Weiss/Manfredi, that probably would not have emerged from a conventional architect-selection process. It was the winner of a competition sponsored by the National Endowment for the Arts. As we try to find new ways to repair nature while accommodating human needs, competitions could be tools of inestimable value.

Competitions can be invited: the sponsor asks only a small number of firms or teams to compete, ones that can assemble unique talents and skills. Or they can be wide open, soliciting designs from any firm anywhere. The design of the Sydney Opera House, among the most famous buildings of the twentieth century, was selected in an open competition, won by a young, at the time little-known Dane, Jørn Utzon.

Competitions for the design of public buildings and new neighborhoods are common in Europe. The prevalence of competitions tends to favor striking designs, innovative approaches, and designers with new ideas—and in this way helps young designers succeed, which overall helps to create a more competitive design culture. Design competitions have become a way to move green innovation rapidly into the mainstream.

Design by competition has its perils. What seems on the surface a brilliant approach may not address all the requirements in detail. Or the requirements and budget are poorly spelled out, which almost sunk the Sydney project. Americans use competitions sparingly, concerned that competitors miss opportunities that would reveal themselves in a more intimate architect-client collaboration. Certainly, this can be true, but technical committees can evaluate detailed performance criteria, while a design jury evaluates the way the project meets the sponsors' articulated needs and how it fits into the city. Of course, no winning proposal need be built exactly as presented. Working closely with the people who will use the building, the architect can refine the design.

The General Services Administration has invigorated public-building design by using invited design competitions. Competitions are one element of its Design Excellence program, which makes use of peer-review panels to vet the designs. Courthouses, for example, need to be publicly appealing and dignified buildings, but experts must also make sure they sequester juries properly, keep judges safe, and hold prisoners securely.

The greatest advantage of competitions is simply to bring in new thinking. Many organizations run "ideas" competitions, especially in the realm of environmentally sustainable buildings, and they are useful to expose a broad public to emerging and innovative possibilities. Since the winning schemes of such competitions are almost never built, the ideas are not subject to trial by cost or ultimate performance, and so ideas competitions too often have limited value.

BUILDING EXHIBITIONS

The United States does little research on buildings, even in the area of energy conservation. You can prototype technologies in a lab—and America should be doing much more of that—but a great building idea can't live until its construction techniques and costs are tested by erecting it in a real place, with real people using it and living in it. A building exhibition is a neighborhood or series of projects that are built precisely to test new ideas. People can see, feel, and touch what new ideas look like. You can find out what they are like to live in. You can try out technologies, tweak them, and replace them. In other words, you can learn from what works and doesn't work.

Building exhibitions are a means to build and test innovations at a larger scale than a prototype. Those innovations can be technical, like new energy-saving concepts, or the project can try to answer difficult questions in new ways: What could a hurricane-resistant neighborhood built on high ground in New Orleans be? How could it fit within the existing pattern of streets and blocks? There actually was such a competition, but it regrettably languishes in the realm of "ideas."[2]

Such projects have a history in Europe, where neighborhoods have been built to test new technologies and ways of living, especially as Modern architecture emerged in the 1920s. In an era of fetid, disease-ridden, overcrowded cities, the Wiessenhof Siedlung in Stuttgart famously showed off well-lit, well-ventilated homes affordable to families of modest means. It introduced functional, modern kitchens and a less-formal, outdoors-oriented lifestyle.

In the 1980s, Berlin launched the International Building Exhibition (IBA), in which dozens of architects worldwide competed to build some three hundred housing projects to inspire new investment in forgotten corners of the city. The housing became influential worldwide because it demonstrated the diverse ways new architecture that served new needs could gracefully energize older, declining neighborhoods. Many knit together blocks that had been fragmented by wartime bombing decades earlier.

The IBA would prove to have unexpected importance. It was conceived well before the city had any hope of reunification, but its lessons were ready-made for application to the much-larger project of knitting the divided city back together once the Berlin Wall came down.

In recent years, the Swedish city of Malmö hosted Bo01, a housing exhibition specifically to showcase environmental sustainability. And a truly vast, nine billion euro "building exhibition" focuses on a moonscape of craters—twenty-two by fifty miles—left by closed surface coal mines in the Lusatia district of former East Germany. Rerouted rivers fill the old mines with water to create a new lake district. It seeks to draw visitors and holiday home builders to a region that's steadily lost population.[3]

About as close as we get in the United States are those "street of dreams" developments that builders erect primarily to test the acceptance of new interior design looks and lifestyle accoutrements. Housing exhibitions could do much more. You could argue that the prototype houses in New Orleans, including the Global Green and Make It Right developments (part 2 opener), constituted a kind of housing exhibition, and to a significant degree, they have had a similarly inspiring effect. Had they been backed by deep research and scaled up with adequate funding, their influence could have run much wider and deeper, and they could have created markets for many of their green tactics.

There are many variants on the concepts I have described. None are perfect, especially in the absence of public trust, of real commitment by government officials, of involvement by civic leaders and local business. Involving everyone with passion, commitment, and ideas in an honest, ongoing give-and-take will engage new ideas and find consensus. Then, do it again and again. In the final analysis, that's how our concrete metropolises will become agile cities.

NOTES

PROLOGUE

1. Kroon Hall information from visit, April 2009; interview with Mike Taylor, Hopkins Architects; Yale University press information; and Mark Simon, Centerbrook Architects. See also James S. Russell, "Yale's Rustic Kroon Hall Fits Carbon Neutral Technology," *Bloomberg*, July 20, 2009; Russell, "Carbon Neutral Now," *Metropolis*, October 2009, 72–79. There are several climate-changing greenhouse gases, but carbon dioxide (CO_2), which results in large part from the burning of fossil fuels, is the most prevalent and damaging and thus is the focus of this book.

2. Information on Dockside Green from author visit July 2008 and interviews with architect Peter Busby and developer Joe Van Belleghem pursuant to Russell, "Green Project in B.C. Burns Sawdust, Treats Sewage in Backyard," *Bloomberg*, August 15, 2008; and Russell, "Carbon Neutral Now."

INTRODUCTION

1. Commercial and residential buildings were responsible for 39 percent of greenhouse gas emissions in 2008 according to the Energy Information Administration's annual report (December 3, 2009). All transportation emissions added up to 33 percent. Coal's contribution to emissions is more than 36 percent, and most of that is used to generate electricity, almost all of which powers buildings.

2. Christopher Leinberger, *The Option of Urbanism: Investing in a New American Dream* (Washington, DC: Island Press, 2009), 35.

3. The World Bank predicted that the annual world gross domestic product in the first decade of this century would grow by one-third. Instead, it almost

doubled by 2008, to $61.3 trillion. World Bank, World Development indicators, January 2010, http://data.worldbank.org/indicator/NY.GDP.MKTP.CD/.

4. The World Wildlife Fund's Living Planet Index expresses the rapid growth in nations' sourcing natural resources outside their borders. In 1961, the global footprint was 8 percent of goods and services traded. It had risen to 40 percent by 2005. World Wildlife Fund, "Living Planet Report," 28, http://www .panda.org.

5. "The N-11: More than an Acronym," Goldman Sachs Global Economics Paper no. 153 (March 28, 2007), accessed via Wikipedia, topic "BRICs."

6. World Wildlife Fund, "Living Planet Index," 2.

7. Steven Solomon, *Water: The Epic Struggle for Wealth, Power, and Civilization* (New York: Harper, 2010). Holland, for example, is deeply concerned about saltwater intrusion according to water management experts and documents presented on a congressional delegation tour attended by the author, May 2009.

8. A combination of climate-regulation uncertainty and rapidly rising demand, especially by China, points the world toward an oil-supply crunch, according to Antony Froggatt and Glada Lahn (lead authors), "Sustainable Energy Security: Strategic Risks and Opportunities for Business," July 2010, white paper published by Lloyd's, the global specialist insurer, available at http://www .chathamhouse.org.uk/publications/papers/view/-/id/891/.

9. Even in landscapes that appear to be healthy, human exploitation alters the ecological dynamic in ways that seem benign but that trigger irreversible harm. Ferocious and mysterious dust storms in the 1930s drove waves of people out of midwestern prairies. They were catastrophic because farmers had plowed under the native sod that held the soil in place. Populations have never returned to 1920s highs, and people continue to leave many Plains counties. Ian Frazier, *Great Plains* (New York: Picador, 1989). Frank Popper and Deborah Popper continue to document Plains depopulation in web pages devoted to their Buffalo Commons idea: http://policy.rutgers.edu/faculty /popper/.

10. Spruce budworm spread, presentation by Daniel Schrag, professor of earth and planetary sciences, Harvard University, at Lincoln Institute of Land Policy, April 2008.

11. Michael Gallis & associates, "Co-Evolution: Creating a New Framework for Shaping Our Future," American Forests Ecosystem Center, US Forest Service State and Private Forestry (2009), http://www.americanforest.org/Co-Evolution/.

12. Pollution alone costs China 10 percent of its gross domestic product, and air pollution alone shortens the lives of more than seven hundred thousand

people every year. "Pollution Costs Equal 10% of China's GDP," *Shanghai Daily*, June 6, 2006; Mun S. Ho and Dale W. Jorgenson, "Green China: Market-based Policies for Air Pollution Control," *Harvard Magazine*, September-October 2008, http://harvardmagazine.com/2008/09/greening-china/.

13. The World Wildlife Fund's "Living Planet Report" shows the degree to which the world's productive capacity and its environmental challenges have intertwined: "In 1961 almost all the countries in the world had more than enough capacity to meet their own demand; by 2005 the situation had changed radically, with many countries able to meet their needs only by importing resources from other nations" (pp. 2–3).

14. Low-efficiency/high-impact discussions by the author with Michael Gallis in 2009. Humanity's tendency to exploit resources to extinction is widely known as "the failure of the commons." A growing literature exists on why such failures happen and on tactics that reverse the failures before the resource collapses.

15. A number of measures help us see the big picture, including the measures of biocapacity and our "ecological footprint." Because each American's footprint is about 22 acres (9 hectares), compared to 6.4 acres (2.6 hectares) for the total human population, America has a long way to go. (The consensus today is that it would take five more planet earths to provide the world's population with a footprint equivalent to America's.) Ecological footprint numbers 2009 from Global Footprint network, http://www.footprintnetwork.org.

CHAPTER 1

1. Author observations and interviews as participant in the congressional delegation tour described, May 25–30, 2009.

2. Coastal marsh loss from Department of Natural Resources, Office of Coastal Management, "Louisiana Coastal Facts," http://dnr.louisiana.gov/index.cfm?d=pagebuilder&tmp=home&pid=99&pnid=0&nid=51.

3. *Lucas v. South Carolina Coastal Council* (91-453), 505 U.S. 1003 (1992), Cornell University Law School Supreme Court Collection, http://www.law.cornell.edu/supct/html/91-453.ZO.html.

4. Roger Pielke Jr. et al., "Normalized Hurricane Damage in the United States: 1900–2005," http://www.nhc.noaa.gov/pdf/NormalizedHurricane2008.pdf.

5. Joseph Ellis, "The Big Man" (review of Library of America's edition of Alexander Hamilton's *Writings*), *New Yorker*, October 29, 2001. Ellis is a prominent historian of America's founding era and is the author of *Founding Brothers* (Knopf), among others.

6. This argument was focused for me by Jerold Kayden, a professor of urban planning and design at Harvard University's Graduate School of Design, in a presentation at the Perspectives on Property Rights, Growth and Regulation conference held at the Lincoln Institute of Land Policy, in Cambridge, Massachusetts, April 26, 2007.

7. See Sam Bass Warner Jr., *The Private City: Philadelphia in Three Periods of Its Growth* (Philadelphia: University of Philadelphia Press, 1968).

8. Tour with Eskew, January 8, 2006; some material first appeared in James S. Russell, "Can Shrinking Footprint Save New Orleans?," *Bloomberg*, January 23, 2006.

9. Kevin McCarthy, D. J. Peterson, Narayan Sastry, and Michael Pollard, "The Repopulation of New Orleans after Hurricane Katrina," Rand Gulf States Policy Institute, Rand Corporation (2006), http://www.rand.org/content/dam/rand/pubs/technical_reports/2006/RAND_TR369.pdf.

10. Volunteer experts from the Urban Land Institute, Washington, DC, made the proposal in November 2005. In a less politically charged form, it resurfaced in Wallace Roberts & Todd, Master Planner, "Action Plan for New Orleans: The New American City," Bring New Orleans Back Commission, January 11, 2006.

11. Amy Liu and Allison Plyer, "The New Orleans Index at Five," Brookings Institute, August 2010, http://www.brookings.edu/reports/2007/08neworleansindex.aspx.

12. *The First Part of the Institutes of the Laws of England, or, a Commentary upon Littleton* (1628).

13. Legendary Supreme Court cases that considered these issues included *Pennsylvania Coal Co. v. Mahon* and *Fountainbleu v. Forty-Five Twenty Five*, discussed in Richard Tseng-Yu Lai, *Law in Urban Design and Planning: The Invisible Web* (New York: Van Nostrand Reinhold, 1988). Other cases developed the idea that pollution harms health and is therefore a "nuisance" that can be regulated without being deemed a "taking," as described in the Constitution's Fifth Amendment, which would require government compensation to parties aggrieved by the regulation.

14. Lai, *Law in Urban Design and Planning*, ch. 7.

15. Lai, *Law in Urban Design and Planning*, ch. 3.

16. The material in this section is derived and augmented from reporting for James S. Russell, "Whose Property Rights?" *Metropolis*, March 2008.

17. Andrea Sarzynski, Marilyn A. Brown, and Frank Southworth, "Shrinking the Carbon Footprint of Metropolitan America," Brookings Institute, May 29, 2008, http://www.brookings.edu/reports/2008/05_carbon_footprint_sarzynski.aspx.

18. Meeting with Van Asche at his farm in Hillsboro, Oregon, January 7, 2007.

19. Interview with David Renhard, an editor at the (Portland) *Oregonian* who has extensively covered land use controversies, January 2007.

20. From interview with Robert Stacey, president of the environmental group 1,000 Friends of Oregon, January 4, 2007.

21. $20 billion figure from "Summaries of Claims" document on Measure 37: http://www.oregon.gov/LCD/MEASURE37/summaries_of_claims.shtml.

22. Jerold Kayden presentation at Perspectives on Property Rights, Growth and Regulation conference.

23. Joel Garreau, *Edge City: Life on the New Frontier* (New York: Doubleday, 1991), 382.

24. Phone interview with Jacobs, January 8, 2008.

25. Phone interview with Stachon, January 2007.

26. Phone interview with David Hunnicut, Oregonians in Action, January 3, 2007.

27. Phone interview with Carbonell, December 11, 2009.

CHAPTER 2

1. Information from "Salmon Recovery Plan Implementation," 2008 data, on Washington State Salmon Recovery home page, http://www.rco.wa.gov /salmon_recovery/index.shtml.

2. Farmlink and Puget Sound Fresh are operated by a nonprofit, the Cascade Harvest Coalition, http://www.cascadeharvest.org.

3. "Salmon Recovery Plan Implementation."

4. On integrating farmland flood control and salmon recovery, see King County's "Snoqualmie Flood-Farm Task Force Report" (January 2008), http://www .kingcounty.gov/environment/waterandland/agriculture/documents/farm -flood-task-force-report.aspx. On integrating salmon recovery and climate change: author interview with Tom Hauger, manager of comprehensive and regional planning, January 4, 2010.

5. The Salmon Recovery Program assessment by the White House, referred to in a May 29, 2009, letter by local members of Congress, is described as "slow."

6. Keith Ervin, "Court Decision Sparks Debate on Use of Rural Lands," *Seattle Times*, March 5, 2009, http://seattletimes.nwsource.com/html/localnews /2008814562_rural05m.html.

7. This section was developed through a visit with Stevens in California in February 2008 and several telephone interviews for James S. Russell, "Blending Nature with Development," *American Forests*, Spring 2007, and follow-ups in fall 2009.

8. Author interview with Briechle by telephone, December 2009.

9. Author interview with Palmer, February 2007, pursuant to Russell, "Blending Nature with Development," and updated January 2010.

10. Ian L. McHarg, *Design with Nature* (Garden City, NY: Natural History Press, 1969), 7–17; numerous works by Orrin Pilkey, who formerly headed the Program for Developed Shorelines, jointly located at Duke University and Western Carolina University, have also sounded the alarm about beaches over decades.

11. Alexandra Wolfe and Blair Golson, "Dune, Where's My Hampton? It's Seceding!" *New York Observer,* August 24, 2003.

12. Ernest B. Abbott, "Floods, Flood Insurance, Litigation, Politics—and Catastrophe: The National Flood Insurance Program," *Sea Grant Law and Policy Journal* 1 (2008): 130, http://nsglc.olemiss.edu/SGLPJ/Vol1No1/7Abbott.pdf.

13. Matthew Heberger et al., The Pacific Institute "The Impact of Sea-level Rise on the California Coast" (March 2009), http://www.pacinst.org/reports/sea_level_rise/.

14. National Oceanic and Atmospheric Administration, "Managed Retreat Strategies" (2007), http://coastalmanagement.noaa.gov/initiatives/shoreline_ppr_retreat.html.

15. "Valmeyer, Illinois," case study on Operation Fresh Start website, dedicated to assisting communities postdisaster: http://www.freshstart.ncat.org/case/valmeyer.htm.

16. Land trusts and transfers of development rights are well-established and widely used tools, with a large literature that considers their use.

17. Yu-Hong and Barrie Needham, *Land Readjustment: Analyzing Land Readjustment: Economics, Law, and Collective Action* (Cambridge, MA: Lincoln Institute of Land Policy, 2007).

18. Natural Resources Defense Council, "Chesapeake Bay's Health Threats Need Federal Remedy," press release, October 8, 2009.

19. Author interview with Frank and Deborah Popper, February 12, 2010.

20. Challenges to farming from the Popper interview and from "New National Park Could Save High Plains in Kansas," an editorial in the *Kansas City Star*, November 14, 2009.

21. Prairie reserve: American Prairie Foundation website, http://www.americanprairie.org; Tom Lutey, "Ranchers Wary of Group's Effort to Create Wildlife Reserve Bigger than Yellowstone," *Billings* [Mont.] *Gazette*, December 20, 2009.

PART 2

1. Harvey L. Molotch, "The City as a Growth Machine," in John R. Logan and Harvey L. Molotch, *Urban Fortunes: The Political Economy of Place* (Berkeley: University of California Press, 1987), ch. 3.

CHAPTER 3

1. James S. Russell, "Along Ravaged Gulf, Young Architects, Nonprofits Lead Renewal," *Bloomberg*, December 26, 2007.
2. Russell, "Along Ravaged Gulf," Author revisited the Global Green houses in August 2010.
3. The Federal Housing Administration, a New Deal program, began making insured loans in 1934. Kenneth T. Jackson, *Crabgrass Frontier: The Suburbanization of the United States* (New York: Oxford University Press, 1985), 203.
4. Joint Center for Housing Studies, Harvard University, *State of the Nation's Housing 2009*, 14–15, http://www.jchs.harvard.edu/publications/markets/son 2009/son2009.pdf. SONH is one of many resources that show the importance of home equity to personal wealth, especially for middle-income earners.
5. Deductible items are enumerated in many places, including "JCS 1–10: Estimates of Federal Tax Expenditures for Fiscal Years 2009–2013," prepared by the Joint Committee on Taxation, Congress of the United States, January 11, 2010, http://www.jct.gov/publications.html?func=startdown&id=3642/.
6. Deductions for homeowners: Canada Revenue Agency, "Topics for Homeowners," http://www.cra-arc.gc.ca/tx/ndvdls/sgmnts/hmwnr/menu-eng.html. Canadian homeownership rates: 68 percent in 2008, Statistics Canada, "2006 Census: Changing Patterns in Canadian Homeownership and Shelter Costs," June 4, 2008, http://www.statcan.gc.ca/daily-quotidien/080604 /dq080604a-eng.htm. US homeownership rate peaked in 2004 at just over 69 percent but had dropped to 67.3 percent by the last quarter of 2009, according to the *New York Times* Economix blog sourcing Census data, February 2, 2010.
7. Cost of homeowner tax benefits from "JCS 1-10." Congress allocated $6 billion to a Neighborhood Stabilization Program in 2008 and 2009 economic-stimulus packages. The $8,000 home-buyer tax credit was later sweetened with a $6,500 credit for existing owners who wanted to buy. The figure for the cost of the tax credit is the author's estimate based on $12.6 billion of expenditures four months before the program expired in June 2010. In that month, experts estimated that the federal government may have bad mortgage obligations on the books of Fannie Mae and Freddie Mac that will ultimately exceed the value of the $780 billion TARP bank bailout program.
8. More information on Leinberger and real-estate finance in James S. Russell, "Follow the Money," *Architectural Record*, June 2003, 98–104, as well as Leinberger's own writings.
9. The nineteen lender-friendly building types are described in Christopher Leinberger, *The Option of Urbanism: Investing in a New American Dream* (Washington, DC: Island Press, 2008), ch. 3.

10. "Second Largest Failure," *Bloomberg* data.

11. According to Leinberger, an accounting methodology called Discounted Cash Flow (DCF) also undercuts the idea of buildings as long-term investments. Christopher Leinberger, "Financing Progressive Development and Affordable Housing," white paper for Brookings Institution, May 2001.

12. Urban analyst Larry Frank had completed a housing survey in Atlanta in 2000, finding that some 37 percent of respondents wanted to live in mixed-use, walkable, transit-served neighborhoods—places that barely existed in the city at that time. The failure of the real estate development industry to respond to this desire he called "clearly a market failure" in an interview on March 20, 2003. "Transportation and Land-Use Preferences and Atlanta Residents' Neighborhood Choices," SMARTRAQ (Strategies for Metropolitan Atlanta's Transportation and Air Quality), March 2004, http://www.act-trans.ubc.ca /research.htm.

13. Author phone interview with Leinberger, August 19, 2009.

14. According to the Congress for the New Urbanism, Fannie Mae and Freddie Mac, agencies that bought a high percentage of mortgages with implicit government backing, avoided loans originated for projects that mixed retail with residential that were in downtowns or mixed-use revitalizing neighborhoods. "CNU Joins Call for Action on Fannie Mae and Freddie Mac Loans," *New Urban News,* January 28, 2010. Loans blessed by Fannie and Freddie usually had lower borrowing costs. The agencies had to be taken over by the government after the mortgage meltdown.

15. Author interview with Davis at Seaside, February 2003.

16. Author visit to Unilever, April 2010, and interview with Peter Schlaier, manager of the project for Behnisch Architekten. Comparison to American usage from "Sector Collaborative on Energy Efficiency Accomplishments and Next Steps: A Resource of the National Action Plan for Energy Efficiency," US Environmental Protection Agency, July 2008, B-1, http://www.epa.gov /cleanenergy/documents/suca/sector_collaborative.pdf.

17. Information from Friedemann came from a presentation he made during an April 2010 tour in Germany sponsored by the Ecologic Institute, a Berlin-based think tank.

18. Russell, "With His Sleek, Ecological Design, Lord Norman Foster Imbues the Reichstag with Germany's New Self-Image," *Architectural Record,* July 1999, 102–13.

19. Friedemann discussed energy codes in terms of German investment norms on April 12, 2010, as part of the Ecologic Institute tour.

20. Though renting can be significantly less than the cost of owning equivalent space, owning at fast-growing urban edges is often correctly advertised as less expensive than renting, after taking tax advantages into account.

21. HUD data shows median new-home prices (ranging from $220,000 to over $300,000) running at or below what a family earning the median income (roughly $50,000 or so over the 2000s) could afford with a 10 percent down payment and a thirty-year fixed mortgage. Average home prices were much higher in most large metro areas, which meant lower-income residents were crammed into older, low-income enclaves—and why those enclaves were devastated by subprime and exotic loan products that could be sustained only under boom conditions.

22. "Federal funding for direct rental assistance has been declining or unstable in recent years," according to Joint Center for Housing Studies, Harvard University, *State of the Nation's Housing 2009*, 30. "As of 2008, 4.7 million renters—roughly a quarter of those eligible—received such assistance. Moreover, spending on low-income housing as a share of the domestic discretionary budget has fallen more than 20 percent since 1995." The primary low-income housing program, called Section 8, has treaded water for years. The Low-Income Housing Tax Credit, which generated cash primarily from banks seeking to shelter income from taxes, collapsed along with the fortunes of banks, though it received an infusion of aid from the Obama administration as an economic stimulus. Its future is unknown at this writing, but there is no evident effort to dramatically increase aid for people who fall much below median income.

23. "By 2007, fully 30 percent of all homeowners were at least moderately burdened, and 12 percent were severely burdened. Even so, the share of renters with severe burdens remained nearly twice as high as that of owners, despite a modest 0.6 percentage point dip from 2005 to 2007." *State of the Nation's Housing 2009*, 26.

24. Joel Warren Barna, *The See Through Years: Creation and Destruction in Texas Architecture and Real Estate 1981–1991* (Houston: Rice University Press, 1992), 31.

25. Groups as diverse as the Silicon Valley Manufacturers' Association and the "Chicago 2020" report of the area's Commercial Club advocate much-expanded affordable housing initiatives as a means of diversifying their workforce choices. Similar complaints were loudly voiced as a major growth impediment for businesses in New Jersey during a planning project I was part of. There is also a large planning literature on metropolitan jobs/housing imbalances.

26. KfW lending from presentation by Christine Willembrook, of the German Ministry of Transport, Buildings and Urban Development, April 14, 2010, Ecologic Institute tour.

27. Author phone interview with Leinberger, August 19, 2009.

28. Interview with Palmer, February 12, 2007.

29. Stapleton community information from its website: http://discover .stapletondenver.com.

CHAPTER 4

1. Tunnel project cost and SR 520 bridge project from Washington State Department of Transportation: http://www.wsdot.wa.gov/projects/viaduct/ and http://www.wsdot.wa.gov/projects/sr520bridge/. I-405 figure is from 2003 estimate of total project, which does not appear to have been updated. Transit plan from "Sound Transit Capital Projects" page of Sound Transit website: http://projects.soundtransit.org.

2. The state's prediction of few new vehicles on the enlarged 520 is predicated on a great number of passengers switching to buses because of high tolls, but the required level of bus service is not guaranteed and tolls have been neither specified nor agreed to.

3. Light-rail timing from published schedule. Rider costs from Larry Lange, "Light Rail's Million Dollar Launch," *Seattle Post-Intelligencer*, July 16, 2009, ridership from Sound Transit tally for April and May 2010 (highest since opening).

4. Frequency of Canada line ridership from published schedule. Airport line ridership: "Canada Line Delivers a Smooth Ride," *Toronto Globe and Mail*, December 28, 2009.

5. Reid Ewing et al., "Growing Cooler: The Evidence on Urban Development and Climate Change," Urban Land Institute (2008), 17, http://dnr.wi.gov /environmentprotect/gtfgw/documents/GrowingCoolerEs.pdf.

6. Iver Peterson, "In New Jersey, Sprawl Keeps Outflanking Its Foes," *New York Times*, March 17, 2000. Author later visited the campus and its surroundings.

7. The proposal by then New Jersey governor Jon Corzine to raise transportation funds through increases on the state's toll roads was heavily debated in 2008 and 2009.

8. The implication of elegantly circular beltways is that cities grow outward evenly, like tree rings. Instead, as famously documented in 1939 by Homer Hoyt, cities tend to grow in uneven wedges, along transportation trunklines. The most rapid and affluent growth extends the "favored sector" of the city (where high-income neighborhoods, universities, and cultural centers tend to cluster) outward into the suburbs.

9. Author experienced this firsthand in January 2007.

10. Washington, DC, growth in proximity to Metro: author interview with Lang, August 2004.

11. Rail emissions from Association of American Railroads citing the US Environmental Protection Agency.

12. First brought to my attention by Vancouver architect Peter Busby in 2002, who designed two stations on the city's Millennium Line. TransLink, the operating company for the line, continued to run surpluses in later years, according to the Wikipedia entry on the Skytrain, referencing the company's operating reports.

13. Ewing et al., "Growing Cooler," 33, 35. Visioning California: Calthorpe Associates, "Vision California/Charting Our Future: Statewide Scenarios Report," revision of May 12, 2010, http://www.visioncalifornia.org and http://www.calthorpe.com/vision-california.

14. Ewing et al., "Growing Cooler," 44.

15. Zeke Hausfather, "Hybrid Car? Or All Electric Vehicle? They All Take Energy? How Should You Decide?" Yale Forum on Climate Change and the Media, September 28, 2009, http://www.yaleclimatemediaforum.org/2009/09/hybrid-all-electric-vehicles.

16. The federal fuel tax has not gone up since 1997, and few states have raised their tax rates either. Congress has spent more than the Federal Highway Trust Fund takes in fuel taxes since 1995. Decline in user-fee support: "Analysis Finds Shifting Trends in Highway Funding: User Fees Make Up Decreasing Share," accessed from SubsidyScope, an initiative of the Pew Charitable Trusts, http://subsidyscope.com/transportation/highways/funding. The analysis reflects data from the Federal Highway Administration statistics, 2008.

17. "Public Road Mileage, 1920–2008," *Highway Statistics 2008*, Federal Highway Administration.

18. Author noticed this trend some years ago following an upgrade on NJ Transit commuter lines. Cutting a half hour off the trip to Midtown Manhattan, realtors said, resulted in jumps in house sale prices of as much as 20 percent. Since then, numerous studies and news reports have documented this trend, even into the downturn: Antoinette Martin, "'Transit Cities Face Roadblocks," *New York Times*, June 19, 2009.

19. $305 billion from $0.25 gas tax rise: Congressional Budget Office accessed from a *Washington Post* editorial: "Tax Truth: We Need to Raise the Levy on Gasoline," July 8, 2010.

20. Tom Lewis, *Divided Highways: Building the Interstate Highway System* (New York: Viking, 1997, ch. 4.

21. Telling you where to drive and live: documents posted on "resources" page for the 2010 "Yes on Prop. 23" campaign that would tie implementation of carbon-reduction tactics to reduction in the State of California unemployment rate. The proposal failed at the polls.

CHAPTER 5

1. Brenda Goodman, "Amid a Drought, a Georgian Consumes a Niagara," *New York Times*, November 15, 2007.

2. Shaila Dewan and Brenda Goodman, "New to Being Dry, the South Struggles to Adapt," *New York Times*, October 23, 2007.

3. Water costs: "Splitsville," *National Journal*, May 3, 1997. The raw numbers may have changed, but the cost difference likely remains the same.

4. An extreme example: extending a water main in rural Southold, New York, almost three miles to a twenty-six-home subdivision where the wells had become unacceptably polluted cost $3.8 million, according to Southold Town's application to the federal government for funding.

5. D. L. Bennett, "Atlanta Water, Sewer Rates among Nation's Highest," *Atlanta Journal-Constitution*, October 5, 2009.

6. Joel Garreau, *Edge City: Life on the New Frontier* (New York: Doubleday, 1991), 382.

7. Brenda Goodman, "Georgia Loses Federal Case in a Dispute about Water," *New York Times*, February 6, 2008.

8. Charles Duhigg, "Clean Water Laws Are Neglected at a Cost in Suffering," *New York Times*, September 12, 2009, part of a series on declining water quality in America, "Toxic Waters."

9. Richard Seager et al., "Model Projections of an Imminent Transition to a More Arid Climate in Southwestern North America," *Science*, May 2007.

10. Visit to Omega Institute, August 2009, where author interviewed Backus; http://eomega.org.

11. John Todd Ecological Design, http://toddecological.com.

12. Treatment wetlands: Wetland Solutions Inc., http://wetlandsolutionsinc.com /wwd_treatment_wetlands.html.

13. Kresge visit June 2006 and follow-up interviews with Joe Valerio, architect, Valerio Dewalt Train; Douglas Farr, environmental sustainability consultant, Farr Associates; and Sandy Ambrozy of Kresge.

14. New York City water reductions: Water Conservation FAQ, from New York City Department of Environmental Protection, http://www.nyc.gov/html/dep /pdf/wsstat02c.pdf.

15. "Watershed Protection" page of New York City's Department of Environmental Protection website: http://www.nyc.gov/html/dep/html/watershed_protection /index.shtml; "New York City" page on the Information Center for the Environment website hosted by the University of California, Davis, http://ice.ucdavis .edu/node/133; Anthony De Palma, "For Bronx Water Plant Being Built 10 Stories Down, a Towering Price Tag," *New York Times*, April 24, 2008; Elizabeth Royte, "On the Waterfront," *New York Times*, February 18, 2007.

16. For more information, see the website of the Philadelphia Water Department's Office of Watersheds: http://www.phillywatersheds.org.

17. Author interview with Glen Abrams, March 2009, pursuant to consulting work on GreenPlan Philadelphia, for the Fairmount Park Commission.

18. Heat island effect information from US Environmental Protection Agency, http://www.epa.gov/hiri/.

19. Charles Duhigg, "Sewers at Capacity, Waste Poisons Waterways," *New York Times,* November 23, 2009.

20. "Philadelphia Combined Sewer Overflow Long Term Control Plan Update," Philadelphia Water Department (2007), http://www.phillywatersheds.org /ltcpu/LTCPU_Section09_Alternatives.pdf.

21. Journalists Forum on Climate Change and Cities, at the Lincoln Institute for Land Management, Cambridge, Massachusetts, April 12, 2008.

22. Congressional delegation trip to the Netherlands, presentation by Vrijling in May 2009.

23. The author saw the flood protections on a congressional delegation trip to the Netherlands.

24. Han Meyer, Dale Morris, and David Waggonner, eds., *Dutch Dialogues New Orleans Netherlands: Common Challenges in Urbanized Deltas,* Sun Uitgeverij, Technical University, Delft, the Netherlands (2008) 36 (Noordwaard), 38 (terp project).

25. Author tour of New Orleans potential water management with Diaz and interview with Waggonner, August 2010. See also James S. Russell, "New Orleans Needs Scenic Canals, Not Billions in Levees," *Bloomberg*, September 3, 2010, and Meyer et al., *Dutch Dialogues.*

26. Louisiana Coastal Wetlands Conservation and Restoration Task Force and the Wetlands Conservation and Restoration Authority, "Coast 2050: Toward a Sustainable Coastal Louisiana," http://www.coast2050.gov/2050reports .htm.

27. "Louisiana's Comprehensive Plan for a Sustainable Coast" (2007), 46, accessed from the website of the Coastal Protection and Restoration Authority of Louisiana, http://www.lacpra.org.

28. Author interview with Paul Harrison, Environmental Defense Fund, and trip down the Mississippi River, August 2010.

CHAPTER 6

1. Robert Fishman, *Bourgeois Utopias: The Rise and Fall of Suburbia* (New York: Basic Books, 1987), 182.

2. For suburbanization of poverty, see Steven Raphael and Michael Stoll, "Job Sprawl and the Suburbanization of Poverty," Brookings Institution, March 30, 2010, http://www.brookings.edu/reports/2010/0330_job_sprawl _stoll_raphael.aspx.

3. Schaumberg information from Brenda Case Scheer and Mintcho Petkow, "Edge City Morphology: A Comparison of Commercial Centers," *Journal of the American Planning Association* 64, no. 3 (1998): 298–311.

4. Robert Cervero, *America's Suburban Centers: The Land Use–Transportation Link* (Boston: Unwin Hyman, 1989). Robert Lang offers forty-four names proffered over the decades: Robert E. Lang, *Edgeless Cities: Exploring the Elusive Metropolis* (Washington, DC: Brookings Institution Press, 2003), 31.

5. Joel Garreau, *Edge City: Life on the New Frontier* (New York: Doubleday, 1991), xii.

6. Edge cities were in part a product of generous tax breaks for real estate development enacted by Congress during the Reagan administration. A tax overhaul eliminated the special treatment, and commercial development peaked in 1986, then rapidly declined into a severe real estate recession that bottomed in 1990–91. Edge cities, and all commercial development, have grown more slowly since.

7. Lang, *Edgeless Cities,* 88–95.

8. Fuerst's e-mail exchanges with author, September 2004. His research was published as chapter 3, "The Impact of 9/11 on the Manhattan Office Market," in Howard Chernick, ed., *Resilient City: The Economic Impact of 9/11* (New York: Russell Sage Foundation, 2005).

9. Street corner schmoozing: William H. Whyte, *City: Rediscovering the Center* (New York: Doubleday, 1988).

10. Percent of small space users: Lisa Chamberlain, "Smaller Offices Being Pushed Out of Midtown," *New York Times,* July 19, 2006. Small space users historically: Carol Willis, *Form Follows Finance: Skyscrapers and Skylines in New York and Chicago* (New York: Princeton Architectural Press, 1995), 154.

11. Richard Florida, *The Rise of the Creative Class and How It's Transforming Work, Leisure, Community and Everyday Life* (New York: Basic Books, 2002).

12. "The Blob That Ate Texas," *Economist,* June 21, 2001. The world learned of the risks and complexity of deep-sea drilling in the Deepwater Horizon disaster of spring 2010.

13. Conversation in 2005. Clem sold Lyme Properties in 2007.

14. Whyte, *City: Rediscovering the Center*, ch. 20.

15. Fuerst, "The Impact of 9/11 on the Manhattan Office Market."

16. Author interviewed Lang at the Metropolitan Institute in Arlington, Virginia, August 2004.

17. Lisa W. Foderaro, "Affluent Town Seeks to Curb Development outside its Borders," *New York Times*, March 11, 2000.
18. Author visit to Orlando and interview with Lauten, planner Bruce McLendon, and others, February 2003.
19. Lang, *Edgeless Cities*.
20. Lauten interviewed by telephone, May 2010.

PART 3

1. Author interview with Drey in Atlanta in November 2005.

CHAPTER 7

1. James S. Russell, "Building a House to Withstand a Hurricane," *New York Times*, August 19, 1993.
2. "The Impact of Planning on Building Energy Usage," in Douglas Farr, *Sustainable Urbanism: Urban Design with Nature* (Hoboken, NJ: Wiley, 2008), 189–92.
3. James S. Russell, "Mayne's Flower Power Federal Building," *Bloomberg*, March 2, 2007.
4. David Cohn, "Endesa Headquarters," *Architectural Record*, March 2006.
5. Tour of Riedburg Primary School, Frankfurt, with Bretzke, April 2010, as part of Ecologic Institute tour. Figures provided by Bretzke. A US reference for Passive House standards: Alex Wilson, "The Passive House Arrives in North America: Could It Revolutionize the Way We Build?" BuildingGreen.com, April 1, 2010, http://www.buildinggreen.com/auth/article.cfm/2010/3/31/Passive-House-Arrives-in-North-America-Could-It-Revolutionize-the-Way-We-Build/.
6. On Manitoba Hydro Place: presentation to author by architect KPMB, as well as their website: http://www.kpmbarchitects.com/index.asp?navid=30&fid1=0&fid2=37#credits. See also Charles Linn, "Manitoba Hydro Place," *GreenSource* magazine, March 2010. Monitored energy performance was less than the design goal, running about eighty-eight kilowatt hours per square meter per year, according to correspondence from John Peterson, of KPMB.
7. James S. Russell, "Ballard Library," *Architectural Record*, May 2006, 158–62.
8. William Morrish, Susanne Schindler, and Katie Swenson, *Growing Urban Habitats: Seeking a New Housing Development Model* (San Francisco: William Stout Publishers, 2009), 76–79, and architects' website: http://www.loharchitects.com.

9. Empire State Building: author interview with owner Anthony Malkin and Paul Rode of Johnson Controls, July 2010. "A Landmark Sustainability Program for the Empire State Building," white paper prepared by the ESB retrofit team (2009), http://www.esbsustainability.com. James S. Russell, "King Kong's Perch Goes Green for $20M as Earth Roasts," *Bloomberg*, August 30, 2010.

10. To my knowledge, there is no nationwide tally of the economic contribution of historic preservation, but if you look at the forces that have brought life back to cities left for dead, the key ingredient has been people who fell in love with old neighborhoods and set about restoring them. Revivals in Washington, Philadelphia, Boston, Miami, Chicago, San Francisco, and countless small cities from Savannah and Charleston, to Main Streets in every corner of the United States, did not depend solely on preservation, but preservationists got there first and sowed the seeds of broader economic growth simply by helping people see value that had too long gone unrecognized.

11. Russell, "Arts Stimulus Ban Is Stupid Economics," *Bloomberg*, February 13, 2009.

CHAPTER 8

1. Author extensively covered rebuilding efforts since 9/11 for both *Architectural Record* and *Bloomberg*.

2. Jeffrey Meltrodt, "Understaffed and Overwhelmed," *New Orleans Times-Picayune,* January 28, 2007. Author confirmed Road Home problems in interviews with officials, activists, and users in February 2007.

3. "Trinity River Masterplan" (2009), http://www.thetrinitytrust.org. Author visited the site of the project and interviewed Trinity River Trust president Gail Thomas in October 2009.

4. Great Park description: Orange County Great Park website, http://www.ocgp.org. Financing: Tony Barboza, "Irvine's Great Park Hasn't Exactly Earned Its Name," *Los Angeles Times,* April 12, 2008. Cost figure from Ken Smith, the park's landscape designer, in Jeff Byles, "Great Expectations," *Architects' Newspaper,* November 25, 2009.

5. BeltLine information from the project's website: http://www.beltline.org. Local news coverage has focused on the city's inability to raise its share of money for the project.

6. Author interviewed Sadik-Khan in June and July 2009 for "So Says . . . Janette Sadik-Khan," *Oculus,* published by AIA New York (Fall 2009).

7. Author conversation with Rachele Raynoff, press secretary, New York City Department of City Planning, June 2010.

8. Factsheet: "HUD-DOT-EPA Interagency Partnership for Sustainable Communities," http://www.epa.gov/dced/partnership/index.html.

9. LEED ND data comes from the "Neighborhood Resources" pages of the website of the US Green Building Council (http://www.usgbc.org) and author interviews with LEED ND principals Kaid Benfield and Sophie Lambert, May 2010.

10. The German equivalent of the US Green Building Council is called DGNB (http://www.dgnb.de). The rating system was established in 2007.

11. James S. Russell, "Berlin Struggles to Reinvent Itself," *Architectural Record*, October 1995, 29–31, 112; James S. Russell, "The New Berlin: What Happens When a City Transforms Itself through Architecture," *Architectural Record*, March 2002, 76–80.

12. Trevor Boddy, "Vancouverism vs. Lower Manhattanism: Shaping the High Density City," presented at the Institute for Urban Design, New York, September 20, 2005, and reprinted on the website ArchNewsNow, http://www.archnewsnow.com. Author also interviewed Boddy in July 2008.

13. Vancouver's EcoDensity initiative: http://vancouver.ca/commsvcs/ecocity/index.htm.

14. James S. Russell, "Where Architecture Is Urban Design," *Architectural Record*, March 2005, 62–66.

15. Author visited HafenCity in April 2010, and the state of construction is depicted as it was at that time. A very large quarter was well into construction on that visit, which will complete close to half the planned buildout about 2012. Information about energy, transportation, and other aspects of HafenCity Planning was derived from "HafenCity Hamburg Projects: Insights into Current Developments," published by HafenCity Hamburg GmbH, March 2010, accessed from the website http://www.hafencity.com.

CHAPTER 9

1. McMansion overbuilding: Arthur C. Nelson, "Leadership in a New Era," *Journal of the American Planning Association* 72, no.4 (2006): 393–406. Nelson was later cited in "Drop in Homeownership Likely to Continue," *USA Today*, August 5, 2009.

2. Author visit and briefing, January 2007, and South Waterfront website: http://www.southwaterfront.com/about/.

3. A skeptic's view of Portland's urban growth boundary: Robert Bruegmann, *Sprawl: A Compact History* (Chicago: University of Chicago Press, 2005), ch. 13.

4. Sheri Olson, "Portland Grows Up—Not Out—with Sienna Architecture Company's Irvington Place," *Architectural Record,* December 2000.

5. Resources for rethinking strip development: Ellen Dunham-Jones and June Williamson, *Retrofitting Suburbia: Urban Design Solutions for Redesigning Suburbs* (Hoboken, NJ: Wiley, 2009); Galina Tachieva, *The Sprawl Repair Manual* (Washington, DC: Island Press, 2010).

6. For inventive multifamily housing, see William R. Morrish, Susanne Schindler, and Katie Swenson, *Growing Urban Habitats: Seeking a New Housing Development Model* (San Francisco: William Stout Publishers, 2009).

7. Author first noticed the house-price transit connection in news reports on New Jersey towns that saw substantial price appreciation after an NJ Transit bottleneck had been removed, speeding service. There is some evidence that walkable and transit-served neighborhoods have lost less value in the 2000s housing crash. Damon Darlin, "Street Corners vs. Cul de Sacs," *New York Times,* January 9, 2010.

8. Despite punishing rents and demographic change, fur, jewelry, and flower sellers are among many wholesale and retail businesses that continue to cluster in defined districts in Manhattan. Brooklyn has developed boutique furniture design and fashion in recent years.

9. The "Incentive Zoning" in New York, before it was repealed, resulted in several Broadway theaters being inserted under office buildings in Times Square, a park no one knows about in Trump Tower, and several glass-roofed, midblock arcades in Midtown.

10. On changing planning priorities: author interviews with Steve van Gorp, Las Vegas redevelopment manager, and Rod Allison, planning manager in Clark County's Comprehensive Planning unit, January 2005.

11. Author interview of Chakrabarti, June 2010.

12. There's a large literature that claims regulations are a key driver of higher development costs, especially for housing. Prominent ones include "'Not in My Backyard': Removing Barriers to Affordable Housing," a report spearheaded by Jack Kemp, secretary of HUD (1991), http://www.huduser.org/publications/RBCPUBS/NotinMyBackyward.html; and much work by planning analyst Anthony Downs. It can be difficult to attribute higher costs to regulations alone, since several factors enter in, especially wealth. Affluent communities of all political stripes tend to welcome regulation that protects property values and "quality of life," costing anti-regulatory forces a powerful constituency. Arthur C. Nelson et al. make the case that regulations only marginally impact costs of housing in *Environmental Regulations and Housing Costs* (Washington, DC: Island Press, 2009).

13. William Fulton, *The Reluctant Metropolis: The Politics of Urban Growth in Los Angeles* (Point Arena, CA: Solano, 1997).

14. James S. Russell, "Can LEED Survive the Carbon Neutral Era?" *Metropolis*, November 2007.

15. STAR Community Index: http://www.icleiusa.org/programs/sustainability/star -community-index.

CHAPTER 10

1. Europe's rejection of American-style, debt-fueled economic stimulus, led by Germany's Angela Merkel, received wide media coverage in 2008 and 2009.

2. The sentiments on government programs expressed in a *New York Times* story sum up presumptions that seem deeply embedded in European outlooks and decision making: Suzanne Dailey, "Safety Net Frays in Spain, as Elsewhere in Europe," *New York Times*, June 27, 2010.

3. Since the real estate bubble collapsed, officials in government and finance constantly warned that recovery would be slow. They were essentially admitting that they saw no obvious basis for renewal.

4. S&L regulations and collapse: "The S&L Crisis: A Chrono-Bibliography," on website of Federal Deposit Insurance Corporation: http://www.fdic.gov/bank /historical/s%26l/index.html. Construction volume from Dodge Construction Index.

5. The go-go bubble (but not the eventual crash) was memorably chronicled by Michael Lewis in *The New New Thing: A Silicon Valley Story* (New York: Norton, 2000).

6. James S. Russell, "475 Brannan Street," *Architectural Record*, June 2000, 162–64.

7. After ten years, the NASDAQ had recovered less than half its peak value: Sam Guston, "Ten Years after the Dot Com Bust, Tech Is Booming Again," AOL Daily Finance website, March 10, 2010, http://srph.it/byHhAE.

8. Joseph E. Stiglitz, *Freefall: America, Free Markets, and the Sinking of the World Economy* (New York: Norton, 2010), offers a cogent description of the housing bubble and its collapse. Alex Blumberg and Adam Davidson, "The Giant Pool of Money," a coproduction of the public radio program *This American Life* and National Public Radio (first aired May 9, 2008), summarizes the same events with extraordinary clarity.

9. Stiglitz, *Freefall*, 19, makes this point, as do many other authorities.

10. Stiglitz, *Freefall*, 182, on offshoring. By 2050, China's economy may be twice as large as America's, with India's equal to it: "The N-11: More than an Acronym," Goldman Sachs Global Economics Paper no. 153 (March 28, 2007), accessed via Wikipedia, topic "BRICs."

11. Ucilia Wang, "China Tops the World in Solar Panel Manufacturing," AOL Daily Finance website, June 3, 2010, http://srph.it/d4wO9u, confirming a comment made on visit to German manufacturer Solon in April 2010. Germany had previously been the solar-production leader as well as the world's largest solar market.

12. High commodity prices—most obviously in oil—helped tip the boom into bust, as owners slowed or halted construction projects in response to prices for steel, concrete, drywall, and copper that were bounding upward by double digits every few months.

13. Stiglitz, *Freefall,* 357, and referencing William D. Nordhaus and James Tobin, "Is Growth Obsolete?" *Economic Research: Retrospect and Prospect,* vol. 5, *Economic Growth* (New York: Columbia University Press, for the National Bureau of Economic Research, 1972).

14. Stiglitz, *Freefall,* 181, 259, is one of many economists. Also, Paul Collier considers economic and political means to avoid exploitation of resources to exhaustion: *The Plundered Planet: Why We Must—and How We Can—Manage Nature for Global Prosperity* (New York: Oxford University Press, 2010).

15. The Lake Washington cleanup was so defining in Seattle that it played a part in Roger Sale's history of the city, *Seattle, Past to Present* (Seattle: University of Washington Press, 1976), 197–200.

16. A conservative thumbnail estimate of the real estate value around Lake Washington is $4 billion.

17. Estimating even the direct costs of air and pollution control, considering primarily health effects for air, and health, fisheries, and recreation effects for water, is an extremely limited way of looking at those benefits, but one EPA used when the renewal of the Clean Air Act (1970) and Clean Water Act (1972) were considered by Congress in the 1990s. Even that analysis showed that air-quality investments were amply paid back, while water-quality investments offered modest paybacks. The water criteria did not assess the most important cost of failing to regulate water pollution: the cost to make water from polluted streams potable for drinking. (Many river cities must filter and sanitize water polluted by upstream cities. Clearly, Clean Water Act actions reduce such costs substantially.) J. Clarence Davies and Jan Mazurek, *Pollution Control in the United States: Evaluating the System* (Washington, DC: Resources for the Future, 1998), 126–35.

18. The lower Cuyahoga River, in Cleveland, caught fire in 1969—not for the first time—and the resulting publicity helped focus the public's attention on the need for clean-water legislation. US Environmental Protection Agency, "Cuyahoga River Area of Concern," undated web-based document: http://www.epa.gov/glnpo/aoc/cuyahoga.html.

19. On energy conservation: Steven Mufson, "In Energy Conservation California Sees the Light," *Washington Post*, February 17, 2007. California Assembly Bill 32 sets the goal of reducing greenhouse gas emissions to 1990 levels by 2020: http://www.arb.ca.gov/cc/ab32/ab32.htm. Vision California: Calthorpe Associates, "Vision California/Charting Our Future: Statewide Scenarios Report," revision of May 12, 2010, http://www.visioncalifornia.org and http://www.calthorpe.com/vision-california.

20. On Empire State Building: information from Anthony Malkin, building owner, on visit, July 2010. On solar shuttle: author visit to Solon headquarters and manufacturing facility, Berlin, Germany, April 2010.

21. John Timmer, "Testing the Vehicle-to-grid Connection," Ars Technica website, February 22, 2010, http://arstechnica.com/science/news/2010/02/testing-the-electric-vehicle-to-grid-connection.ars. In a presentation in April 2010, Andreas Kraemer, director of Ecologic, a German think tank, claimed that electric cars could one day provide twenty times the reserve grid power now available.

22. Smart grid, controls, electric cars: David J. Leeds, "The Networked EV: Smart Grids and Electric Vehicles; First Stop, California," in GreenTechGrid, industry news website, February 23, 2010, http://www.greentechmedia.com/articles/read/the-networked-ev-smart-grids-and-electric-vehicles-first-step-california/. Home control systems for load shifting: presentation on "E Haus," prototype demonstrating German KNX protocol as well as Gira controls, Germany-based consumer home controls, in Germany, April 2010. Both support Internet-based load shifting. These update the kinds of home-control systems in the United States that have been available and have steadily improved since the 1990s.

23. Much of the building technology described in this book was developed outside the United States (though as late as the early 1980s, America was a greentech leader). High-speed rail technology is imported, as is much transit technology. Hybrid-car power trains were mainstreamed in Japan. Several business leaders have called for large increases in US research: John M. Broder, "A Call to Triple U.S. Spending on Energy Research," *New York Times*, June 9, 2010.

24. Paul D. Gottlieb, "Growing without Growth: An Alternative Economic Development Goal for Metropolitan Areas," discussion Paper for the Brookings Institution Center on Urban and Metropolitan Policy, 2002. There's also a new research focus on shrinking cities that seeks a stable economic basis for European communities that are aging and losing population, and for American industrial cities that have failed to find new engines for either economic or population growth. The work has identified means to shrink more gracefully

but in my view has not yet made a persuasive case for nurturing wealth or well-being in the absence of at least some long-term population gain.

25. David I. Stern, "The Environmental Kuznets Curve," *International Society for Ecological Economics Internet Encyclopedia of Ecological Economics,* June 2003, http://www.ecoeco.org/pdf/stern.pdf.

26. Keith Bradsher, "China Fears Warming Effects of Consumer Wants," *New York Times,* July 4, 2010.

27. Collier, *The Plundered Planet.* Stiglitz, in *Freefall,* 405, also endorses using energy-exploitation proceeds to build low-energy infrastructure and also mentions Chile. Norway has pledged a 40 percent reduction in carbon emissions by 2020, the most ambitious of any developed country, and will finance measures largely with revenues from oil extraction. Alex Morales and Marianne Stigset, "Norway Offers 40 Percent Emissions Cut, Biggest among Developed World," *Bloomberg,* October 8, 2009.

28. Alice Waters, of Chez Panisse restaurant, was an early champion of what has come to be known as slow food. Eric Schlosser's *Fast Food Nation: The Dark Side of the All-American Meal* focused on industrially processed food (New York: Harper Perennial, 2005). Michael Pollan contrasted the heavy use of oil and corn in food production with local and organic food in *The Omnivore's Dilemma: A Natural History of Four Meals* (New York: Penguin, 2006).

29. The founding of the Slow Cities movement—*Cittaslow,* in Italian—is attributed to Paolo Saturnini, once mayor of Greve, in the Chianti region: http://www.cittaslow.org.

30. Frances Mayes, *Under the Tuscan Sun* (New York: Broadway Books, 1997), and numerous other titles by Mayes and others popularized the lifestyle, landscape, and food of Tuscany. Italian product design, with brand names from Olivetti to Alessi, triumphed from the 1960s but has been challenged in its dominance by other European countries and Asian makers. Its major fashion houses are international powerhouses, but personal friends in the business say the specialized textile crafts that supported Italian fashion dominance, from high-end textiles to shoes, neckware, and beadmaking, are rapidly being decimated by lower-cost producers, mainly outside Europe.

31. Bike culture in Portland, local-food cultures in California, and Brooklyn's nexus of designers and producers of specialized food, furniture, and clothing are "slow city" hubs in America, even if not explicitly so. Environmental writer Bill McKibben endorses local economies as a global warming solution in *Deep Economy: The Wealth of Communities and the Durable Future* (New York: Times Books, 2007).

32. Jane Jacobs, the brilliant urban analyst, coined the term *import replacement* to denote the process by which localities evolve by replacing imported goods

with locally produced ones that can compete by capitalizing on unique local skills and resources: Jane Jacobs, *Cities and the Wealth of Nations: Principles of Economic Life* (New York: Random House, 1984).

33. The Living Building Challenge, a project of the Cascadia Green Building Council that demands net zero energy consumption, limits the radius from which materials can be obtained to a maximum of one thousand miles.

34. "Sustainable Energy Security: Strategic Risks and Opportunities for Business," July 2010, white paper published by Lloyd's, the global specialist insurer, available at http://www.chathamhouse.org.uk/publications/papers/view/-/id /891/.

35. European agricultural subsidies: Pietro Nivola, *Laws of the Landscape: How Policies Shape Cities in Europe and America* (Washington, DC: Brookings Institution, 1999).

36. A deep literature has developed on environmental economics, valuing "ecosystem services" and integrating them into human endeavor. Driving down resource use forges "natural capital," for example, in Hunter Lovins, Amory Lovins, and Paul Hawken, *Natural Capitalism: Creating the Next Industrial Revolution* (Boston: Back Bay Books, 2008).

37. GDP measures "growth" that erodes rather than enhances well-being: Stiglitz, *Freefall*, 259. The triple bottom line is often attributed to business consultant John Elkington. A significant literature has grown around the idea and its implementation.

38. Ed Blakely, New Orleans rebuilding czar in the late 2000s, told me that green construction techniques had been identified by studies as a powerful potential driver of the city's economy.

EPILOGUE

1. James S. Russell, ed., *The Mayors' Institute: Excellence in City Design* (New York: Princeton Architectural Press, 2002). See also http://www.micd.org (Mayors' Institute) and http://www.govinstitute.org (Governors' Institute).

2. *Architectural Record* magazine and Tulane University hosted the "High Density on the High Ground" competition in New Orleans in spring 2006. James S. Russell, "Designing the Future of New Orleans," *Architectural Record*, June 2006, 114–23.

3. Jess Smee, "The Watery Future of East Germany's Coal Mines," *Spiegel Online*, September 28, 2010, http://www.spiegel.de/international/germany /0,1518,717855,00.html.

INDEX

Figures/photos/illustrations are indicated by a " f ."

Island Press | Board of Directors